Europe on Saturday Night

Europe on Saturday Night

John Gould

Down East Books

Camden, Maine

Published by Down East Books
An imprint of The Rowman & Littlefield Publishing Group, Inc.
4501 Forbes Boulevard, Suite 200, Lanham, Maryland 20706
www.rowman.com

Unit A, Whitacre Mews, 26-34 Stannary Street, London SE11 4AB, United Kingdom

Distributed by NATIONAL BOOK NETWORK

Library of Congress Cataloging-in-Publication Data is available on file

Library of Congress Control Number: 68030877

ISBN: 978-1-60893-552-9 (pbk. : alk. paper)
ISBN: 978-1-60893-553-6 (electronic)

♾™ The paper used in this publication meets the minimum requirements of American National Standard for Information Sciences—Permanence of Paper for Printed Library Materials, ANSI/NISO Z39.48-1992.

Printed in the United States of America

This is my first book since
Terence
came into our family, so I mark it pleasantly to him,
but this is not the same Terence who once wrote:

*There is nothing more unjust than a man
without knowledge of the world: he thinks nothing
is right except what he has done himself.*

Disclaimer

One time Joe Starbird shot a coot and wounded him. Every time the coot would dive Joe would grab up an oar and take after him, and every time he came up Joe would shoot at him. If a coot decides to be stubborn you can plan on all day. Joe went away over to Small Point after this coot, and along about dark he came rowing home. After all this the coot was hardly more than tail feathers and beak, and Joe said, "This ain't much of a coot, but I went a long ways to get him."

And this ain't much of a book, but we went a far piece after it. Yet, after setting down some of our impressions and experiences, it seems to me there is much in this which the Great American People should know. I suppose this is the nearest I ever came to preaching; and having produced some other books in different vein perhaps I should apologize when this one thumps the pulpit and exhorts.

But Dorothy says I don't need to feel that way.

— J. G.

Europe on Saturday Night

On or About

The original settler in our family sailed from Hull, in England, somewhere around 1615, and found the North Atlantic so distasteful none of his descendants had wanted to get on a boat since. When all the others in his migration went to catching and cutting fish he took to carpentering, and when he went anywhere he walked. He spoke so emotionally about the sea that none of us followed it in the great era of down-east ships, clippers and windjammers, but stayed home to be carpenters, farmers, even bankers, and those who couldn't do anything else went into the ministry or taught school. We have been, since 1615, a land-bound family. My own father, once, was crossing to Prince Edward Island on the ferry, and he became violently seasick about twenty feet out and went around explaining to the other passengers that it was a family ailment. The Northumberland Straits, that day, were smooth as glass, but Father had inherited hatred of water. His trip was only the third time in over two hundred years any of us had been on a boat.

In 1758 one ancestor started for Louisburg on Cape Breton Island with the Boscawen forces, and the first time the ship put in towards land he went ashore and walked the rest of the way. He would get ahead of the expedition and have to wait, but he took part in the business at Louisburg and then walked up to Quebec City for the encore. But he was once on a boat, and he didn't like it. Then my own grandfather, enlisting in Company I of the 16th Maine Volunteers to free the slaves, got hauled to Fall River on a train and put on a boat. He had to stay on it all the way to New Jersey, and he always said that short ride on the water took all the fun out of the war and he often wished he would get shot so he wouldn't have to sail home. He didn't have to, and came back to Maine by rail where he lived a long and useful life growing tomatoes, keeping bees, and staying home.

This whole land-bound attitude is inconsistent with Maine. We had a whole glorious era when deep-water vessels were plopping into the tide from every hayfield, and Maine men were sailing them around the world. It was nothing to say goodbye to a friend in Portland, and then see him next time in Bangkok. But not us — our only traveler of note was an uncle who went "out West" and homesteaded a ranch in Dakota Territory. Every other home in town had sea chests full of Spanish laces, Eastern silks, Eskimo boots, and assorted mementoes of the Seven Seas, but all we had was a Sioux warclub hanging on the dining room wall. That one passage from Hull to New England had been enough, and the violent distaste for the ocean had been handed down to the tenth and eleventh generations.

So it was noteworthy when I, and my farmer's bride, announced that a trip to Europe was contemplated and we would shortly sail away for four months, or until our money ran out, and put an end to this foolishness about the ocean. Immediately all our friends and all the tourist

4

agencies told us our whole premise was as ancient as the ancestor — they said we ought to fly, that flying is the only way, and we would save time. But we didn't think so. We had a silly fancy that we would like to step aboard a vessel here in Maine, as one might have in days of yore, and dare the gods of wind and storm. The more we thought about it the more enticing it became, and the more we wanted to do it the more everybody said we couldn't.

We do still have ships. The old drawings and photographs of our harbors, showing masts thick as spills on porcupines, are museum pieces today, but Portland and Searsport still get occasional vessels other than the unromantic tankers. Pulp and paper, potatoes, titanium, china clay, and other random cargoes come and go, and freighters do have space for passengers. And this is the way people used to travel. They'd look up and down the docks and find a vessel going where they wanted to go, and then they'd wait for her to sail. We made inquiry, and for the next couple of months learned a great deal about the modern tourist business, finding out what Americans do when they travel, and finding out what not to do. It got so when somebody suggested something we decided to try something else. This was to be our vacation, and we wanted to do it our way. We wanted no reservations; we wanted no tours. We wanted to avoid anything that would label, define, advertise and stereoplate us as "American Tourists." At least forty times, when travel agents begged us to fly, we answered patiently and with dedication, "We want to visit between airports."

The minute you step into a travel bureau and ask for a freight ship you learn how guided, conducted, prepaid, scheduled, all-expense, programmed tours stranglehold the American. Every agent we approached had the same answer — "But you don't want to go that way!" Then came the sell. We could have five days in Algiers; ten days in Paris. We would save time and money, and there was an opening. We would come back to the farm and sit by the old-fashioned wood fire in our fireplace and eat an apple and pop some corn, and we felt alone and unbefriended in a mad, tumultuous world of rushing and running where time is only to be saved and travel is best when it is soonest done. Every time they told us about the speed of jets we wondered if they knew what "cruising" ought to mean.

Probably too much of our times has passed us by, and hasn't found us up in Maine. It was thirty-five years ago that we came as newlyweds to our old family farm and rooted ourselves in. In that time the United States has become a nation of movers, and roots are no longer important. You can live in Kansas, or in a trailer. And our cities have become a national problem. To us, happy on the hundred acres cleared by forebears, there have been few pressures. Every April we tap the same sugar maples that my great-grandfather tapped, and this begins a year that has been our way of life. The children came and we brought them up, and one day along in there somewhere I told my wife, "As soon as they're educated and married off, we'll go on a trip and see the world."

Kathy was married in June, and the happy couple larruped old Sam until he woke up and clattered the buggy out of the dooryard according to traditional going-away capers. With the lawful tears of a bride's mother wetting her bosom my wife turned to me and said, "Okay, let's pack!" For some reason she hadn't forgotten. We did pack, and we spent that next winter getting ready. We had plenty of time — the same twenty-four hours in

6

every day that everybody else has — and we got teed off every time a travel agent tried to speed us up, whip us into line, and convert us into typical American tourists.

You see, travel agents know nothing about freight ships. They will, if they can't sell you a champagne flight, concede to a passenger liner and get you a booking, but you floor them with freighters. Freighters are not scheduled and always sail "on or about." The American has become precise and his wants specific. No right-thinking American wants to start a vacation "on or about." But the travel agents all said they would see what they could do, and waggled their heads. Weeks later they would report that nothing had turned up, and would we reconsider the jet? So we wised up then, and went to Portland to see Ralph Leavitt.

If you want to sail on a freighter you don't go to the glass-fronted tourist bureau with its gay posters of Tahiti and Antigua, the Tyrol and Lorraine — you go to a ripe, ramshackle building on the waterfront, and you ask somebody like Ralph Leavitt. Ralph's grandfathers sailed those old Maine ships, and today he deals in maritime affairs and can tell you without looking what time the tide serves. To him "on or about" is an old story. He remembers his grandfather's telling how he had to bribe the lighters that brought out guano on the West Coast, and if the skippers of guano ships didn't bribe enough they would sit there at anchor for as much as four months. Four months is quite an "on or about," but Ralph understands such things and travel agents do not. Ralph said our desire to sail from Maine was sentimentally laudable, but traffic doesn't move that way. Maine is a first port, and steamers go on to New York and Baltimore before heading back to Europe. And there's a $10,000 fine if a foreign-registry vessel carries passengers between Ameri-

7

can ports. We could go to Baltimore to embark, but he suggested Montreal. We asked about American-registry freighters, and Ralph spread his hands discreetly. So we said all right — Montreal.

After that things began to happen. While all the travel agents continued to call us up to say that nothing was available we began hearing from shipping lines, and before long we had any number of choices out of Montreal, which is nearer to Maine than New York is and easier to get to. We sent a deposit and knew that we would finally get to go — on or about. Our vessel was to be the motorship *Wolfgang Russ*, out of Hamburg by the Ernst Russ Lines, and the agent was the Montreal Shipping Company, Ltd., far down on St. Nicholas Street and nowhere near the glass and chrome travel bureaus in uptown Montreal. Correspondence was with a Mrs. E. Kroeger, passenger agent, who turned out to be a native of Pilsen but long a Canadian, a veteran handler of freight-ship riders who does everything to make them happy except kiss them goodbye — and after we met her I could have endured that, too. Charming, efficient, and completely aloof from the mad, hurry-up pace of modern travel, she eventually took us to the dock and wove a magic spell until the rusty, paint-splotched, salt-crusted *Wolfgang Russ* looked like the finest ship afloat and all her lumbering derricks were peppermint sticks.

So we knew we would go and we got ready to go, and all we had to do was wait to be told which day was closest to "on or about."

Champagne and Au Revoir

When my wife and I first began loading the canoe on a truck and heading for backwoods Maine to snag a trout and sleep under the stars her preparations were extensive and her baggage likewise. It wasn't hard to convince her, shortly, that one cocktail gown was enough, and after a few trips she dispensed with that, but it was years before I got her down to three handbags and a purse. Even when she knew she would spend four days in the same pair of pants she would bring skirts in case, so I wondered how I would make out when I applied my woods-trail rule to foreign travel — take only what you can pick up and lug in two hands.

Amazingly, she came up with two suitcases into which she got everything. For weeks she would bring something from a closet, stand by the open suitcase to ponder and deliberate, and then hang it back in the closet. She took far less gear to Europe for four months than she takes for a weekend at Caucomgomoc Dam, and when all was packed she said there was still room if something came up at the last minute. We got our passport, and we got our travel checks. We also combed some banks and picked up a small amount of foreign money — a good thing to have

9

if you get to a place after the exchange windows have closed. And when Mrs. Kroeger finally wrote and said the on-or-about had been nailed down to one or the other of two weeks we made ready for the big bon-voyage party due us. Our children, with husband and wife, made the arrangements. The six of us went to Flatiron Pond, caught a mess of trout, and had a cookout. Probably the only bon-voyage party ever held at Flatiron Pond, and the only time a champagne cork popped that high in Franklin County. The bottle was chilled in the cold, bubbling spring at the water's edge, and we quaffed from white agate cups. The lawful limit at Flatiron Pond is five fish a day per person, and thirty trout snuggled in one fry-pan is a handsome Maine memory to take abroad. We would embark to sample the foreign cuisine, and this would be something to measure up to. The sun was blood-red in its Kennebago glory over the West Range when we came out of the woods and started for Montreal and our rendezvous with on-or-about.

Thanks to Expo 67 a great many United Statesers learned that Montreal is a great Western city. Since the 27th proved to be on-or-about the 24th we had three more days to practice our French, and Mrs. Kroeger said we would find the *côte d'agneau* at Le Petit Havre restaurant better than anything in Paris. She was right. We stopped in at the church of Bon Secours and left a coin to propitiate our voyage — as mariners are wont to do and have done for years. And on the 27th we carried our suitcases to the dock and found the *Wolfgang Russ* loading pallets of tinned green beans in an interminable routine of ups and downs that threatened to exhaust Canada's supply. Before the St. Lawrence Seaway was finished a good many vessels were built specifically for it. One more coat of paint and they couldn't get through

10

the locks. The *Wolfgang Russ* had been to Chicago and Toronto, and as Montreal was the last port she was taking on anything she could get to fill the holds. There were some raw hides, as well as the beans, but they had to take the beans first and everybody was sad, because hides pay a better tariff than beans do. They told us they had one hold full of Canadian whiskey, and another loaded with fertilizer.

Just upriver from us, at the same pier, was a Soviet grain ship, and she was a beautiful thing. She was new and clean-painted and had the hammer and sickle on her stack. Our German crew greatly admired her. To us, indoctrinated well against anything Russian, she was something of a surprise. That she had come down from the Great Lakes, passing through multimillion-dollar locks and channels the United States had liberally financed, and was trading unconcernedly with friendly Canada, seemed to belie some of the things we had been hearing at home. The passengers who looked down from her decks at us seemed no different from us looking back, and we were astonished to learn that we could have sailed to Europe on her, and that in Canada the Russians advertise for business. But there were going to be many more informative lessons in the weeks to come — an American has much to learn. A tug pushed the Soviet ship into the channel, and another moved the *Wolfgang Russ* into her wake. But she was faster than the *Wolfgang Russ* and we were soon left behind. We didn't look at her much after that, because the sunset we had seen over the Kennebago mountains had followed us to Canada, and now the skyline of Montreal was silhouetted against a fire-red sky, with the *Schraubenwasser* of our vessel catching the color and kicking up crimson. It would be raining ten days later when we got to Hamburg, but they say it always

11

rains in Hamburg and everybody there has a sore throat. In those ten days thousands and thousands of typical American tourists would fly to Europe and back — every hotel room reserved in advance and every bus stop cleanly clocked. They would all have a wonderful time. Meantime, we would slog along at an optimistic twelve knots over the bounding North Atlantic — which none of our family had seen since 1615.

The steward came to interrupt our sunset to say, "Dinner is soon, would you care for a Steinhager or a Kirschwasser?"

Six days later, after everybody was well acquainted, he told me that he had expected me to ask for a Manhattan or a Martini. This would be another of those lessons. I told him this would have been impossible. "You see," I said, "my wife didn't pack a cocktail gown."

Our Own Yacht

The real, honest reason for a ship trip is adjustment. We came to Europe with ten days of getting ready, and that much time to get over being Americans. We know what tourists are, typical or otherwise. Maine has been in the vacation business a long time, and almost anybody is interrupted now and then by rusticators who say, "My good man, can you direct us to a decent restaurant?" We are told by our publicity experts that it is good business to respond kindly to these people because they are spending good money amongst us and elevating our economy, and that we are wise to leave a good impression. So they will come again. But there doesn't seem to be any publicity expert who takes the tourist to one side and explains to him that he shouldn't walk up to a State of Mainer and say, "My good man . . ."

One time Lester Titcomb was piling pulpwood at the fork in the road, and there are two signs there, one pointing each way, and they both say "Portland." A tourist came along and stopped, and called at Lester, "My good man, does it matter which road I take to Portland?"

Les said, "Not to me, it don't."

But I could tell that woman something about Lester she wouldn't believe. One time a New York editor was coming up to see me and he missed a turn and wound up in Lester's driveway. This fellow was a gentleman and a scholar and a good judge of flesh, and he wasn't the kind who thinks he needs to be saluted just because he is a tourist and passing by. Lester took to him, and asked him to look at his cellar. We sat around all evening waiting for the editor to show up, and we didn't know where he was until Lester called and said they were just finishing supper and they'd be over as soon as they drank dessert. So, we understand some of the nuances, and we approached Europe with restraint on our sense of importance.

We particularly resented the advice of one travel agent, who said in addition to our travel checks to take along a handful of plain United States dollars. He said we'd find we'd run into perplexities where a good American greenback was a sure key to the hearts of the natives. We didn't take any dollar bills, and we never needed one. We left home at home, and we studiously avoided looking like the sport-shirt set who see a lobster flopping on the wharf and ask if it is fresh. The kind who let you know immediately that they are from Connecticut.

And we most certainly didn't buy any guidebooks. We've seen too many places approved and authorized and recommended and accredited, and we wouldn't stop at them on a bet. I always liked the sign on a roadside lunch stand at Oquossoc — "The Place Duncan Hines Missed." It sizes up our opinion. And the story about Billy Hill down at Mount Desert Island — Billy ran a lunchroom, and a man came in on Clam Chowder Day and wanted an Oyster Stew. It just wasn't the right day. After some loggerheading, the man laid his cards on the table and said, "Mr. Hill, my name is Duncan Hines, and I publish a book listing good places to eat. Now, if your oyster stew is as good as they tell me, I'll put you in my book and you'll be famous coast-to-coast."

Billy said, "Don't make no damn's-odds who you be, Mister, today is clam chowder day, and I ain't got no oyster stew."

Finally Duncan Hines left in a huff, slamming the screen door, and when Billy told about it that evening somebody said, "What did you do, Billy?"

Billy said, "I went right over to the cash register and I rung up 'No Sale'!"

Even better is the yarn about Bud Russell at the Kennebago Lake Club. Bud runs the best summertime dining room in Maine, and every spring he sends in his food orders and big trucks stock him up. He always orders his pickles from the H. J. Heinz people, and one spring on opening day the chef came in and said, "Buddie, we don't have a pickle in the place — the Heinz order didn't come through."

14

So that evening Bud was mixing drinks at the bar for a few frozen early fishermen, and a man steps up to the bar and says, "Good evening, Mr. Russell, I'm from Duncan Hines."

And Buddie says, "So where the hell are my pickles!"

So we didn't feel we should spend our time looking at things somebody else has decided we ought to look at, and which are seen by everybody who buys that book. Maybe we'd find some no-sales. We did take our French and German dictionaries — not the handy instant-culture kind that teach you how to ask for a room with a bath and please wipe my windshield, but our college models. We did not take a camera, and hence approached everybody without a Polaroid-Kodak complex. Everything helps. When we stepped aboard the *Wolfgang Russ* a deckhand looked at our two suitcases and said, "Is that all?"

When the *Queen Mary* and the *Queen Elizabeth* were retired from trans-Atlantic passenger service there were many sentimental regrets. About the same time the great liner *United States* shifted the emphasis in its advertising and instead of fast service began offering "a leisurely cruise of three and a half days." We couldn't care less. On the *Wolfgang Russ* we wandered pleasantly down the St. Lawrence River, watching things go by. The Isle of Rabbits, where hares breed so relentlessly that men go out every fall and salt down great casks of meat. The high ramparts of Quebec City, still alight in the early morning. We saw where the clear, cold water of the Saguenay reeves out into the gray St. Lawrence and draws a straight line down the channel for miles. We went by Baie Comeau, where the Canadian naturalist Napoleon Comeau lived and wrote one of the great English books — although he never heard a word of English spoken until he was fifteen. Napoleon Comeau is forgotten in Baie Comeau today, and the statue in the park is of Colonel Robert McCormick of the Chicago *Tribune* — it shows him running rapids in a bronze canoe. You can't see the canoe from ships passing in the river, but you can see the pulpwood piles to be chewed up for *Tribune* newsprint.

When we neared the open ocean and passed Belle Isle we heard the first engineer explaining to a German passenger that Belle Isle is named for Alexander Graham Bell, the "American" inventor of the *Fernsprecher*. I spreched-up at that, and said Mr. Bell had really invented the telephone in Ontario, according to Ontario, and that Belle Isle is so-named because the lighthouse has a bell in it. They nodded, and I hope this has become standard in the *Wolfgang Russ* lore. We also taught the chief engineer how to play cribbage — he would count his hand in German, translate it to English, peg the holes, and say, "I zink."

Passengers on the *Queen Mary, Queen Elizabeth* and *United States,* if they paid the long price for first-class passage, might sit at the captain's table and brag about it when they came home. On the *Wolfgang Russ* our cabin was larger, better equipped and more congenial than a cabin-class stateroom on the *United States* — and we sat at the captain's table every meal. The chief reason freighters take passengers at all, we decided, is to provide company for the captain, who has nothing to do and desires companionship. The manner in which Mrs. Kroeger arranged the company suggests this, and we remembered how she had adroitly filled us in on Captain Eichhorst's likes and dislikes. The captain spoke fairly good English, and when a passenger asked him what he did, specifically, on a ship that seemed so well organized

16

he answered, "I am just like the President of the United States — I do nothing."

He took rum in his tea. The bottle stayed by his chair at table, and when the tea was served he gave it a good lacing — without offering any to his passengers. After he had taken some he would lace it again, and shortly his cup of tea was strong enough so he was influenced into a bilingual recitation that shortly ran out of English. When, a couple of days into the Atlantic, radar picked up an iceberg, he descended from the bridge personally to invite us all up for a look. It was a small iceberg, and already below the cold-water line, so it wouldn't last much longer. We saw it on the horizon most of the day.

We were eight. A professor from a western college and his wife, on their way to spend a year in Spain. A young German from Hamburg, Volker Jacobsen, who was learning the shipping business and was a free-riding passenger. An older woman from Berlin who had been visiting a daughter on Cape Cod — she kept to herself mostly and I think the sea bothered her. Then Herr and Frau Willi Lemm — he is an artist in Bad Neustadt, and had been commissioned to go to Canada and do a portrait. While there he had made over fifty landscapes in the wild region north of Lake Superior, and in midocean he exhibited them for us — begging us to remember that they were not yet finished. He painted in his cabin every day. And ourselves. Two spoke only English; two spoke only German — others had some of both. I was the only one who knew any French, and on the whole voyage I had only one chance to use it. When we dropped our last St. Lawrence *pilote* and he swung down the ladder to the pilot boat, his briefcase around his neck on a strap, he was cascaded from above by *auf-Wiederseh'ns,* to which he answered with ingratiating French politeness, "Auf Wiedersehen, eine

gute Reise!" It was then that I yelled down, "Au revoir!"
He stopped dead on the ladder as if somebody had shot
at him, and looked up. He broke out in a big grin. "Au
revoir," he called back. "Bon voyage!"

Frau Lemm, the artist's wife, looked at me as if I had
the erudition of a Harvard president, and she said, "You
speag Franch!" I said oh, yes — but I was soon to learn
from fifty million Frenchmen that they thought otherwise.

German food is not to be lumped with German-
American food. The hog's knuckles and sauerkraut of
Jake Wirth and Lüchow, and of the old city of Milwaukee,
is nothing to go by. Germans do have hearty fare, but
their cooks are equal to dainty refinements by any standards, and for ten days on the *Wolfgang Russ* we had
every chance to make this discovery. Dorothy has asked
me not to state how many pounds she gained on the trip
over. The ventilator from the galley came through our
passenger deck, and between meals we could surmise on
the next. The four meals each day were substantial and
delicious, and we learned immediately that the principal
occupation of any healthy German is digestion. Since we
set our watches ahead an hour every other day, as we
gained on the sun, the four meals sometimes covered a
span of only twenty-three hours. Table was served with
every politeness, and no deluxe cruise ship ever offered
finer menus. In ten days we had no repetition except for
fillet steaks, which Captain Eichhorst also liked for
breakfast — and to us, who had been brought up on the
Heavy-Western-Beef philosophy, a European fillet steak
proves interesting and makes you wonder. I offer one
day's food on the *Wolfgang Russ* (the translation is
mine):

Breakfast:	*Grapefruit*
	Cornflakes, fresh milk
	Eggs any style
	Fillet steak with mushrooms
	(pfifferlinge)
	Assorted breads
	Various cold cuts
	Cheeses
	Coffee, tea

Noon meal:	*Cream of mushroom soup*
	(not canned!)
	Breaded pork chops
	Spinach, potatoes
	Peach melba
	Mocha

| Tea (3:45 P.M.): | *Coffee, tea, cakes* |

Dinner:	*Shrimp soup with croutons*
	Frankfurters with salad
	Roast venison
	Red cabbage, duchesse potatoes
	Fruit compote
	Coffee, tea
	(Wine throughout)
	Fruit bowl

On a German vessel, the bridge is the place where the officers eat between meals. In one sense you don't save any money traveling on a freighter. The fare is not that much less. But in ten days a passenger can eat up a lot of money, and you couldn't dine ashore for that price —

let alone have three thousand miles thrown in. It all boils down to time. But if you take that time it emphasizes the distance — and you can't truthfully equate travel without the factor of miles. The ocean looks much bigger from the middle than it does from Pemaquid Beach — and Europe is an ocean away. Breakfast in New York and lunch in London is an illusion, and we are thankful for the *Wolfgang Russ* — most Americans desperately need ten days on a *Wolfgang Russ* to get over their absurd, pell-mell rush to oblivion. We sat quietly, gazing over interminable water, fumbling with a strange language, guessing what the ventilator was cooking, not opening, for dinner, and leaving our homeland far behind in distance and in thought. We would not step foot in Germany as from a jet — still sanctified with red-blooded American constitutional privileges. When the dockside derricks of Hamburg waved us a welcome, we would be ready. It was raining when we first looked upon Saint Pauli — would everybody in Hamburg have a sore throat?

When we did step ashore that morning we looked back up at the tedious old *Wolfgang Russ,* already half emptied by the cranes of Hamburg, and we set our suitcases down and made a little moment of it. Dorothy said, "It was just like owning your own yacht!"

In Hamburg San' Paul-lee

When you sail by freighter
you sign away all rights. You agree that you have been
warned of every hazard, including explosives. That you
understand there will be no physician, barber and stenog-
rapher on board, and that if sudden death strikes you
down you will go quietly and not complain. This done,
you set sail and learn that everything possible has been
done to make you comfortable. No ship afloat, even those
with full-color advertising in the shiny magazines, does a
better job. Built to haul payloads, the freighter is designed with the limited passenger accommodations balanced in the center of the vessel — where roll and pitch
have the least effect. Today's freighter is completely
equipped with safety and navigation devices. Our room
on the *Wolfgang Russ* was as large as the average American sitting room, and much bigger than cabin-class state-
rooms on the big liners. Even the artist and his wife had
excellent accommodations, and they were put in the
"Hospital." Not because they were ill, but because the
hospital is rented out too. It was a little comical to see
the sign "Hospital" over the door and look in and see all
the paintings of Canada leaned up on something to dry.

Mrs. Lemm is a gym teacher in the Bad Neustadt schools, and said that during the Nazi days they had a rough time of it. My guess is that Herr Lemm has a great talent.

It turned out that we did have a barber aboard. John Wenrick, the professor, happened to mention that he was pretty fair with the clippers, and Horst Zandech, the engineer, produced some. About everybody who needed one got a haircut before we approached the Elbe River. And it turned out, too, that we had a doctor — sort of. He was everybody. Volker Jacobsen, the young man learning the shipping business, had caught himself a wracking cough. This young man amazed us — here we were in our middle age setting out to tour amongst other languages, with hardly more than hello-and-goodbye ability, and this young fellow who had yet to complete his university courses launched merrily into English with us, jubilant at his ability. We were to see a good many young people like him — delighted at knowing something. Too many times, back home, we got the feeling our young folks today look upon learning as something square, if that phrase is still in style, and never really approach learning with enthusiasm. Volker showed what it is like to be glad to know something. But anyway, he had caught a cold, and he hacked and whooped all over the place, and in lack of a doctor everybody on board kept giving him suggestions for a cure. He patiently tried every suggestion, drawing on the pharmacy kept by First Mate Adolf Aselmann, and without effect — proving the old saying that nature cures the disease and the treatment amuses the patient. Also proving that you can get along without a doctor aboard.

Every afternoon the radio officer would bring down the news. This came to him in dots and dashes from the great afternoon newspaper in Hamburg — Axel Springer's

IN HAMBURG SAN' PAUL-LEE

Abendblatt. We were to run into Springer's influence on
German affairs many times, and this was our introduction. Twice, out of respect for the non-Germans aboard,
this boy laboriously translated the whole sheet into English, looking things up word for word in a dictionary.
Most of it came out dubiously. One story said, "Today
gives it much concern totally unsuspecting in Bonn re-
garding numerous problems relating to government."
After we thanked the boy he would dash back up to his
wireless, and if his translations were small he at least
gave us assurance his technical abilities were good. He
said he was studying English because he wanted to mi-
grate to Canada and marry a girl in Toronto who had
refused to go to Hamburg to marry him.

After we had sighted the Outer Hebrides, and gone
past Heligoland into the wide mouth of the Elbe, our
freighter became a sporty place. To eight of us this was
arrival in a far place after a safe crossing, but to thirty-
five crew members it was coming home after seven weeks.
When the first pilot boat pulled alongside, Captain Eichhorst, complaining that last night's beer had been too
warm and his stomach was upset, went to bed. The "nothing" that he had been doing for ten days was all done.
Immediately all the deckhands began experimenting
with the beer to find out what had been wrong with it.
Back home in Maine we have a holdover from antique vir-
tues known as the "Maine Christian Civic League." It is
headed by a dedicated and devoted cleric named Benjamin Bubar, whose purposes seem muddled to many
but whose zeal is above reproach. He wages constant war
on sin, and is particularly mad at alcoholic beverage. I
never heard that his membership list was smoked out, but
he claims to represent a lot of people, and our legisla-
tures always shudder at his approach and kowtow to his

23

remarks. Partly because of him, Maine has a hodge-podge of liquor control laws, most of which are as antique and outmoded as glass lamp chimneys, and many of which are complete absurdities. So any Mainer who goes to Europe and sees how they handle booze has his eyes opened.

Now, on the *Wolfgang Russ,* our steward was seeing that everybody made out, and shortly a deckhand who had merely bowed with me every morning now climbed to the passenger level and became real chummy. As he swung up the companionway, keeping time with his beer, he was singing, "In Hamburg San' Pow-lee . . ." It is a good song, and I could see true and unashamed emotion flooded his heart. Saint Pauli is the waterfront of Hamburg, where sailors come home, and it has many songs. This sailor shook hands again and again, communicating the fervency of his friendly nature, and although I couldn't understand everything I appreciated the high regard in which he esteemed me. Other sailors were shining shoes and pressing pants, and now that the professor had cut everybody's hair the chief engineer cut his.

We soon passed the west end of the great Kiel Canal, and moved up the river past the industries along its banks. The pilot had reduced speed, and evening came upon us before we arrived in Hamburg harbor. There is a restaurant there, with windows looking upon the traffic, and all day long a man sits at a phonograph and plays the national anthem of every ship that goes by — a loud speaker booming it off over the water. For the *Wolfgang Russ,* coming from Montreal, he would hardly play the "Star Spangled Banner," which is a softening thought, but it turned out he didn't play anything. It was dark and late, and he had gone home for the night. We were told we would not go ashore until morning, but the customs men would be aboard early. The night was like trying to sleep on a speedway — derricks loudly unloaded the beans, hides, whiskey, fertilizer and all, with floodlamps everywhere and from all angles the toot of tugs casting on and casting off. Hamburg never closes.

Breakfast was magnificent. The wives of the officers had come aboard as soon as we tied up, to spend the night, and now we had a bevy of beautiful north German girls around the table. And three German customs and immigration men joined us — each in a handsome green uniform with the traditional high-crowned Teutonic cap. Each customs man had, by his place, a bottle of the best French cognac — a small token of friendship and esteem from Captain Eichhorst, who had recovered. Tourists who have been rousted off a passenger liner or a plane upon arrival will not have seen gay disembarking parties like this one at 8:00 A.M. We had not, in ten days at sea, exhausted the larder of the *Wolfgang Russ,* and the steward hopped around. We had everything except a girl that jumped out of a cake, and the radio officer had put on a tape that orchestrated appropriate music. Many a toast was offered and accepted, frequently and warmly we were welcomed to Germany, and special greetings were conveyed from the Free Hanseatic State of Hamburg. Some of the toasts were enunciated again just in case we hadn't heard them the first five times. I confess, very sadly, that the Rev. Benjamin Bubar's name came to mind off and on, as it did all during the next months, and I wondered how he would like a welcome to Germany, and what he would say at the sight of sworn public officials tippling before foreigners and before breakfast. This was but a logical down-east reaction to the confrontation of conflicting philosophies, and that morning we were all very philosophic. I also wondered if the passengers were getting off the *Queen Mary, Queen Eliza-beth* and *United States* all right at Le Havre, Southampton, New York.

Clearing customs is a favorite topic with tourists. Some have troubles, some have none. Ours was hardly worth mentioning — we drank a leisurely breakfast with beautiful women and dashing officers, with soft music and gay laughter, and when we got through we shook hands with everybody, walked down the limber plank to the dock, and found our suitcases sealed and passed. The steward had retrieved our passport from the officials and handed it to us when we tipped him. From the *Wolfgang Russ* we could still hear the tinkle of Mozart, the lilt of feminine glee, and possibly the clink of crystal, sort of. The customs men were settled in, we decided, for a long day's duty which, however demanding, would prove pleasant.

"In Hamburg San' Paul-lee . . ." I sang, and we got into a taxi.

We Pay a Call

For thirty-five years our vista has been the long meadow and orchard through the big kitchen-sink window, and Hamburg is a big city. Our taxi took us to the heart of things — the Hauptbahnhofplatz. Here we confirmed our boat trip home at the travel agency, and then we had to find a hotel. Here began our wonderful associations with everybody we were to meet — and we are sorry, but we cannot report that anybody insulted us, cheated us, seemed uninterested in us, or shouted at us to go home. Several times, now that we tell about our trip, seasoned travelers have said, "Oh, yes — we stayed there; that's the place we had such poor service." It never happened to us. Our very first presentation was a sample of all those to follow. I looked across the Hauptbahnhofplatz at all the hotel signs, and I decided to apply at the Continental — for no reason whatever.

In most German cities the railway station is still important — the Bahnhof. Because Hamburg has more than one, the principal station is the Hauptbahnhof. And the square in front of it is a constantly busy place. As I walked across, leaving Dorothy to sit on the bags until I found a room, I practiced what I was about to say.

The first great hallucination of the American People is one repeatedly bolstered by the travel bureaus, who say, "Oh, nowadays everybody speaks English!" This is hogwash, but it does a great national disservice. We live with the educational delusion that languages are unimportant, and if you ask a boy why he's studying French he says he needs it to get into college. Not one of our Maine teachers colleges gives any foreign language, ancient or modern, and we consequently have no public feeling that speaking a foreign tongue is an accomplishment. The young Volker Jacobsen on the boat butchered English until sometimes we couldn't make out a word, but what is important is that he did it without embarrassment, and with great pride in being able to. We talked about this, wishing some of his intellectual ambition could be communicated to schoolchildren back home, and we

27

made up our minds we were going to do the best we could to get along with as little English as possible. Around Maine, French is common enough so we felt secure with it. Some say Canadian French is no good in France, but this is not true. It can even be an advantage, as we soon found out. I didn't believe my college German would be too helpful — but, again, this is not true. I could remember something of sentence structure, and at least I knew how to pronounce it. I didn't shine as a German student, but all at once the "ist" verbs began coming back to me, and the first time I saw a sign that said "Ausfahrt Freihalten" I laughed just as we used to laugh in class — a German can say "Fahrt" right out in public and not know what it means. And our few days in Montreal and our ten days on the boat had sharpened our ears a little, which helped a lot. Dorothy was getting so she could understand what was meant when she didn't know what was said. And I had done a little review work with the grammars. It took me about as long to cross the busy Hauptbahnhofplatz as it does to spell it, and when I came to the desk in the hotel I asked for a double room with some confidence.

But things don't always happen just so. I expected either a yes or a no, but this clerk said, "übernacht?"

Professor Ham was never very proud of me in the old days, but I think he must have smiled with pleasure in his retreat of eternal rest, suddenly aware that all had not been hopelessly lost. I floundered a bit in undergraduate memories, and came up with that "vowel modified in the plural" list. And I said, "Zwei Nächte, bitte." And from then on I never hesitated again — I would come as near to anything as I could, and like Volker Jacobsen I let it go at that and beamed at my skill. In America, where Education is judged not by what it does but by what it

28

costs, there is abundant need for the people to know of the intense personal satisfaction that comes when, as a result of schools, you can step up to a man in his own country and speak to him, however badly, in his own language.

We stayed three days in Hamburg, feeling things out. We walked along the Alster, saw the botanical gardens, and took some refreshment in Saint Pauli. We inspected the ancient church. And the second day we got on a bus and rode up through Harburg Kreis to call on some people — cousins of friends back home. It was a three-hour ride through the orchard country, and beautiful. Ed Herling, our mailman on the R.F.D. route, told us if we happened to be in that vicinity we should call on his mother's people, so we happened on purpose, and stepped from the bus in a prosperous village with neat stone and brick homes. We didn't find the street right away, so we popped into a grogshop to inquire, and stayed about an hour after a Polish fellow who spoke English found out why we were in town and then introduced us to the assembly.

When we came to the cousins' home a sandy-haired young woman answered my knock, and I could only say, "Herling, Herling!" The poor thing took on a frightened look, and then dawn broke. "Aus Amerika," I said. She said, "Ja, ja!" We were invited in, and spent the afternoon with people who live between airports. She telephoned across town to a sister, and the sister came with two children — three bicycles — and the beer was brought out, and afterwards the tea and cakes, and I got a lot of help from the small boy, who was studying English in school and had thoughtfully brought his dictionary. We gave them a good report from their cousins in Maine. Somehow we had the feeling that their cousins in Maine

pictured their German relatives a little patronizingly —
as if the luckier branch had moved to America. That
night I wrote a long letter from the Hotel Continental to
our mailman back home, and tactfully I tried to correct
this impression. His cousins were well off, fat and handsome, in a modern home with all appliances and gadgets,
in a delightfully landscaped neighborhood. They would,
indeed, probably think the Herling home in Maine was
outmoded. When we left they made us promise to come
back, which we never did, and they walked us to our bus
stop. The youngsters ducked and shook hands, and the
two sisters kissed us *auf Wiedersehen*. We thought our
first sally into the privacies of Europe had come off rather
well.

Breakfast Beer

German coffee is excellent.
They blend and roast after their own fashion, and use a
lot of steam machines, but the average cup is better than
at home, where — let's admit it — you can get a poor cup
of coffee without looking too far. One of the German
coffee companies advertises, "The German housewife
makes the best coffee in the world" — we found that out.
And we ate the European breakfast of hard roll, marma-
lade and coffee because it went with our room, until we

learned to do what the Germans do — eat when you're hungry and have what you want. On the morning we left Hamburg we ate sausages and beer at 6:00 A.M., and this proved not only interesting but nourishing.

The train for Wolfsburg leaves the Hamburger Hauptbahnhof at 6:45, so the clerk in the Continental Hotel got us up in good season and pleasantly revealed that he had learned to speak excellent English since we had arrived. He said when we returned to Hamburg he would have a room for us, and he held the front doors open while I took out our suitcases. "Auf Wiedersehen!" he called, and since we were already three days in Germany we saw no need to smile when he added, "Eine gute Fahrt!" It was still raining in Hamburg, and we threaded carefully through the traffic across the square.

Even at that hour the railroad station was thronged, and those who were not exactly going and coming were standing at counters eating breakfast, and we looked around and saw that they were having sausages and beer. The well-oriented tourist will of course strive not to be conspicuous, so we stepped up and ordered the same. It is not, truthfully, anything I would admire to develop into a major habit, but Dorothy said she would like to set it down in her memories as a great once-in-a-lifetime experience. Then I went to the wicket to get two tickets to Wolfsburg, and when the girl looked up I enunciated distinctly and asked for two tickets to Wolfsburg.

She said, "Where?"

I repeated, "Zwei Fahrkarten nach Wolfsburg, bitte."

I was very careful to make it "fulfsburkh."

It was all Greek to her; she leaned forward and tilted one ear and asked me again.

"Fulfsburkh," I called, "Volkswagenfabrik!"

She understood. "Ach!" she said, "Foylesbeersch!"

"Ja," I nodded, "Foylesbeersch." Somehow in college they hadn't dwelt too much on dialect, and down in Bavaria we were going to tell people how to pronounce Wolfsburg in Hamburg and they would all laugh.

For anybody from Maine, where railroad passenger service died years ago, a ride on a German train is better than reliving your youth. If you are due in Hanover at 9:42 and you look at your watch and it says 9:42 — get off, because you're there. Whenever we had a train on time in Maine it was yesterday's train. And because of our early breakfast and its nature, we soon explored the toilets, and found that with sensible German approach the railroad doesn't provide two conveniences simply because there are two sexes. We had already begun to document ourselves on the general subject of German plumbing, and this was added to the notes. We sped along, finding the German countryside beautiful and interesting, and presently came to Hanover, where we took part for the first time in that great German sport known as *Umsteigen*. There are two words in German every tourist must learn, retain and obey — one is *Umsteigen* and the other is *Umleitung*. *Umsteigen* means to change, and whenever anybody on a train yells "Umsteigen" everybody gets off. An *Umleitung* is a detour, a traffic will-o'-the-wisp that led us many a merry chase into remote sections of West Germany where the tourist was unknown and we became a great curiosity, with profit to all. German highway workers have a way of marking an Umleitung off o'er hill and dale and then going away forevermore. At Hanover we Umsteigened, and presently came to Wolfsburg, where we spent the rest of the day in the patronizing atmosphere of the great VW complex.

Hitler, back when he was largely considered a pleasant fellow, got the idea of making a low-priced automobile that would put the German people on wheels. It wasn't unlike Henry Ford and the Model T. The factory was at Wolfsburg, and because in the socialized scheme everybody owned it, nobody did. When war enveloped everything, the automobile works was converted to military uses and presently the British, French and Americans bombed the hell out of it. But after the war VW's appeared again, and today the vast Volkswagenfabrik is the world's third largest motor vehicle manufacturer. One oddity of their success is their small volume of profit. Newspapers in Germany like to run editorials calling on the government to do something, because everything runs pell-mell day and night and nothing seems to get laid by. But the whole area around Wolfsburg is VW and everybody lives off it, and the town supply of electricity comes from the plant, and so on. We arrived to buy an automobile, and found our whole trainload of passengers had the same idea.

Indeed, railroad travel is largely one-way — people come on the train and drive off in a VW. A free bus meets all trains, and our poshest hotel staff could go to the VW plant and learn about reception and service. On the bus passports are inspected, and there is some cloak and dagger security — but what interested me was the variety of languages spoken. These VW customers come from all over the world, and the bus driver was talking to each one — when he saw our United States passport he shifted from Arabic to English as smoothly as his VW bus shifted from third to high. When we got to the plant we were escorted into a cafeteria lounge, and while our purchase papers were being processed a pleasant young lady showed us seats and asked what we would like to have. She quickly added, in a way that showed this to be a rehearsed recitation, that the drinks were on the house, but were also nonalcoholic — VW couldn't have its customers driving away in a drunken stupor. We suggested coffee, which she brought, and it was excellent, and it was at this point we first became utterly ashamed of being Americans.

We saw them coming through the door — two couples looking like a brass band and advertising in all directions, "Look at us! We are Americans!" They carried paper sacks with red letters that said, "Tax Free American Cigarettes," and below that the imprint of an airline. They were talking altogether too loudly, with much haw-hawing and tee-heeing, and they looked around as if they expected everything they saw to look funny. Dorothy said, "Oh, oh!" and we both lowered our heads and tried to look absent. The four made a beeline for a table, draped their coats unasked over an odd chair at another table where three Spaniards were quietly waiting for their automobile, and one of the men raised his hand and shouted, "Hey, waitress!"

Next to our State Department, here is the greatest hindrance to American popularity abroad. No matter how many thousands of reasonable tourists we export, one batch like this creates the bad impression and makes us all look like numskulls. The waitress came instantly to their table, with no expression whatever on her face, and brought them four coffees. And then we heard the louder man call out, "Hey, waitress — you said you had some American coffee, this isn't American coffee!"

The girl explained to them patiently that it was a percolator coffee, not the steam-driven kind, and that under the circumstances it was the nearest she could come to pleasing them, and she was sorry. "Well, it's a lousy cuppa coffee," said the man. We noticed that everybody else in the place was making believe he didn't hear anything, busy with something else. The waitress said, "I'm sorry," and moved away.

The word *gefallen* is not easy to construe; it means "to please," but instead of saying "I like him" you turn it around and say, "He is pleasing to me." So I had to sit there a minute and wrestle with my rehearsal, and then I went up to the counter, put my hand on the girl's arm, and I said, "We like German coffee, may we have some more?" Then I said, "You know, we're not all like them." She smiled. And said, "I should hope to hell not." I said, "You seem to have facility with the vernacular." She said, "I ought to — I lived three years in New Jersey."

So I said, "Then, you know what I mean, bring us some more coffee and visit a minute." This was a mistake — the four Americans heard us talking English with the girl, and they moved in. "Hello," said the loud one. "Hear you talking English! Name's Anderson. Milwaukee, real estate — what's your line?"

There was one more outbreak. We'd been there perhaps an hour, enjoying everything except the Americans, and they had been with us maybe a half hour, and Anderson reached up and grabbed the arm of a VW man going by. He yelled, "Look, we haven't got all day — if I don't get my car pretty soon I'm going to make trouble for somebody!"

And, do you know, the funny thing is that he got his car almost at once. It was the quickest way to get rid of them, and the whole efficient VW organization moved into high gear and almost at once Anderson & Co. had gone. The girl brought us more coffee, and she said, "For Americans, you don't seem to be in a hurry."

"Wir haben Zeit," said Dorothy.

She said, "We don't see many patient Americans."

35

Spaniards, Australians, Africans — they got their cars and drove away. We lingered, perhaps because we were fun to have around — why not? — and one by one the girl brought VW officials to meet us, and they would sit and visit for a cup of coffee, and we had a most delightful afternoon. Our VW came in due time, we were instructed in its operation, given our papers and maps, and a dozen people shook hands with us, wished us *auf Wiedersehen* and *gute Fahrt*. We drove fifteen kilometers, found a guesthouse and descended for the time being.

The Anderson party had boarded a plane at Milwaukee, changed to a jet in New York, and flown nonstop to Frankfurt. There they boarded a speed train for Wolfsburg, and they came to the VW factory without a wink of sleep since leaving home. Now, with a new car, they had five days to tour Denmark, and they were going to do it if it killed them. We sat in our little guesthouse fifteen kilometers from Wolfsburg and thought about them pushing toward Copenhagen, and how they would loudly narrate their experiences back home in Milwaukee, and we could look through the door into the kitchen and see our cook lovingly nudging our supper along. We were the only guests, and he, too, had time. It was a delicious supper — scrambled eggs with those tiny mushrooms called *Pfifferlinge,* fried potatoes, sweet fried ham, and a great green salad which tourist pamphlets say Americans mustn't eat because it disturbs the functions. The cook came in to ask if everything pleased us.

It was 10:30 P.M. when we got up from the table, and it had been a long day since those featherbeds in the Hotel Continental in Hamburg. "It grieves me," said the cook, "but we do not have overnight rooms; however, I have telephoned and in Gifhorn the hotel is waiting for you. Auf Wiedersehen!"

36

Gifhorn was but a short ride, and we came into town to find the streets jammed with a parade, bands playing and a midnight crowd milling all around. We could see the hotel, and a struggling policeman was trying to straighten out traffic in front of it. We pulled up beside him, and he frantically waved us away. But then he noticed our automobile and he said, "Is new?"

Yes, I said, is new, and we have a room in this hotel — how do we get in to park?

The gay function was some kind of a veterans' rally, and the whole celebration was moving into a big hall directly behind our hotel, but the policeman stopped everything until he had found us a place, and then he helped us carry our bags in. There was a snarl a mile long in no time, and all night we listened to bands and speeches — and we remarked that Gifhorn sure knows how to welcome the stranger.

The bar-girl in the hotel was indeed waiting for us. By the telephone on the wall was a blackboard, and scribbled on it I saw, "Room 2, Englishman." She reached up on the rack and gave me the key for Room 2. "Sleep well," she said.

In Room 2 the featherbeds were deep and wide as a dreamland cloudbank, and although with the drums and loud speakers it wasn't the best night for slumber in Gifhorn, we made out fine — really pleased, considering everything, that we had been billed as Englishmen. Nobody in Denmark, we were willing to bet, was going to make that mistake with the Andersons.

A Delicate Topic

The green salad which disrupts the functions, and against which so many pamphlets warn, is the best introduction to German plumbing — and unless you successfully acquire the *Durchfall* you will not get the most out of your trip. The tremendous technical skill of the German people, otherwise extending in all directions, deserts them completely when they start piping something, and you notice this almost at once. I have asked a great many experienced travelers if they were prepared for the German toilet, and they have said without exception that no agent, no book, no pamphlet gave them an inkling. This is to be blamed, naturally, on the general reluctance of American conversations to speak freely about taking a dump. We don't talk about that, but we circumlocute by warning against green salads and drinking water and we never come to grips. This is a shame, because the minute you land in Germany the common hopper of commerce becomes an intimate item, and anybody who has ever defecated with any kind of regularity across the German Federal Republic knows that a little forewarning would have been a big help. Olympic track champions have never set the time of an

38

ordinary tourist who, after enjoying a green salad, has to find the "00" in the dark, cool corridors of a German inn, and that is when you realize the travel bureau should have been more open-minded about discussing bowel movements. But we are the victims of an ingrown national euphemism where toilets are called rest rooms and the extremely useful word *pissoir* is never heard.

The German people are inherently clean. Back home, we used to smile at the filling station sign "Clean Rest Rooms," because it conveys left-handedly that many are not. Finding an untidy toilet in Germany is an occasion for amazement, not just because the management keeps them clean but because the public helps. The place is washed down, well ventilated, and always acceptable to the most fastidious. True, those who take the scheduled tours may not run into the things we did, but off the beaten path when you begin to meet the people you find the whole subject exciting. First of all, you do not walk into an inn and ask for a room with bath. There are such rooms and they can be had, but this tags you straightaway as an outlander and it is wiser to come by a bath a little later. Mostly, this request forces the management to explain, however it is said, that you are away from home and don't be silly. The room that you get will be large and comfortably furnished, with good mattresses and fluffy featherbeds that are worn on top of you — not under you as back in old-time Maine. There are no sheets as we know them, but the featherbed is buttoned into a clean cotton sacking of sheet material. The room will have a washbowl with faucets marked hot and cold — which may mean something. Often it means hot and cold. There will be no flush toilet and no bathtub. If you find that there are two washbowls lined up side by side, you can wonder why, if they went to the expense of two more pipes, they didn't leave one washbowl out and put in a hopper, but this good question has no German answer. They try, sometimes, to tell you that the building is old, and plumbing came later, but then you will find brand-new hotels with the two washbowls. Two washbowls is not, really, a bad idea for tourists. You can launder shirts, socks and stockings in one and keep the other for ablutions.

Water is no longer a doubtful commodity in Europe. Tourists tell me the pamphlets still urge caution, and sometimes thus explain the use of beers and wines, but today the Germans have as good water as we do and they still drink beers and wines. In parts of Swabia they say lack of iodine contributes to goiter and there is considerable traffic in bottled spring water, but home in Maine one of our more durable industries has been the packaging of Poland Water and I don't know what reason they give for that. The good, clean, bracing aroma of chlorine rising from a bathtub is not an American exclusive — you can smell that in Europe, too.

Now and then in Germany you will find a pussy-bath, which you always find in France, and to anybody from Maine, at least, they have considerable fascination, whether you use them or not. So, instead of a room with bath you will find the essential plumbing is mostly at a distance and is shared. If you want a good hot bath you will speak to the management or chambermaid, and in some of the older and more delightful hotels this turns out to be a monumental matter. In one German hotel the girl told us we couldn't have baths because the bathroom wasn't ready — we found it had been stored with garden tools and chicken wire, and the tub was full of flowerpots. But that was the only time, and in all other places we had baths if we asked, and with two washbowls in our room we could always make do anyway. When you ask the maid or the manager for a bath, if this is your first time, you may think they didn't hear you. But when you know the routine you return to your room, undress, get on your robe, and wait. A tap comes at your door, and the girl leads you down the hall, sometimes up or down stairs, to the bathroom. Once she took me through the lobby, and I bowed at everybody and kept going. Once in a while you will still find a chambermaid who holds a thermometer in the water and then lifts it up so you can see if it is the right temperature, and if you can remember whether you multiply or divide by 5/9ths, and if you add or subtract 32, you can quickly convert centigrade to Fahrenheit and tell. If the young lady hangs around it is only to make sure you have all you want, and in my experience they always left discreetly before I stepped in and scalded myself.

Such a bath is usually put on your bill, although today many a hotel considers the bath *"mit."* It is maybe a mark, and well worth it. The instant you leave the bathroom the maid strides in to give it a thorough cleaning, scouring the tub. Soap and towels are supplied in Germany, and the word for towel is *Tuch.* In some parts of Germany where dialect is exciting the word *Tuch* can be misheard as *Dusche,* which means the little flexible hose you hold over your head to get a shower. It is fun to ask for a towel and have the girl come running in to show you how to use the *douche.* You wouldn't want it otherwise.

So the several bodily functions are kept apart, for there is no flush-hopper in a German bathroom. That is, in the hotels where, as Dorothy put it, the fun is. The hopper is in a small room just big enough for it, usually at the end of a corridor and on an outside wall so it can be vented and cooled. We never found a toilet where the

41

little window to the outside, always left open, gave on to anything besides blank walls and roofing tiles — they are placed with care. If, on a cold morning when exposure seems rugged, you close such a window, the girl will come running the moment you leave and open it again. Some mornings at higher elevations I was touchingly reminded of the old days on the farm when the convenience was on the far end of the barn and we went out wearing mittens.

The piping for any German flush toilet will throw an American plumber into hysterics. The normal feed is a quarter-inch tube, about, and this imposes considerable time between flushes, so waiting for the reservoir to fill often takes longer than waiting for the toilet. In a great many of these small rooms wallpaper is put up after the plumbing is done, and to keep the pattern continuous the decorator just papers right over the pipes — an interesting, if undulating, effect. And behind each and every hopper in Germany stands a little device, often ornamental as well as functional, where you find the long-handled swab brush for cleaning down the porcelain. There isn't a toilet in Germany without this item. True, we have these at home, but a tidy housewife manages to keep them less evident, and with American plumbing they are less needed. Because the German hopper bowl is differently designed.

In our domestic American hoppers the contribution is insinuated directly into the aqueous material, and when the flush mechanism is activated a great dispersal occurs. We get action. It is possible, and actually customary, to use an American hopper without contaminating the porcelain. But a German hopper is made with a little shelf that comes at the point of maximum traffic, and during maneuvers there is no more than a light dew of water on this shelf. The shelf extends forward, toward you, and the

42

exit is straight down. The effect being, you see, that nothing is done in secret. When you arise, a fine feeling of great accomplishment coursing through you, what you have accomplished is right there staring back lovingly, and you feel like clapping your hands and crying, "Good boy!" As the case may be, for this toilet is for men, women and children as they come. Back home what you leave behind is gone forever in functioning finality, but in Germany there is a lingering effect. The bowl is so constructed that the flush, when you flush, doesn't really do very much and you have to hang around after the crime to destroy the evidence.

We found one hotel where the pull-chain was outside the room, so we'd step outside to pull and then come back in to see what happened. They have pull-chains, thumb-levers, push-buttons and pull-up knobs, and sometimes just a valve on the pipe to unwind — but such is the piping and the manner of flow that zeal is lacking. After you have done all you can you grab the brush and police the joint, and you see why the brush is ubiquitous. All over Germany in every other respect you admire their skill, their intelligence, their efficiency — and then wonder about their plumbing. I believe the Brush Cartel has a deal going, and gives the plumbers a cut.

The toilet is variously marked. The term "WC" is common and in all languages means water closet. In hotels where rooms are numbered the bathroom and toilet may be "0" and "00," particularly in Bavaria. The German word for a toilet is the logical *Abort*. They also use the French word *pissoir* commonly, which properly warns the ladies away. Off dining rooms and bars there will often be sexed toilets designated as *Damen* and *Herren*, and *Herren* doesn't mean her'n. You will see "er" and "sie," and sometimes just two pictures, one male and one female. Such is their freedom from our puritanical incumbrances that they do not make light of any of this, except in Bavaria, and the common toilet signs in Maine, pointers and setters, would not seem funny in Germany. Not that they're too funny in Maine.

And this is a good thing to know. The general subject of elimination and the European attitude towards it needs contemplation by the tourist, and they are never crass and rude and comical about it, but sensibly straightforward. More could be added to this exegesis by considering other countries, but it is Germany that has the reputation for love of efficiency and admiration of mechanics — and it is in Germany that you ask why they stick to what they have. It is something you sit and think about.

Never a Farmer

The best hotels and the best food in Europe is in Germany. What makes this sweeping generalization correct is the great number of hotels you find in all parts of the country, and you need have no hesitation about any of them. We can, and will, mention places in other countries where food was equal to the German food — but day in and day out, town after town, Germany is set up with an ideal hotel situation for the vagabonding tourist. And you will find that these small places where the fun is, and where the people worth meeting pop in for their beer — the places you would like to go back to sometime — are family operated and cater almost altogether to local purposes — the tourist is not important to them. The pity is that so many who go on scheduled tours miss the pleasure of these small inns, and put up instead at city hotels and places geared to handling the foreigner. Things happen, instead, when the local gentry collects, and the football team pops in for its post-game celebration. I recall one hotel where the young woman said yes, she had a room, but no, she was sorry — she never rented rooms on a Saturday night because it was dance night and the place was too noisy. She would feed us and find us a room in another hotel — but dance night was no night to spend with her. I suppose some tourists, misunderstanding, could have gone along and told later how they were uncivilly refused a room — and thus missed the unforgettable experience of dance night in Gasthaus Adler.

Nearly all these smaller hotels observe one day a week as rest day, and the place is closed. The day varies, so there is always one hotel in the area that remains open, and there is no need to let *Ruhrtag* bother you. If it is rest day a sign on the door will say so. If there is no sign — pull in where the driveway says "Parking for guests only." Along about three or four in the afternoon, a logical time for wise tourists to begin looking, you will find the big dining room and the beer hall polished and empty. Except for a rich brown-gravy smell that is typical of these hotels there is no immediate evidence of occupancy. But the brown-gravy smell, coming probably from the pot of goulash soup in the kitchen — that is the commonest denominator — is a far finer welcome than any greeting from a doorman or bellhop. And, of course, there is no doorman and there is no bellhop.

What you do next is critical. You can thump the little handbell on the bar, which is intended for that, and wait until somebody appears, which he will do almost at once. Or you can just make yourself at home. I found it was pleasantest for all if I just wandered out into the kitchen, and sometimes upstairs, until I found somebody stacking empty beer bottles, or slicing carrots, or waxing a hall, or sometimes just reading a newspaper by the window. These people live in their hotels, and time after time the husband turned out to be cook and his wife the barmaid and waitress. When I found somebody I would ask for a double room, in German, and almost every time this was the total extent of all negotiations. Yes, I could have a room.

The Statler-Hilton organization goes through a lot of foofaraw the German innkeeper avoids. The man has said yes, so what else is there to say? Now you go to your automobile and get your wife and your bags, and you both carry them up to your room, and you are all set for some of the greatest hospitality and care you can find anywhere. Sometimes the owner will carry your bags up, sometimes he yells "Gretchen!" and a pretty little fifteen-year-old girl appears *schnell-schnell* and trots up with them as if she had a daisy in each hand. Sometimes an aged *Putzfrau* staggers in and she'll do it. Mostly, if you choose to try to fit into the scene, you will do it yourself, and you size up each hotel as you arrive. Elevators are hard to find, and we discovered that any hotel with elevators usually had tedious Saturday nights.

After the war, when wandering peoples were a problem, Germany had strict rules about registering at a hotel — you had to show your papers, prove who you were, and your whole biography went down on a form, with a carbon copy to go to the police, but as so often happens with strict rules in time, the opposite became popular. Now you merely write your name if they ask you to register at all. Many times we signed as we left, or later in the evening, or the next morning. Sometimes they will hand you a key at the bar, sometimes you find the key to your room in the door — and many times we went up to pick out our own room. Indeed, some places we selected a room before we found anybody to ask about one. The key is always attached to some kind of a great big blob, so you can't very well put it in your pocket and wander out of the hotel with it. You are expected to leave it at the bar every time, and it gets hung on its hook. But you soon discover that every time you come back for it the barmaid says it's *"oben,"* and you go up to find your room unlocked and the key in the door — the chambermaid has tidied up. At first you may have some wonderment about your valuables while you were at the museum or taking a boat ride. But these people are completely honest, and we never ran into anything otherwise. What we did, we soon left the lock open, left the key in the door, and never gave security a thought. We never lost anything.

The same with wardrobes. There are few closets, and every hotel room has a wardrobe with keys. We never locked one. You never need to. I remember one place I left a handful of loose coins on a table, and when we came back the maid had done the room, and she'd piled my coins up neatly for me.

Whenever we were asked to sign a register upon arrival, I would put my occupation down as "Farmer." You have no idea how much good-nature this generated — because in Germany no farmer would ever sleep in a hotel room. The very idea was hilarious, and every time I did it the innkeeper would laugh. Later, as my German improved, I refined it a little and I would set down "Torfbauer." A *Torfbauer* is a peat farmer — poorest of the poor and lowest of the low, whose land is useful only to be cut up and sold for fuel. None of the innkeepers ever believed I was a farmer, let alone a peat farmer, and they would chuckle with me and become affable and friendly. Many an evening, after that, we would be partaking of the merriment around the dining room, and people would look at us and smile, and it was because the innkeeper had told people of our little joke.

In these hotels an American tourist must never mistake restraint for indifference. They will leave you strictly alone, but at your slightest request they will respond beautifully. Sometimes when you think you are being ignored they have anticipated you and are merely waiting for you to ask. One evening at table I said to Dot that we ought to get a couple of bottles of Coke to take up to the room. So on our way up I stopped at the bar and asked for two bottles of Coke. "They are already in your room," the girl said. The waiter had overheard us at table. Little things like this happened all the time — but much of it, I'm sure, was our own approach, and the care we took to be friendly, and never pushy and demanding.

In these small hotels we often asked the waiter to let the cook make us something — instead of picking from a menu. And sometimes we'd see the chambermaid scoot out a back door, cross the street and thump on a storefront that had long since closed for the evening. The cook needed something to please us and he sent out for it. Since Dorothy was on a recipe-hunting expedition this gave us a chance to stick our heads into the kitchen to convey our thanks, and the next thing I knew Dot would be stirring a pot of oxtail soup and tasting from the spoon. After you have roomed yourself, coming down to dinner at a proper hour can be a surprise. The dining room, so dark and empty when you went up, is now full of people. We got no figures on the dining-out habits of the German people, but it must be high. There is no "quick lunch" aspect to this — most of the guests have settled in for the evening. They come by ones, and they come by families. If it is the headquarters of the football team there will be one table in a corner reserved for it — with trophies and photographs on the wall. There are many clubs, but not at all like our Rotary-Kiwanis-Lions stuff. Commonest is the shooting club, which dines and drinks and then rises one by one to shoot at targets on the dining room wall with an air rifle. In some places we saw bowling clubs, and members get up two by two to go out to the alley, roll a box apiece, and come back to their beer and sausage.

As an evening wears along a warmth is generated, and as strangers we found ourselves very easily included. A glass would be lifted at a neighboring table with, "Zumwohl!" We would respond, "Sehr wohl!" Then we would be four at a table. The highest we ever hit was thirty-five people, but that included a football team. One of the greatest sights in Germany is to see a waitress adroitly handling the orders of thirty-five different people at one table, never missing a trick, never giving the Steinhager to the Kirschwasser, and making change out of the leather pouch under her apron. She has to lift her apron to get at the pouch, and as the evening progresses and the pouch gets fatter, she begins to look like a pregnant kangaroo.

A supper in a brown-gravy German hotel is as far from an American meal as Germany is. "Please, eat while it's hot," they say, and you may finish your plate before anybody else at table is served. Almost everything is cooked on order, and no cook will send a plate to table until everything is to his liking. Nobody is in a hurry, and the table is yours as long as you care to sit there. Conversation is as important as food. And no waitress or waiter has yet been known to plunk down your tab as if asking you to pay up and leave, when he or she thinks you have had your meal. Not even upside down. They'll bring it soon enough when you ask for it, and not until.

Many times we ran into the Manhattan-Martini ideology. Whenever we got chummy with a barkeep, who is just the landlord usually, he would ask us about Manhattans and Martinis. At home we're perfectly able to get along indefinitely without either, but they seemed to have the idea all Americans live on them. Some of them had taken the trouble to learn how to mix these drinks, and were all ready should any American tourist stop by. Now they had some American tourists who didn't want any. But the mixed drink is something the American tourist wants to leave at home. We learned, for one thing, to ask always for the local beer and the local wine. There is parochial pride, and we had done a nice thing.

One night I asked for two Cokes to take to the room to drink later if we got thirsty, and the landlord would have none of it. No, sir. He would leave the Cokes in the cooler, and when I wanted them I would ring my bell and he would bring them. They would get warm on the bedroom table. I woke up drier than an August sermon about three o'clock, but I didn't have courage enough to touch the button. If I had pushed, he would have risen from his featherbed, pulled on a robe, gone down to the bar, got my Cokes, taken them to the kitchen, found a tray, added glasses, put on a bottle opener, come up to our room, and served us. Then he would have gone back to the bar and added 20c to my bill. It wasn't worth it, and I thirsted until breakfast.

Not one German hotel ever showed us discourtesy or lacked in warm, friendly hospitality. In almost all of them we made friends and passed happy hours with German people who ignored our feeble attempts at their language and politely helped us with syntax and vocabulary, and often invited us to their homes. A Berlitz course is a good thing, but a good substitute is the friendly application of a little Asbach — which is a German cognac of unestimated linguistic facility and a fine cement for international goodwill. Its best effect is in its native lair. After a brown-gravy supper.

And a Wedding, too

Back home we drove a Ford station wagon and didn't know much about foreign compact cars. People with a Saab are supposed to make fun of VW's, and so on, and once in a while somebody is supposed to shout, "Buy American!" but the subject had passed us by. Now, setting out for Holland and Belgium in a new VW, we found we had made a good choice, and that the brand name is important. We'd not only bought a car but joined a tourist club. The experience with the policeman in front of the hotel at Gifhorn is merely a sample.

The next morning the crowds had gone and the convention was over, and just across the way was a hardware store. I wanted to buy some good German skinning knives to bring home to my trail cronies in the Maine woods, so I went in and found they had two. I picked up a couple of dozen of them before we came home, but was never able to get more than two at once, and often a store would have but one. This introduced us to another wonderful German word — *Fahrtenmesser*. A *Messer* is a knife, and this means a traveler's knife. It's the same thing that we call a hunting knife, and I figured my friends would like to own one from Germany — particularly when they heard what they are called. So we came out of this store and found seven Germans standing around our new VW, and at first glance I thought it must have caught fire or something. They were just looking at it — it was a new model just off the line and they hadn't seen one yet. I lifted the front and rear hoods, demonstrated the four-way flashers, tooted the horn, and gave them the four-dollar show. Then we put in our suitcases and took off, and they stood there wishing us a good trip and waving goodbye. But in this demonstration I found our directional lights weren't working, and as a result learned how to read the VW map the VW people had given us in Wolfsburg. They had given us road maps of all Europe, and now I found that unless a town has a VW agent it doesn't get on their map. Thus the camaraderie of the VW membership began to show up, and we pulled in at the next town on our map to get the directional lights fixed. There was no charge, and the friendly mechanics gave us suggestions about what to see and how to get there, and we learned that touring problems are best left to the VW dealer, and never mind about American Express.

The only definite date we had was to meet George and Betty Morrill in Munich for the Oktoberfest, and that was weeks ahead. We planned to lazy through Belgium and Holland, find a place to leave the VW in Calais, and go the boat trip to the United Kingdom so we wouldn't have to do any British wrong-side driving. And come noon of the day we left Gifhorn we had our first picnic. We went shopping, while the man fixed our lights, and got some bread and cheese, a little cold meat, a bottle of wine and some sweet pastries. And a Bingen Pencil.

Once upon a time the Bishop of Bingen called his monks and priests together for a powwow on church matters, and at one point the suggestions were so good the Bishop decided to make some notes, and he asked for a pencil. Nobody in the whole assembly had a pencil. But a few minutes later the Bishop felt like a drop of wine, and he called for a corkscrew. Every priest and monk immediately handed up his corkscrew, and to this day a corkscrew is called a Bingen Pencil. I asked a girl in a store for a Bingen Pencil and she said, "Ja!" Then I asked her what the correct German word might be, and it turns out to be the logical one — "cork-puller." You can't ask any language to be more logical than that. The cork-puller came to 15c, and the bottle of wine to 35c — and we began a noonday custom that gave us a lot of pleasure. Each day we'd pull up under some trees, or along a canal, or by a beetfield, unlimber our Bingen Pencil, and lunch. It was inexpensive, and as we were having hearty dinners every night it was sufficient.

We came that afternoon into Nordhorn, and we thought Gifhorn to Nordhorn made a good journey. The hotelman said he was having a big wedding party that evening, and we might find the place noisy until about 3:00 A.M. Having had bands in Gifhorn the night before we thought this might be a pleasant change, so we moved in. The wedding was a huge success. If Consolidated Tours could include a good wedding in every all-expense, ten-day package it would be a good thing. The third time I kissed the bride the new husband seemed concerned, but her father was a good sort and I didn't want him to think I wasn't grateful. He kept insisting Asbach, which is very fine for toasting brides, and nobody seemed to care that we were three thousand miles from home and mooching. Three o'clock came before we hardly knew it. "How do we explain this to the people back in Maine?" Dorothy asked. The next morning we shopped around for a gift to the bride, and we had it delivered with our best wishes for a long and happy life.

At Nordhorn we also attended our first market day. These things come in different towns on different days, and we saw dozens of them. Held on the ancient market squares, they complicate overnight parking if you don't pay attention. For if market day is on Wednesday, and you show up Tuesday evening, you don't want to leave your automobile even close. I don't know what they do to you, because we never got caught. Long before daybreak the farmers and hucksters move in, and I would not want to be the tourist who tampers with this tradition. In Nordhorn we saw the women going with their string bags and we followed them to the marketplace — where we bought some apples and pears. The apples didn't have too much flavor, but the pears were sweet and good. The flower stalls were beautiful, and we noticed that almost everybody was taking home some small bouquet — I liked best the fat lady riding a bicycle through traffic with two long-stemmed bronze mums, unwrapped, across the handlebars. Standard chrysanthemums were retailing at less than $2.50 a dozen — great blooms as big as a sun. Nordhorn gave us our first chance to see the German public out in numbers. They are a purposeful people, striding straight ahead, but always courteous and always orderly. They dress well and look good in the aggregate. We were to see Paris, and even London's Carnaby Street, but here in Nordhorn we saw good-looking people well turned out who didn't need to nod at anybody. The German woman, although often heftier, dresses stylishly until you get to her shoes — she likes sensible footwear, and even in party clothes she goes like a Black Forest hiker.

There were some men at the Nordhorn market, of course, but I don't remember too much about them.

Our First Britisher

About the only filth you'll find in Germany is around their roadside picnic areas. They have huge signs up that say "Bitte Sauberhalten," but most of those we paused at were littered and sometimes noisy smelling. And as we left Nordhorn on our way to Holland and Belgium we struck the scrub-brush hour — almost every building we went by had some woman out with a pail and mop, washing even into the streets. There is no sign of what our own vote-seeking politicians would call poverty, but at one place we came upon a cluster of shacks that caught our attention — it looked like a squatter settlement along the tracks. They turned out to be toolsheds for communal garden plots at the edge of town, and as it was the clean-up hour they were all getting soap and water! But if we thought Germany was nasty-neat — then we came to Holland.

This was our first confrontation with customs officers — at Hamburg the steward had managed for us and we never really came to grips and valises. For long years we had listened to others tell of wild experiences with European customs and immigrations, and we wondered how we'd fare. But Europe has advanced the spirit of inter-relations even more than the practice of it, and the Economic Community has made border hopping a cinch. Since every motorist must have liability insurance, which boils down to a document called the "Green Sheet," we had been told by the VW people to protect this with our lives. We held the Green Sheet up for the Dutch customs man and he nodded, smiled, and waved us on. We were miles into Holland before we realized he hadn't stamped our passport — hadn't even looked at it — and we had no souvenir of the crossing. After that we always asked for the rubber stamp at the boundary, and such is the informality of today's border guarding that this request was often a big nuisance. They'd have to go and hunt around and find a stamp, and then a stamp pad, and later at Denmark the man said he forgot his stamp that day and couldn't help us, but would gladly sign his name.

Holland is lovely. Tidy to a fault, with no evidence of poor housing, and, except for Belgium, the wonderland of flowers. We saw the wooden shoes and paused by canals to watch the boats, and did the things in Holland one is supposed to do. And we saw the other side of Holland — the miles upon miles of vast industry which clashes with tulips and the quaint headgear of the girl on the Old Dutch Cleanser can. We have a Philips plant in Maine, and some of our friends work at it, so we had positive instructions to stop at Eindhoven and say hello to this and that executive of the company — men who at one time or another had been in Maine. I'm sure none of our friends who work for Philips in Maine have much of a notion what Philips is like at Eindhoven. In the United States industry likes to farm things out — if you need a bolt to fit something you are making you get a bolt factory out in Indiana to make it for you. But if Philips needs a bolt, they set up their own bolt factory, and because they need a lot of things they have a complex that goes on and on and is not really much of anything a sensitive tourist wants to dwell on. Nor is Eindhoven the Holland you go to see. We were glad the day turned out to be Saturday and we couldn't get to see anybody.

But here began to churn in us the Great Doubt. Everybody remembers the big hullabaloo in 1967 when George Romney came right out in honesty and said he had been "brainwashed" about Vietnam, and the press and television and the Washington big-shots all gave him a hard time. Well, you don't have to circulate very long in foreign places before the Great Doubt wells up in you, and you understand just what Romney meant. The American People know more things that aren't so than anybody else in the world. We continue to believe the most absurd things, and are so completely and intensely brainwashed that ninety percent of those who read this very sentence won't believe me. I remember when Bob Hope went to Russia and came home with some motion pictures the Russians had "permitted" him to make, and he showed them on television. One sequence showed a suburb of some Russian city with television antennae sticking up from every roof, and Hope called attention to the aerials. Then, after a Bob Hope pause he sprung his gag line and he said, "No sets!"

What incredible ignorance on the part of Hope's great national audience led him to believe that this would prove funny to the American People? What has had to happen to us, as a nation, to make us laugh at Russians because we are told they all have television antennae, but have no television sets? Multiply this a thousandfold as you move about in foreign lands and begin to see how things really are, and you come up with the Great Doubt. You think on the smug provincialism of your own homeland, a great nation which seems to feel nobody else anywhere else really has anything. You feel sorry for Romney. And having seen the VW plant, and now some of the Philips layout, we began to realize a good part of our touring was being devoted to a deflation of the Good American Supposition. Aerials without sets? Of course the Russians have sets. How many Americans are immediately willing to believe that when it comes to television reception our domestic sets are rather poor? It's a matter of light scanning, and we do not project as clear a picture as they do in Europe. In Europe they say, "Oh, yes — we perfected television technically before we geared for production." At the time we were there color TV had not been perfected to their liking, and consequently the time-payment public had not gone through a period of blue Indians and green Negroes, which was the American price for premature production. One look at Eindhoven and you suspect perfected color transmission will soon be available to Europe.

It is, or it should be, an abashing experience for an

58

American to learn, after years of brainwashing, that there are some areas in which we do not necessarily excel, and that our judgments are not always unanimously admired abroad. The Bob Hope theology that we are "slumming" if we travel is not a happy companion, and there are many times when we should be more humble.

Belgium, again, asked to see our Green Sheet, and after Holland, which has much tourist publicity, we found Belgium greatly undersold. We thought the Germans did much with flowers, and the Dutch even more — but we never saw posies until we hit the tuberose begonias of Belgium. Time and again we stopped our VW to get out and walk among them. We told a man they were beautiful, and he said, "Yes, and they are beautiful by ones." Every plant, lost in the profusion of Belgian miles, was even so nurtured by ones. I have never seen any crop so beautiful as the Belgian begonia bloom.

Somewhere between Westmalle and Schofen we came upon "The Bellhouse" and it remains a standout amongst our European inns. Some insight into Flemish came when the German *Glocke* showed up as *Klokker*. We are convinced the Klokkenhof Bredabaan is Belgium's best. It sits a little back from the highway in a horseshoe grove, and we drove in to park by the side. I stepped in to be greeted by a young man in full dress — white tie if you please. He bowed, and I could see the casual manner of gaining a room in Germany no longer would do. I expected German would answer, and it did, and he conveyed us to a room as modern and comfortable as anything to be found in a Holiday Inn or a HoJo. I have never been "roomed" anywhere with such full diplomatic charm, nor was anything at the Klokkenhof to be less delightful.

Belgium has the greatest per capita beer consumption

figure in the world. With legends of Bavarian thirst oft-heard, I hadn't expected this. We wandered from our room, after brushing up, out onto the patio and terrace, where we found some Belgians trying to set new records, with the floral surroundings and the warm afternoon sun congenial, and we bowed pleasantly to some of them and took a table. Stouter, perhaps, than the Germans, but equally well dressed, these people delighted us with their conversations — although we had no idea what they were saying. The slightest whisper came from the deep belly, and while things had a German tone they were anything but. With memories of "Foylesbeersch" for Wolfsburg we knew already what can be done with words, and we harkened to Flemish in amazement. The young man in the dress suit, tails whipping behind him, came to oblige us and asked for our passport as we signed his register for him. He had not guessed our origins, and when he saw the United States eagle he immediately used English — a straightforward, smooth, cultured English that showed no trace of labor. He brought our beers, and as he served other customers we heard him not only talk to them in his own language but also in French and German. I have known hotel clerks at home who have all they can do to talk one language.

The afternoon passed delightfully, with birds singing amongst the roses, and at dinnertime we made twenty-two at table. Our young man, tails still flying, served us all, and except for a chambermaid he was the only staff we saw. As if he had nobody else to worry about he met us at the door, seeming to know precisely when we would come through it, and he escorted us in stately dignity to a table. We have never seen, anywhere, a dining room so impeccably served. And while we were King and Queen, he lavished equal attention on the other twenty. Nobody had to ask for anything — it was at your hand before you asked. We had an aperitif, soup, poultry, vegetables, salad and dessert — and sat there two hours. He selected a wine, and without our asking he brought us final cognacs. At one point Dorothy said, "I think I'd take a bit more chicken," and before I could reach for the silver tray over the small flame he had it by her side and was selecting just the piece she wanted. Naturally we acted throughout as if we were accustomed to this all the time, and never did otherwise at home — but I never did get fully second-natured about tasting the wine. I always felt conspicuous about it.

Well, in Maine a cheap bottle of Chianti costs over two dollars in the state stores, and if you want a wine that merits the tasting routine you'll drop real cash. And in Europe, since we always asked our waiter to select a wine, I had a two-way taste job. Not only to see if it was good, but to see what each waiter thought was our kind. These could be demanding decisions for somebody who knows one wine from another, but for me it was only a formal rote and after I'd gone through it I didn't know much. But I did gain this: I decided all the wines were good and all the waiters geniuses.

With tea, beverages, dinner, room, bath and breakfast, and free parking as well as wear and tear on the waiter's tails, our bill for one of our finest visits in Europe was pleasantly modest. I gave the boy two $10 travel checks, and he gave me some change. Although his bill included tips, I felt a warm wave of philanthropy mount during the sweet sadness of parting, and I pressed a few extra coins in his hand. He closed the VW door for Dorothy after shaking hands with both of us.

As Eindhoven had tarnished the charm of Holland, we found Ostend did this for Belgium. It is a big resort, and as it lies just across from England it draws the holiday trade. An American is not so noticed there. We stayed long enough to see the place and get its feel, but it was not our kind of fun. We thought we'd pay our respects to the invasion beaches, and I stepped into an alehouse to inquire the road out of town to the Dunkirk area as a place to begin. Here we met our first Britisher, and he set the pace for our upcoming visit to England.

Here were three men in white jackets behind the bar, and before it was this sandy-haired fellow with brushy moustache, wearing tweeds, and very busy propitiating the long evening ahead. There was nobody else. Three waiters and one customer. The waiters looked up, expecting me to order something, and as the tweedy one drew on his glass I said, "Would you set me on the road to Dunkirk?"

At this the tweedy chap turned with a look of utter scorn and he called at me, "Queue! Queue!"

As soon as we got to England we realized what a preview this had been — today when a baby is born in England they teach it first to cry, "Queue!" The submissive knee gently flexed to royalty is nothing to the submissive standing in line that has rendered the British docile. Britons, never to be slaves, are slaves to the foolish queue. The three waiters glanced at the poor little Britisher in his tweeds and his cups and began to laugh, and one of them told me the way to Dunkirk. As I left I hove a coin on the bar and said, "Buy him a Mickey Finn!"

Manitoba Neighbors

Twice in our lifetime our country has risen bravely to the occasion and, at great expense and without hope of reward, has sallied forth to solve the problems of Europe. I can remember being handed a small flag and lined up with my classmates in grade school to march to the railroad depot and see the soldiers go to fight the Kaiser. That was the last great war that had good songs, and while we tots waved our flags at the doughboys we sang "Keep the Home Fires Burning While Your Hearts Are Yearning." I can remember other home-front activities they thought up. Food stamps. Mother told me to stand by a certain tree and not move until she came back, and then she went to buy a pound of sugar with ration stamps. After the war we had a million-aire move into our town and they said he made all his money on sugar during the war. And I remember a man in a uniform who came to school and said he was a major in the army, and the soldiers were really having a bad time of it in the trenches and to help them we would all have to be very thrifty. He was going to give us a recipe for bread that he wanted us to take home. He wanted all our mothers to help win the war by baking this bread. So he wrote the recipe on the blackboard and the teacher gave each of us a clean sheet of paper and we took the recipe home. My mother looked at it and said, "Humph!" She said it was a much more expensive loaf of bread than the kind she baked anyway, and since my mother was always the world's best bread baker we let the war run along. And I can remember knitting washcloths for the soldiers. The teacher gave us all a set of needles and a ball of string, and every day for so many minutes we'd sit in school and knit on a washcloth. When you're nine or ten years old these things don't fetch a war too close, and from the 1917–18 affair we also remember, "Where do we go from here, boys? Where do we go from here? Across the sea to Germany to drink the Kaiser's beer!"

Yes, and the next time when I was past the critical age and had productive acres on which to grow essential foods we saw more of the same. We contracted to plant a big field of beans, and then couldn't get any tractor gasoline. Every time a tank truck came and dumped gasoline at our local filling stations people who were not growing beans would go and fill up, and by the time we got to town with our cans the gasoline was all gone. They gave us ration tickets for gasoline, but you had to run around and locate your own gasoline. I had two five-gallon cans, and two or three five-gallon tickets a week would have done just fine, but when I signed up with the War Production Board to grow beans the Office of Price Administration sent me seventeen thousand tickets which were all good for one gallon apiece, if there had been any gasoline. They told me to be sure and sign each ticket as I used it, and I said I thought it was much better back when we baked Victory Bread and made washcloths. I don't think we had seventeen thousand gallons of gasoline in our whole community all during the war. The reason I mention this is because we came from Ostend down towards Calais, and we stood on the beaches of Dunkirk and had thoughts.

It is not cheerful to stand thus in tranquillity and reflect on history. I remember this happened to my grandfather. When he was an old man he went back to Gettysburg one time and reflected. Until then he had always talked about Gettysburg as a hero should. He had been in the first day's action, and the historian says, "At dusk the gallant 16th Maine withdrew, if 34 officers and men may be called a regiment." Grandfather used to tell about it, and how he fired his musket sixteen times that day, ". . . and every time I saw my man." I have the musket still, with his initials carved on the stock, and it stands in our front room corner as memorial to one of mankind's bloodiest idiocies. But after Grandfather revisited the battlefield of Gettysburg he never talked about it again in just the same heroic way. Tears would drop onto his beard and he would change the subject. So, Dunkirk.

Campers and picnickers were having fun amongst the concrete and what debris is left, and out on the beach were bathers. It was to be the same with us wherever we saw the relics of war — cemeteries for the brave men who died for France, or the brave men who died for the Fatherland, or the brave men who died for democracy and liberation and freedom. In those lands this all goes back to the Huns and the legions of Caesar, and it is still there with the maneuvers of French troops in the Vosges Mountains and the mighty installation of the United States at Kaiserslautern. In Ostend we saw the bare knees of gay English girls pedaling their Irish mails gleefully about the Belgian resort, and we came along past the grim memories of Dunkirk to busy Calais, where we would pay French money to ride on an English ship.

Along the canals we saw people sitting under umbrellas as if dramatizing some of de Maupassant, but we didn't see any of the long poles snag a fish, and suddenly we came to the French customs. Before we could get the window rolled down the man caught sight of our Green Sheet and waved us through, and I said, "Vive la France!" Nobody knows why we have a town in Maine called Calais, which we pronounce "cal-lus." Settled in 1779, our Calais has no derivations from the French city. Many Old World place names were selected by early Maine settlers for no reason at all — which accounts for Berlin, Madrid, Lisbon, Norway, Paris, Jerusalem, and many another. And as we expected to visit many European places with Maine names we had come prepared. On statehouse stationery our governor had composed and signed a formal document introducing us "to whom it may concern," and we were goodwill ambassadors in his name.

Calais would be the first place we could hand out one of these, and we wondered if maybe we would get the key to the city and be honored at a banquet. But our entry into this fine old city turned out to be less than magnificent — we promptly got revolving the wrong way in a rotary, and when we stopped, a large and conspicuous policeman was precisely beside us. I am not by nature scairt of policemen. My mother always told me if I got lost to find a policeman. The policeman is my friend. This one proved my mother correct. In my best Canuck I apologized, stated with misplaced *le*'s and *la*'s that I was a stranger in the land, and with great presence of mind I said I was looking for the service of the Volkswagen, s.v.p. I spread my hands in a Gallic gesture that threw us on his mercy, and he broke into a grin and said, "Where did you learn the French?"

66

This is a good question. I learned my French in school and college, but it has been embellished constantly by the presence in Maine of some three hundred thousand French-speaking Quebeckers. It is the kind of French where you go into the store and say, "Avez-vous des flashlight batt-ree?" It is a French that has been separated from Mother France by three hundred years of naturalization in a foreign place — where a staircase is still a "ladder," and if you say thank you they will answer, "B'envenu!" I don't know if *je vous en prie* and *n'a pas de quoi* are understood in Waterville and Biddeford, but I would be accounted highbrow if I used them there. To the policeman in Calais I could easily have answered, "Back home in Maine," but nobody in Europe knows anything about Maine. They know Chicago and Hollywood and New York, and the Grand Canyon and Niagara Falls — but never Maine. But the French of course know about Quebec, so I told him I lived near Montreal. He nodded, and then shook his head and said, "Tch, tch!" Thus we were welcomed to Calais.

This policeman was tall, and while he directed us to back into a driveway and turn around, and then how to get to the Boulevard Victor Hugo and the VW agency, it occurred to me that the VW has another touring feature. It is so low-slung that everybody who tries to give you directions has to stoop and stick a head in the window. In Europe, where direction-giving can run into half-hour sessions, this is a distressing position to hold. So this policeman taught me to stop, set the hand brake, get out, and conduct inquiries erect. This is much better, and at times it led to invitations to step in and continue the discussion over a wine. Back in Maine pointing down the road for a tourist never becomes the social event the

French are able to make of it, and because this policeman was tall I caught on early.

Again, although now in a new language, the VW man was all the tourist bureau we needed. Yes, he would keep our VW while we were in England, and he thought we were wise to leave the wrong-side traffic to the *anglais*. He would perform the service checkup while we were gone, and he would take us to the boat when we were ready to go. He knew of a hotel, and suggested some restaurants and said we would find Calais exciting.

I don't see how a tourist would otherwise find our hotel in Calais. He said to go out the road to Paris, but not beyond city limits, and on the left we would see a tobacco shop. It might be lighted and it might not, but just behind the sign that said "tobacco" we would see another small sign reading, "Hotel." We drove past it twice before we saw it, and it was not lighted. It was a sign at least one foot long. The door below it was locked, but the hotel was plainly a part of the tobacco establishment, which was also a bar, and when I asked the bartender if he had a room he said yes and nodded toward the corner. An inside door led to the same stairway gained by the locked outside door. He gave me a key to Room 4, and the same key unlocked the outside door. Very simple. We found our room fresh and clean, even newly painted, adequately plumbed, and our window looked out on a group of Old World back yards, chicken coops and window ledges hanging with flowers. Nobody asked us our names, and nobody waited on us. There was room on the street for our VW. We bathed, got into eating clothes, and came down in due time to find out if France was to receive us with the cordiality we had already enjoyed in three other nations.

The bar was busy. We nodded at folks, watched a

card game at a corner table, and I patted a small boy on the head who was having a wine with his mother. He was five. Back in Maine he would have to be twenty-one. But he looked healthy and intelligent, and so did his mother. I watched, and when they left hand in hand they didn't stagger at all. Neither did we, and after an hour or so with the neighborhood people we struck out to find a restaurant. We found one and had an excellent French meal, falling in with two young men at the next table, and when we came back to our hotel the bar was closed and our landlord was tidying up. In a few minutes he came up to our room with three cognacs, which we hadn't ordered, and he visited with us to make sure we were happy with our room. He said he had some relatives in Manitoba, and wondered if we knew them. He thought their name was Sansoucy, but if his mother were alive she would know for sure. It was long ago. Goodnight, he said, sleep well.

We did, until a rooster crowed and I thought I was back on the Maine farm until I looked out the window and saw the back yards of Calais. So we had an early start on our preparations to visit Merrie England.

Another Policeman

There will always be an England. She will go on and on in two ways. One is in the hearts and minds of all people everywhere who trace their origins back to the tight little isle and judge her by Magna Carta, muffins, Shakespeare, Sherlock Holmes, Richard of the Lion's Heart, and such things. But as you come to England looking for Alice down a rabbit hole and the cakes of King Alfred, you find the cards are scattered all over and Alfred is long gone. England, as per our tweedy friend in Ostend, is a long interminable queue of patient people lined up to find out what they're waiting for.

England is the refresher course for College English 1–2. It is the complete answer to the oral exam at the end of the senior year. You can't turn a corner without bumping into something you once studied. But all the treasures and all the memories and all the history have been left with an odd kind of custodian who can be as rude and baffling one moment as he can be charming another. The first problem of the tourist is language. In the *New Yorker* the British Travel Ministry advertises that "they speak your language." They don't. We never found out

70

what they speak, and they had as much trouble with me as I had with them. The first Britisher to brush me off was a policeman at the dock in Folkestone, and after our charming French officer in Calais this was a bitter welcome to the land of my ancestors. I simply asked him what we should do now, to come to London, which was not a bad question all in all, and he stared me down and walked away. I began to think perhaps my ancestors were smart to leave. Nobody else in any other country ever stared me down and walked away, and some of my questions were pretty silly, but it happened often in England. It got so I hated to approach anybody, and then — bang, somebody would throw an arm about my shoulder and walk me up the street gibbering in his native tongue and bring me straightaway to the place I was looking for, and awsk if he mought do hanything helse and then bumble away calling cheerio until I didn't know what to think. Our general conclusion is that the British are the craziest people in the world and make a specialty of it. "Oh, he wasn't being rude," somebody told us. "He just didn't know what to say, so he left." He's the only cop I ever knew without an answer.

The Merrie England the tourist brings with him is there. It is prominently displayed and you have no trouble finding it. The countryside is beautiful until you get weepy. The little inns and the pubs are all they say. The British museums and ancient landmarks make you gasp. The railway system is tremendous, if bumpy. No London cabdriver minimizes. The Underground is sensible, and the two-deck buses a delight. We thought the food was fine, although from things that had been said to us we hadn't expected it to be. Perhaps a Maine bringing-up is a good introduction to English food — we know what boiled vegetables are. Tea at the Dorchester is a mighty

71

display of pomp and ceremony, but we thought a kind of mental seediness went with it and we came out thinking we used to have such at the old Bellevue in Boston, but we let it lapse and it's gone forever.

Any American needs a trip to England to see the queue. We stand in line sometimes, and know how to take a turn, but we have nothing in the United States like it. You aren't in England long before it offends you and you wonder how it persists. They tell us it all started during the war, but this doesn't explain why they keep it going. They tell you it is just a custom, but we saw a policeman enforcing a taxi queue at Victoria Station, so it does have lawful standing. Our guess is that the queue is England's state of mind. Creeping socialism has had them in thrall for so long they have lost their spirit of aggressive democracy and have no public outlook except to stand in line until somebody does something for them. They queue up placidly, and then moan editorially because the United States is stealing their doctors and their airline pilots. That the United States is merely attracting talent which can no longer function happily in Great Britain is no answer to their perplexity, and they queue up again to go to the toilet. After a certain amount of queuing you feel like getting up in Hyde Park and making a speech about it, but you find you have to stand in line to get a soapbox.

Two queue incidents were completely ridiculous. I was in line for a toilet, and an old gentleman behind me was clearly in more hurry than I was. He was gritting his teeth and shifting weight on his legs until his turn came, and I motioned him ahead and said, "Please, sir, be my guest!" He shook his head and refused. He would disgrace himself in public before he'd break the queue.

The other came at the ticket window when I went to buy our trip back to France. By the time I got to be

72

second in line we had four minutes to train time, and I heard the man ahead of me inquire about a tour to the Middle East, which he wanted to take with his wife the next February. "My train leaves in a moment," I said. "I wonder if I may cut in?" It wasn't the man, it was the ticket agent who snubbed me up. "This gen'man will be some time," he said. "You'd best queue at another wicket!" It is an absolute, uninvented fact that if you stand before a closed shop door in London one or two Englishmen will presently show up and queue behind you, instinctively and unquestioningly. It is fun to do this, and then wait for somebody behind you to ask what the queue is for.

You might as well ask why they change the guard at Buckingham Palace. They do, and it must be seen. Getting the replacements through the crowd of tourists is no minor maneuver. While we were attending this ceremony we heard somebody say, "Is the Queen in residence?" Somebody else said, "No, she's in Scotland." Somehow the practical security reasons for a full guard when the Queen is not at home seem thin, but your heart leaps up at the spectacle and they always change the guard. We expect the queue will remain an honored British tradition in the same way.

On the boat coming from France — and the Channel was smooth as glass — we suddenly realized we were surrounded by Italians. One whole family was having trouble with customs declarations, and we helped them fill in the blanks. Some had been to England before and had taken a holiday back to Italy, some were coming for the first time. The answer is that the domestic help situation in England has been taken over by Italians. All the legendary talk about English butlers and upstairs maids and nannies has gone by the board. The servant class in

England has been emancipated and social uplift has opened a market for foreign labor. Arthur Treacher is an anachronism. The boat was crowded with cooks and chambermaids and waitresses, and when we came afterwards to Edinburgh we found out how all this works.

We asked a taxi driver if he would suggest a small hotel where we might mingle with some Scots. He said the Claremont was excellent. It proved so. But the waiter was Italian, and his buddy was the cook. If we had expected porridge and haggis, we got lasagne which was served by Pepi with a flourish and gave some latinity to our first evening in Scotland. The owner of the hotel was Scot enough, and on Saturday night a considerable group came into the lounge until Pepi was hopping smartly to take care of them. We fell in with two couples, and from them learned that the Claremont was a popular spot for certain regular Saturday night customers, and they would be delighted to have us join them. Thus far the meals we'd taken at the Claremont had been in a second-floor dining room, but we learned the Saturday night set went down two flights, instead, into a cozy retreat where eating, beering and dancing went on until precisely midnight. The chance to join some real Scots at their frolics, nipping their dew, eating their bonny bannocks and tripping their wild strathspeys was eagerly embraced. We did close the place promptly at midnight, agreeable to both a Scottish and a State o' Maine rule that there shall be no sinnin' after hours, but other than that we decided the evening was less Scottish than we deserved after such a long trip — there was more lasagne, and the weird, wild Scottish dance into which the company threw itself with abandon was the current version of the twist.

But Edinburgh is not Scotland, and London is not England. When we bought railroad tickets in London the man asked us which part of Scotland we wanted to go to. I said it didn't matter. He said, "Well, mind you see Glasgow, but Edinburgh is a better introduction to Scotland — I think I'll suggest Edinburgh first. If you'll go to the other end of the counter the very good-looking young man at the first window will sell you your tickets."

So as we walked up to the other end of the counter he did, too, and when we got there he was the very good-looking young man himself, and thinking this compensated beautifully for some of the disinterest and rudeness we'd seen around London I played it straight. "Ah, good morning," I said. "The jolly, good-natured chap at the other end said you would sell me two tickets to Edinburgh."

"Edinburgh?" he repeated.

A train ride back and forth is a wonderful way to view the utterly beautiful and lovely English countryside. You can see a good deal more from a train window than from an automobile — particularly a low-slung VW. Back in Maine we landscape roadsides, and at great expense give the motorist a chance to see. In the old days we always had an appropriation for "cutting bushes," but now they squirt herbicides. But in England the growth of all roadside puckerbrush has been cultivated assiduously since the days of Boudicca, and an automobile ride is about as scenic as crawling through a raspberry patch on your hands and knees. From a train you can see off some.

Not only that, but the British National Railway merits attention. Howling into the trackyards of London at ninety miles an hour is an occasion for prayer, and if just one of the thousands of switches should stick a little bit there would be a mess. Since the railways are government operated, and now and then the workers strike against the government, you wonder how stupidity and genius combine to bring you in safely on time. Noticing that it works all right, you then see it collapse in the system of selling reserved seats in the coaches. For a small additional charge you can have your seat saved for you, and before each train takes off somebody has to go through it and put little markers on all the seats thus reserved. The great mentality that can program a high-speed train through 128,000 proper switches directly to the right platform has never figured out how to put little markers on the right seats, and the first twenty or thirty miles of every trip are spent straightening this out. They have the compartments, and everybody who is looking for a misplaced seat climbs in and then climbs out again, and people who had not reserved a seat do the same hoping to find one that isn't marked. It could be a folksy time if people were in a comedy mood, but in England the mood is otherwise, and it's really a surly disturbance. Every time the train stops the whole process begins again.

The dining car routine is amusing. On state-owned railroads the profit-and-loss factor isn't important, and back in the United States the railroads always whined that they lost money on diners. In England the meal is served when all the seats are filled up, and after everybody has left they tidy up and get ready for another batch. The idea is to feed people well and reasonably, as a public service, and not to lay by any ten percent for the stockholders. We ran into but two menus — lamb and gammon. The only other time I ran into gammon was in Hi-ho-says-Anthony-Rowley. Gammon is ham, and in a British dining car is superb. Beverages may be had.

Coming down from Scotland on a Sunday train, we shared a diner table with a dear little old lady who had been to the Isle of Skye to visit her relatives. She told us

Gaelic had been her native tongue, but she had left Skye as a girl and in London had met and married a gentleman in commerce. His business took him the world around and he amassed a fortune, and just lately he had died. She was well-heeled and kept a house in London, but traveled a good deal. She tried to run up to Skye regularly to visit her family. Now she was returning to London and she said, "My family was loth to have me ride on a train on Sunday."

"Oh, yes," she said, draining a double Scotch in a gulp, "our people on Skye are dedicated sabbatarians. The only thing they permit themselves to do on Sunday is attend church. They tell me I am sinful because when I am home I never go to church with them. And it is a sin to ride on a train on a Sunday. Did you know that?"

I said my own ancestry was such that I had heard of sabbatarianism, but mainly it meant we couldn't play cards or dance.

"Yes, I know," she said. "But I have traveled a great deal and I'm afraid I'm no longer a true daughter of Skye. They ask me why I won't go to the kirk with them on the sabbath, and I tell them, 'I don't believe God can understand a prayer in Gaelic.' "

"I should like to buy you another oos-ki-baw," I said.

She said, "It's oos-ki-bay, and you may." I never knew how it was pronounced, and I've wondered if God took note that I bought a double whiskey for a converted sabbatarian on the Sunday train to London.

On another train we found a pretty young girl black as the ace of spades between us, and we talked along for miles before she found out we were from the United States. Instantly she looked up and said. "But I'm Indian — I'm not Negro!" There was a whole great sadness in that — until she learned we were from the United States there had been no need of explaining anything.

A great part of England no longer concerns the English. If an inn makes you think of Mr. Micawber there is generally somebody around who by indifference manages to take the fun out of it. From Edinburgh I insisted on a bus trip to Dunfermline, and I had my reasons. Here The Bruce was laid to rest, and many a Scottish king, but it wasn't for that. It was because of Sir Patrick Spens, who with the Twa Corbies and Fair Margaret and Jock o' the Green, had pretty much begun my boyhood interest in the winged word, and ever since I was old enough to read I could rattle off:

> *The king sits in Dumferling toune,*
> *Drinking the blude-reid wine . . .*

I guess we took as much of England and Scotland to England and Scotland as they offered us when we got there. Anyway, I waxed poetic with the girl who sold me my bus tickets, and she shrugged and said, "I guess that was before my time." I guess it was. There is a fingerboard in Dunfermline which points to Abedour, if you are interested.

Our disappointment in the mood of the English hardly kept us from enjoying our visit. We didn't get off on any wrong foot, and we never felt we were unwelcome or resented. It's not that kind of a mood. It seemed to us, and still does upon reflection, that the British are terribly mixed up and in a great national state of mind which comes close to a funk. Whatever has happened to their ancient pride and glory is a degrading thing. They harp about their economy, lament losing their empire, prestige and prosperity, and stand stolidly in line to see what happens next.

78

Our gayest moment west of the Channel was an evening at the Paladium. The theater was polished and shining, and everybody was in high anticipation. Harry Secomb was the big attraction, but the bill had several others equally good. The jokes were elderly and I remembered most of the punchlines from the good old Doc Rockwell vaudeville days. It was interesting to find that a good family joke can be Englished into a bathroom gag, and that toilet paper is funny in London. But it was a bright, memorable evening, and it was good to see some English people in hilarity. Perhaps Shakespeare started something, after all.

Kitty-cornered across from the current ghastly American Embassy in London, we saw the lovely old home where John Adams, our first minister to England, lived. Not long ago it was suggested that the United States buy this building and use it for a little American museum, a chance for Londoners to step in and get a taste of us. Congress had something else much more important to ponder, and the idea didn't hatch. So today the home of our first minister to England is the Japanese Information Centre.

And it was a thrill to stand at night and look across Regent's Park and see the perpetual lamp maintained where the Baker Street Irregulars think Sherlock Holmes lived. Do you remember that Sherlock Holmes story in which he sits in his room, momentarily baffled by the evidence, and smokes shag in his pipe until Dr. Watson comes in and believes the place is on fire? It's part of that noble tradition that all tweedy Britishers puff great briar pipes. Well, the whole thing is an economic impossibility. Pipe tobacco is so fraght-flee de-ah in England that only the extremely wealthy can afford a pipe a day, and none of the tobacco is fit to smoke. The warmest attention I got from anybody in England was when, about ten times a day, some tobacco-hungry Britisher would overcome his chaste inherent timidity and sidle up to me and inquire what I was smoking. I still had some pipe tobacco I'd brought from home, and eager to grasp at any evidence of English friendliness I would offer some. They'd cram a pipeful, touch it off, and mumbling thanks would move off. Mine was a popular brand I can buy at home for $1.25 a pound, and before I wised up to the English tobacco situation I had most of my supply mooched away.

It was disturbing, after we had left England, to reflect that most of the people we got close to had been bribed into thawing by tobacco and drink.

What about Swans?

Twice on our trip — in London and in Paris — we touched fingers with friends from home, both connected with our foreign service. In London we visited Max and Manya Grossman. Back in the happy days of the old Boston *Post* Max was a featured writer on the Sunday department, and he used to do two stories every week. One was signed "By Max Grossman," and the other was signed "By Patrick Sullivan."

In Boston this was a good idea. The style was the same in both stories, and anybody who knew Max could tell at a glance that he did them, regardless of signature. He was one of the greatest of the American Sunday writers, and besides holding down a full-time job with the *Post* he was also head of the journalism department at Boston University. Later he became provost of the new Brandeis University, and after 1945 he went to Frankfurt with the American Occupation of Germany. Since then he has been with the State Department in Japan, Colombia and Washington, and now is Information Officer in London. A distinguished career. Max had his embassy duties, and at the moment some complications were bothering him, but Manya dropped everything to show us a good time.

But both in London and later in Paris we found the life of official diplomatic service people revolves around their own national communities, and that a good part of this is because of rules, stated, implied or imagined, which derive from the job being done. Max and Manya live in a split-level Nash apartment off Regent's Park, a building better known because Wally Simpson lived there, and some of the effect of being in London is dissipated when you look up on the wall and see a Vermont sugarhouse painted by Emil Kessler — another old Boston *Post* alumnus. But even so, with Manya and occasionally Max guiding us we got to see London much sooner and more easily than we should have on our own. They took us to Carnaby Street, for a starter, and as the miniskirt was then a hot item we made no objection. But the most you can say for the miniskirt in Carnaby Street is that it reveals only English legs, and even to the terminus this is nothing to make me froth at the mouth. Carnaby Street made me think of something Dick Reed used to say about a Maine town far down in Washington

County — that if you put a tent over it you'd have the biggest bawdy house in the world.

With Manya we found a pleasant upstairs restaurant, and an interesting man joined us at the fourth chair. He was English but had been a business accountant in Argentina for many years and was back home for a brief stay before a transfer to Nigeria. He said he was appalled at the things he found in England, and was glad to be leaving soon. For years he had longed to come back, but his England was gone. He said he found the people no longer interested in doing a good job well, and that the public attitude has the young people bewildered. He felt the older people had lost influence and control, and were now condoning the aberrations of youth as some natural consequence of affairs. He almost wept as he said he had decided never to come home to England again. So we didn't think some of our impressions were too far afield.

And then we came to the swans. On the Thames. Certain swans belong to the Queen, and some do not, so the Queen keeps a head swankeeper and thus another great tradition is supported at public expense and probably to no purpose. Each season the swankeeper separates the royal swans from the profane and vulgar commoners, but what he does then wasn't cleared up for us. As something of a custodian of poultry myself, although strictly a barnyard man, I suddenly had the graceful swan swim into my ken and my curiosity, and I mildly inquired what the Queen does with a flock of swans around the palace all winter. I never heard that anybody ever ate a swan, or poached their eggs, and all at once I wondered why they are managed so strictly and what the Queen wants them for. I never got a good answer. All over Europe we saw swans in every river, moat, canal and park, and I would ask whatever becomes of swans, and nobody could tell me. All agreed they enhance the scenery, and so do I, but that's it. There seemed to be enough swans on the Thames for everybody, and no great public necessity for telling one from the other. I'd like to know how the Royal Swankeeper tells. And I hope, occasionally, a low-bred swan sneaks by. They told us the swankeeper job is a high honor and pays well, but I wouldn't want to think my own worldly success came from distinguishing one swan from another.

Max and Manya finally put us on the boat train to Dover and we watched the chimney pots of Elia run out until we were amongst apple orchards again. We dozed and as any train rider does we tried to make music from the wheels on the rails. Nobody could tell us why the English match their rails, length for length, side by side, so you get both bumps at the same time. On other railroads you can lull back to the clickety-click and there is a tempo and a rhythm until you make up words and say them over and over. On an English train the rails just go bump-bump-bump, and nobody ever dozed and said, "You-tickle-my-toes-I'll-tickle-your-toes" all the way to Dover.

We Get a Speech

We presented our official State o' Maine credentials to the City of Calais on our way back from England, and had quite a time doing it. We had found the British customs the most formal yet, and the man asked us quite a few questions. I commented that he was making more of it than we had run into on the Continent and he said, "Yes, but you see, we are not in the Common Market yet."

I said, "What do you mean — 'yet'?"

We wondered if the French would use retaliatory tactics, but we found they did not. At Calais, on the return to France, we had trouble finding the customs people at all. When we got off the boat from Dover the entire facilities of the International Company of Sleeping Cars and the Grand European Express were drawn up on tracks between the boat and the dock sheds, and we had all we could do to keep from being herded aboard to go to Barcelona, Vienna, Tel Aviv and the Orient. We, having an automobile waiting for us in Calais, were the oddballs. Every few feet somebody in a uniform would try to get us on a train, and we climbed over cars, went around engines, and walked miles before we could thread

84

through the tracks and get into the building. Here a classy young lady in a customs inspector's uniform seemed surprised to see anybody, and quickly scrawled with chalk on our suitcases and said, "Hokay." So much for the Common Market.

But now in the waiting room we found a glassed-in booth which was the harbor office of the Calais Chamber of Commerce, and we still had our governor's message to the good people of the other Calais. We stepped in and found two men who were calmly relaxed, looking as if they had succeeded in finding a hermitage where the world had ceased to intrude, and as if they couldn't believe that somebody had finally found them. I conveyed greetings, presented my scroll, extended a transoceanic handshake, and they looked at me as if I had carrots sticking out of my ears. The great moment seemed over. I couldn't imagine how I would go home and convey to our good governor just what, if anything, had happened. So far the two men hadn't even stood up. We began to back out, for the office was hardly large enough to turn around in, and just then they stood up. They reached around and took down their suit coats and slowly, methodically, put them on and straightened them up. One man snapped his cuffs, flipped his lapels, stepped forward about two feet, and launched into a speech with gestures and elocution. He welcomed us to Calais and spoke of the long-range plans for improving the harbor facilities, improvements which would shorten docking time and greatly reduce the expense of loading and unloading, a comprehensive and ambitious program which would place Calais in the forefront of the maritime cities "du monde." He begged us to call on if in any way the Chamber of Commerce could assist in matters of trade. He charged us to return the warmest and most sincere greetings to our governor and the people of Maine, and particularly the happy citizens of that beautiful community so fortunate as to be named, also, Calais. This went on for about twenty minutes, and then both men began pulling out desk drawers and loading our arms with booklets, pamphlets, maps, prospectuses and statistical summations — all the promotional material they had. Then we left.

We meant to bring all this stuff home and show it to Judge Dudley and other good people of Calais, but as our trip ran on we found other souvenirs more important. Pamphlet by pamphlet, across Switzerland, Austria, Italy — we left the stirring story of Calais on hotel-room tables.

At the VW agency they shook our hands, welcomed us back, and brought our car all shined, greased, gassed and checked off in the service booklet, and we noticed the mileage had run up just about enough for a weekend in Ostend. We guessed that is why they charged us nothing for washing and storage. And he said it was a fine little car and he thought the new seats were more comfortable than those last year. Mobile again and not needing trains and buses we studied the maps and took off — having nothing to do but wander along toward Munich. George and Betty Morrill had left Maine about the same time we did, and we agreed to meet them in Munich and attend the Oktoberfest — for six months we all had reservations at the Pension Olive in Swabing, because if you don't plan ahead you can't get near a bed in Munich during Oktoberfest.

We turned east off the Paris road, and soon were bug-eyed at the French farmland. I knew France produces much food, but the great rolling fields to the horizon were unexpected. And the machinery at work in the fields ruined any charming notion I might have had that Millet's gleaners could still be seen, waiting for evensong. When you presume that Iowa has the patent on corn, a French farm landscape brings you up short. Here and there were crews spreading fertilizer — and not the piled-up kind from a barnyard so famous to France, but white commercial fertilizer that hove great clouds of dust in the air. Too much in our American bringing-up leads us to suppose Europe is crowded and close, with "huddled masses yearning to breathe free" and "wretched refuse of your teeming shore." It's a shock to find potato fields that make Aroostook County's look piddling, and signs along the road, "Deer Crossing." Here, through north France moving toward the Rhine, we were in one of the richest gardens in the world. Towns were small, and we came to one that seemed to be called "Haut," but haut-what I couldn't learn. A sign said café, and the place looked like a hotel. We were about to sample our first country tavern in France.

But this hotel was nothing new to us. We have them in town after town along the Maine-Quebec border. Food, drink and rooms in the French flavor. The family lives upstairs, everybody waits on table, everybody answers the bell, and everybody does everything. A woman with a baby in her arms came from the kitchen and cordially welcomed us. She showed no surprise whatever at my peculiar French, but the next day her curiosity burst forth and she asked. We were the only roomers that night. By German standards the place was not polished up to the last notch, but it was neither dirty nor untidy. It did not have, and no French hotel ever has, the brown-gravy smell we had admired in Germany.

At home I go a month, sometimes, without ever putting on a necktie, but on this trip I wore one most of the time, and always for meals. When I got it straight we went down for the preprandial exercises and found a few local folks had wandered in. Amongst the tables was a soccer game — a thing like a pinball machine that two people can operate and make the players kick a Ping-Pong ball around. The European game of "football" appealed to me, and I suspect it's really a better game all around than our American variety. But these indoor soccer games are common, and the one here was getting a good workout. Not, however, from the customers — the children of the innkeeper's family were playing it for free. One of the children was in skirts and we thought she was a girl, but he was a boy. He could play the game like a fiend, and when the action got brisk the Ping-Pong ball would light out across the dining room and all the children would chase it down. Customers nursing their wines would cheer and groan as scores were made or missed, and it made an exciting kind of cocktail hour. One of the smaller children was a squealer, and every once in a while she'd screech out in a way that made your ears flap, and once when she was chasing the Ping-Pong ball in our direction she let go, and I grabbed her arm and said, "Tait-twee!"

If I had suddenly jumped up and sung "La Marseillaise" in Yiddish it wouldn't have produced a more electrifying response. I'd heard mothers on Mill Street yell that at their children, but the tipplers of Haut evidently hadn't heard exactly that inflection. All turned to look at us, the children stopped short at their play, and the squealer did just what I had asked — shut up. Then a young man with white fertilizer on him got up from his table, bringing his wine, and asked if he could sit with us. He wouldn't shake hands because his hands were dirty from his work. I'd gather that everybody who frequents that tavern had been wishing for a long time the squealer would quit, and in one swoop of outlandish French I had done the trick. The young man wearing the fertilizer wanted to know in what part of France anybody said "tait-twee." After a few words he turned to all the other customers and announced, "Cana-dar!" I asked him if he were a farmer and he said no, that he only worked on a farm. A nice distinction where landowners are the gentry.

Upon rising to go everybody wished us good chance and said *au revoir*, and for supper we had steak and potatoes, a fine green salad that upset our functions, and a wine to remember. Speaking of that green salad, we shortly found that many French toilets do not supply tissue — information that is definitely not better late than never. The next worst experience is finding one where the paper is outside the room and you are supposed to tear some off before you go in.

This hotel had a sign outside inviting folks to bring their own food. Amongst frugal farm people this seems cordial, and I suppose the inn expects to sell a drop of wine and find its profit that way. It made me think of Grammy Baker who once had some kind of an errand in Boston, and she carried her lunch in her handbag. Come noon she went into Filene's restaurant and laid her sandwiches out on a table and began to eat. A waitress came, but one look at Grammy Baker was enough to make anybody back off, so the waitress merely said, "Do you have all you need?" Grammy said, "No, I'd like a cup of hot water." So the waitress brought a cup of hot water and Grammy took a tea bag from her purse and made a cup of tea. It was amusing to think that in Haut, France, Grammy Baker would feel right at home — as, of course, she had felt in Filene's.

The noisy children were soon in bed, and we had a

quiet, restful night. Breakfast included croissants, but the coffee was worthy of a Milwaukee complaint. The dining room was hung with brilliant copperware, and the mother took each piece down for us to admire. They were her pride and joy, antiques and ornamental. "One can buy copper today, but not like this," she said. Before we drove on from Haut Dorothy brought her notes up to date. I see that she put down, "Very different from England and Scotland — having fun again."

The Rhine Again

There wasn't a mile across France that didn't give us much to look at, and we came to the Vosges Mountains entirely unprepared for their beauty. Somehow you get prepared for the Black Forest, but in some ways we found les Vosges more appealing. We hadn't driven far before we began to think about "poverty." Back home we were entangled in massive efforts to alleviate squalor and bring people onward and upward — we had even brought our public thinking along until tax collectors regard television sets as "necessities" rather than "luxuries." So we would drive into a small French town and find a woman doing her laundry by hand in cold water at a public trough. A pipe came down from a mountain spring into great stone tubs. I pulled up alongside and said to Dorothy, "Now, I don't ever want to hear you complain again."

The woman was larruping the laundry, and looked up to smile at us. She seemed cheerful, and probably considered herself lucky that she didn't have to lug water in buckets. She dropped one corner of a shirt and waved to us when we drove along.

At Amiens we found another kind of French "poverty" — the largest ecclesiastical edifice in France. Here for our first time we touched the never-ending lore of Joan of Lorraine, for in this cathedral she sat beside the dauphin as he became Charles VII. As had happened so often in England as we approached the shrines of our culture, we stepped into the cathedral already awed and quite ready to be favorably impressed. Then we felt, and saw, the shoddiness. There are too many pigeons and too few pavement cleanings. There are rich red rosy gules cast on damp flagstones from high galaxies of glass, but the place is chill. Everybody present is hushed in huddled smallness before everything — please, says a small sign, remain in reverent attitude in the presence of this monument. The effect is glumness and graveyard silence. I guess the Pope has never heard a batch of Freewill Baptists blat forth the opening hymn in the worn clapboarded crossroads church — where the presence of God peps things up and everybody is glad. If God does understand prayers in Gaelic He must also wonder why the cathedral at Amiens always sends Him a sad message. For all the glory of leaded red transepts, costly beyond computation and famous the world around, anybody looking for uplift and comfort would do well to go into a hothouse. We came out depressed, yet we had just seen one of the half-dozen things in Europe that must be seen. It is beautiful, lovely, historic, mighty, massive and monumental. We put a coin in the slot, hoping some poor priest in cold sandals would pray for us, and perhaps be glad we came. The great spires stand high and they were still in the sky when we were far beyond Amiens in the warm, lush countryside We saw many another great church, and most of them were the "biggest" something or other, but certain feelings we had at Amiens persisted always.

Then there were the battlegrounds of World War I, with the cemeteries honoring forever the gallant dead. They were from all nations, and they were forever dead. We came to the grave and memorial to Marshal Foch where he dealt with the Germans in 1918 — offering them a wine of the vintage of 1870. The railway car in which the Armistice was signed is enclosed with a short run of tracks, and a wooded park surrounds the monument. Another place of silence. It is impossible to tour this region without emotional response — rows and rows of crosses, and something of the futility and idiocy of war begins to seep through the schoolbook definitions. Back in 1917–18 we knew all about these places — here the doughboys slept in the mud and built up for the great Black Jack Pershing slaughter that became the heroic offensive of the gallant victors. Here, again, in the full-color rerun, is the Maginot Line, its absurd concrete bunkers and parapets in hayfields and corn patches, itself a memorial to military genius, and lunacy. From those beaches below Ostend across France to Luxembourg and the Rhine our peaceful tour was intruded upon by the sadness of monument after monument, and the birthplace of Joan of Arc hardly cheers you up.

I suppose the rude manger in Bethlehem, and possibly the log cabin in Kentucky, are similar symbols. In Domremy, peaceful and serene, the Maid of Orléans first drew a breath, and first heard the saints. For one about to

92

become so embroiled, and no pun is intended, the rude
beginning too easily suggests the Christ, and even the
Lincoln. At Amiens we had seen the scene of her ultimate
mortal victory, under the splendor of God and God's
work, and here in Domremy we could stand and reflect on
all the meantime. You don't tour France without frequent meeting-up with La Pucelle and her career.

It was here in this region, however, that we had our
thoughts quickly turned from the emotional and depress-
ing by the discovery of *le sapin qui pisse*. We were riding
along slowly to admire the scenery, and from the corner
of my eye I caught a sign that I thought said, "Au sapin
qui pisse." A *sapin* is a fir tree, and back in Maine we have
a lot of them. But it also has, like so many French words,
extra meanings — to "feel the fir" means to have one
foot in the grave. Casket wood. *Pisser,* of course, has only
one meaning. What I thought I had seen seemed improbable, so we kept on going. But presently we saw another
sign that said the same thing, and now we definitely had
to go and look at *le sapin.* Up a side road we found it.
Some joker had piped a mountain spring down in such a
way that the pipe came out of this fir tree a couple of
feet off the ground, and a little pool had been arranged.
It wasn't unlike one of our springtime sugar maples with
a spile in it — except that maples drip and this fir was
running full tilt. It was, indeed, *un sapin qui pisse,* and
it was doing a dandy job of it. It amused us to find this
kind of tourist attraction in the first place, but even more
when we found a stationery store in the next town had
an ample display of picture postcards showing the oddity
in full color. We bought a whole batch of them and I
mailed them that night to our friends in the Maine pulp
and paper industry. You can still find them stuck up in
wangans and bunkhouses. Maine has a great lore of

manly deeds, but we never produced a tree like that.

For the time being, our last picnic in France was half-way up a long, winding hill in les Vosges. It was a beautiful spot, and we could look down on hairpin turns coming up from a small town. As we chewed our bread and finished our last drop of French wine we could see a double-bodied truck come through the village and start up the long climb. It was too far below us to be heard, but gradually as it patiently churned upwards we could hear the diesel grind. It was an hour later that it came past our picnic spot, hardly moving in lowest-low, and we fell in behind it to make the rest of the upgrade just as slowly as it did. From the top we would descend into the Rhine Valley.

We had already crossed the Rhine once, on our way to England — far down where it is widest and busiest. We would cross it many times again, and see almost all of it one time or another. It is one of the great rivers of the world, changing its mood as it flows. Its crags have their tales, its vineyards are backdrops for chugging Dutch barges that churn the water to foam, it nurtures smoking industry and it offers placid scenery and quiet resorts. But most of all, as we came to it now, it is the great dividing line between France and Germany — a link and a barrier, one of the most complete and absolute transitions that can be made. There is nothing in all creation so different as a Frenchman and a German. The whole manner, mores, philosophy and customs change as abruptly as a switch turns a lamp on and off. In the width of the Rhine River we moved one to the other, completely and wholly. A stately German official, who wouldn't know how to shrug his shoulders if he took lessons at the Sorbonne, looked in our VW window and said, "Guten Morgen."

94

Time and again people ask us which country we prefer
— not only as betwixt France and Germany, but of all the
places we visited. This is not a valid question, and has no
answer. We weren't trying to find out which nation we
liked the most, or least, but were trying to learn about
each by itself as it came along. We can give you a diatribe
about Italy, and will, but this also is not valid. It is not
valid because it imposes American opinions as a basis for
judgment, and I'm sure all Italians believe Italy is best.
And when you cross the Rhine River you are not journey-
ing between two comparable countries. Rather, the re-
portable oddity is that in the span of one short bridge
you go so very far.

We were to come back to France; now we were coming
back to Germany. I held up my Green Sheet and asked,
"Freiburg?"

The customs man said, "Geradeaus!"

And to the Danube

From Colmar in France to
Freiburg in Germany takes you across the haut-Rhin, so
to speak, and then you come to the Schwarzwald. Here
you will buy a cuckoo clock, take some Kirschwasser, and
soak up the lore and legend of what turns out to be a
good-sized woodlot under expert management. My wife

and I have pushed a canoe into Allagash waters and lived with it for two weeks, and you might think the Black Forest would have little to excite a couple of veteran Maine woodsmen. It doesn't work that way — God made the trees in both places, but no Mainer ever sobbed with emotion about his wilderness the way any German goes to pieces over the Black Forest. And at a place called Hirschsprung we got the message and fell under the spell.

The forests of the Vosges Mountains in France had almost convinced us, but as Joseph Conrad said about Bangkok, there is the extra-special connotation of the Schwarzwald. Hirschsprung is a pass, a gap, a gorge, a gulf in Vermont, through the rocks at a high point in the hills, and atop a crag is a great bronze stag, which is what *Hirsch* means, and in Maine such an animal would go about 180 pounds dressed and just miss the "Big Buck Club." Every tree, stream, rock and crevice in the Black Forest has its story, and here the stag is said to have leaped the gorge one time for some reason we didn't have German enough to understand. It was a good jump. It was, truthfully, remarkable. I asked somebody what was chasing him, and a language deficiency followed. When we came up this long grade to Hirschsprung, and could first see this poised stag, the presence of a crowd startled us. It was something like crossing Seboomook Dam on the way to Caucomgomoc and finding a Red Sox baseball crowd at Beanpot Pond. We pulled off the road, with a courteous German policeman helping us, and we got out to roam the paths and mingle with the Germans who were there to pay homage to their blessed Black Forest.

This is a high and remote place. It is rugged and wild. But it is laid out like a city park with paths, bridges and signs. A tumbling stream is provided. Refreshment and souvenir booths are available. And up and down, back and forth, walked the Germans in ecstasy, all hushed under the magic spell of the Black Forest. We saw families complete with a dog on a string, and lovers all alone in a crowd, and even purposeful loners striding along. The dominant tree is a black spruce. We don't have the same tree in Maine. There isn't much down wood, and the floor of the forest is fairly neat — they give out permits for scavenging fuel. Forestry in Germany is rigidly controlled, and one man told us about the French. The Black Forest area was under French occupation after the war. The Russians had the east, the British the northern industrial area, and the United States all the scenery. France went to cutting timber. All at once a mountainside would be stripped, each tree with its poltergeist and connotations, and the French would haul the boards off to France. The ax-happy French outdid any Paul Bunyan stunt, and every time they stroked a tree they cut into the heart and vitals of every honest German. I suspect if this had been done by the Hungarians, or the Swedes, or even the Greeks and Canadians, the Germans would not have been so mad, but to have the French do it was criminal. I can show any German a Maine timberland tract where ten times the wood was harvested, and in fifteen years the saws will be back, but this would be no solace. Their precious Black Forest was abused, and the stag certainly did leap the gorge. It was about like leaping from Maine into Vermont, and he must have been in the air all of twenty minutes.

We avoided the German *Autobahnen*. They are trunk routes, as good as any highways in the world, and they are toll-free. There are no speed limits and a purposeful German can open his Mercedes-Benz up to 140 kilometers an hour or better and keep all appointments. We also avoided the lesser through routes and wherever possible took the byways. We came into Donaueschingen abruptly and by a back road, and we paused there to pay respects to the Danube.

The Danube, which is anything but blue, is not called the Danube. It is the Donau. The source of this river, which flows easterly to become greater and more international than the Rhine, is supposed to be in a walled-up spring behind a church in Donaueschingen. Actually, the Donau forms from a couple of Black Forest streams, but at this late date nobody knocks the Donaueschingen fairy tale. As if in deference to a greater river, the Rhine makes a swing from Constance to Strasbourg and the Donau rises within the circle — at its origin the Donau is not too far from the Rhine. And after you have followed the Donau from its spring to Passau, and crossed and recrossed it in wanderings about Germany, and hear the word pronounced reverently, you realize that Donau is a far prettier word than Danube.

You don't have to be in Europe long before you find out many such things. I remember some years back that Russian cartographers began producing maps of the world for use in Russian schools, and one day they came up with a map of Maine. On this map our capital city of Augusta was "Ogaste." The foolish editor of one of our Maine newspapers did an editorial about this, and asked the Russians how they would like it if we made a map and misspelled Moscow. Since Moscow in Russia is not Moscow, travelers soon see just how foolish this editor was — and many a place is called something else when you get there. So we went to the well of the Donau and cast our coin in the pale green water to propitiate whatever it is you propitiate there, and we wondered who finally comes and retrieves the coins and how much they get per take. I suspect it may be the church and the upkeep of the well is a sound investment. Later, when we were to see the en-larged Donau at Regensburg and Passau, and so on along Austria, we wished we had thrown in a box of good American chain-store detergent — something that would bubble and fuzz and blub-blub-blub right down the drain and ride like a white Ajax knight clear through to the Black Sea and sweeten things up. With enough wash-day blue the tawny Donau might indeed become the Blue Danube. True, it might kill all the fish and wildlife while doing it. But there — we have a few rivers in Maine, too . . .

By the well, just as with the stag on the rock, things are believable. The Donau is the second longest river in Europe; only the Volga, which the Russians call the Volga, is longer. Down its course the Donau becomes the Duna, and Duna becomes Dunarea, and real old people call it the Ister. It flows on and on with romance and traffic, accumulating waltzes and kuck as it goes, and a spare French franc is well spent at the source.

We Join a Club

Moosehead Lake in Maine is forty-eight miles long, entirely within the state, and in warm weather you must troll deep to take a togue. The Bodensee, Germany's biggest body of water, is forty-six miles long and smells like a hornpout pond. It amounts to a wide place in the Rhine River. If we had a tenth of the resorts of the Bodensee on Moosehead Lake everybody would be complaining about overcrowding, and the Legislature would be entertaining an appropriation to clean out the algae. The Germans have to share this lake with the Swiss and Austrians, and when the Swiss speak of Lake Constance they refer to the exact same body of water. We were saving Switzerland for later, so we motored down the east side of the Bodensee, Friedrichshafen and Lindau, and got our first view of the serious-minded Germans in vacation mood. They act as if they are going to have fun if it kills them. They walk and ride and eat and drink, and must need weeks of rest after every outing. The Bodensee, besides all the hotels and restaurants, is famous for the little white boats that sail all over the place — most of them being floating restaurants. You don't have to give up eating between meals. From Constance you can eat your way across the lake to Meersburg, have dinner, and then eat all the way back to Constance.

After inspecting the Bodensee we took back roads toward two other famous German resort lakes, the Ammersee and the Starnberger See, and somewhere in this general area we discovered the Tittisee. It is a pretty little lake, lined with dining Germans and souvenir shops, and they had some beautiful souvenir sweaters that caught my eye — they had "Tittisee" in big letters right across the front. Dorothy said she thought she wouldn't like one.

This southern section of Germany is beautiful, and we fell in love with the big herds of beautiful Brown Swiss cows. In Maine the leading dairy animal is the Holstein, because she gives a good flow of milk in which the butterfat is adequate to meet the requirements. The Channel breeds don't give so much and their milk has a higher butterfat, but they come next after Holsteins. However, we do have a good many Brown Swiss in Maine, and they are a beautiful animal. Friendly eyes and open countenance, and a fairly heavy animal. Herd by herd, taking them as they come, the Brown Swiss is the pretty one, and here in southern Germany they range in good numbers. And their bells make some of the sweetest music in the world.

We heard the bells first through the open car window, as if some distant carillon were attempting all the hymns in one great medley, and the sound came from a herd of Brown Swiss well up a hillside field. Presently we came to a herd closer to the road, and I stopped to lean over the fence and inspect bossy's bell. It was a good six inches across the mouth, with a lead clapper, and it was not one of the sheet-metal kind we use in Maine, but a high quality cast brass or bronze. In the casting certain esoteric figures were raised, one of them a Christian cross, and I judged these to have superstitious reasons. Furthermore, while at home we always belled one cow with the idea that if we found one we'd find them all; here every cow in the flock had her own bell. For long miles we listened as the whole countryside tinkled for us, and we decided we'd buy some of these bells to take home for friends who could best use them — for cottage or camp they'd make a wonderful come-and-get-it.

Several times we paused by farm homes to inquire, but our German wasn't that good. Everybody seemed pleased that we admired the bells, and also that we had good taste enough to admire the cows, but the women we approached shook their heads at the idea of selling any bells, and we

got the idea they were priceless family heirlooms handed
down from cow to cow over centuries.

In one town we hit the right day for the market, and we
stocked up with bread, wine, sweets and a bunch of new
grapes which we washed at a town trough, and soon after
that we came onto one of the best picnic spots we saw.
A little dirt road ran off the highway, across a long field
facing a valley, and the fringe of woodland beyond looked
inviting. When we got to the woods we found some settees
there so we figured we were invading no privacy, and if we
were it must be all right. We laid out our snack and were
just about to begin when a VW like our own came bounding up the dirt road and pulled in, and a couple with a
small daughter joined us. The man hopped out and called
"Mahlzeit!" at us, and then began one of the most amazing demonstrations of compact logistics I've ever seen.
On television Wild West shows I've seen a man ride off
into the sunset alone on a horse, and then they show him
camping out with more gear than a horse could haul.
They could learn something from this German. They
began taking things from the VW the way a magician
takes things from a hat, and soon had a table, lounging
chairs, footstools, sets of dishes, great interlocking containers of food, and above everything a gay yellow and
black umbrella about ten feet across. This couple of old
Maine campground veterans learned about picnics right
there. The whole rig, which set up to nearly half the size
of the old Sparks Brothers Circus, was designed and made
in Germany to fit into a Volkswagen, and every joint
worked and every cleat fitted. They laid out enough food
to last a driving crew on the West Branch a month; it
included beer, wine and cognac, and we noticed they
didn't give the little girl any wine. Only beer. When they

102

were disposed and deployed the young man turned to us and in very slow German so I would understand he said, "There is nothing like the open countryside to make a good appetite!"

Our cheese and bread, with kuchen and a 35c wine, seemed meager, but I managed to keep cheerful, and I lifted my glass and said, "Guten Appetit!"

"Thank you," they said, and fell to with a High German chomp and smack that echoed down the lovely valley like pistol shots. They were still there, eating away, when we shoved the cork in our bottle, backed around and took off for Mindelheim. One of the great pleasures of Europe is to hear a German eat.

Mindelheim, halfway from the Bodensee to Munich the way we went, is a fine old city with walls and a great flavor of welcome. We drove about, looking things over, and finally parked by the Gasthof zum Stern, which I found in the usual condition of midafternoon desertion. But there was a brown-gravy smell, and I followed it to the kitchen, where I found a girl up to her armpits in dishwater, scouring away at gleaming kitchen pots that couldn't possibly be made any cleaner. "Ja," she had a room, and she went back into the dishpan. After we settled ourselves in she came up to ask if the room pleased us. It did, and we fell in love with Mindelheim and the inn and the folks who run it, and we stayed there until we had just time enough to get to Munich ahead of the Morrills.

The hotel is owned by a grand old grandmother whose proportions gain on her as they descend. She needs a large chair. She wore long black skirts, and any Hollywood casting director would put her precisely where she is — as the motherly owner of a good inn where people come and have pleasant evenings somewhere in Germany.

Her son was killed in the war, so his son in turn is inn-keeper — but you soon see that Grandmother has a tight rein. The grandson's name is Hermann Fischer, and we promised him we would send our friends. When we came down to supper, again as usual, we found the dining room well filled and a jolly evening well under way. Hermann flourished us to a table and went for our Kirschwasser, and Grandmother arose from her place in the corner and came over to welcome us and wish us a good appetite. I motioned for her to take a place, and she sat down as if glad for a chance. Now and then she would get up and go to another table to wish good appetite to other diners, but she always came back to ours, and she labored patiently until she found out all about us — and we found out about her.

Midway of the evening a drinking club came in. Sixteen students, each wearing the club's white cap, were carousing in the alehouses of Mindelheim, and having already been to about half of them they had the Gasthof zum Stern next in line. Grandmother jumped up when the first white cap poked through the front door, and with more agility than her heft promised she got to him and grasped his hand warmly before he was quite inside. Then she welcomed each student as he came in, getting her hand kissed each time, and motioning them on toward three tables the waitress had shoved together to make one. It was right by ours. I wondered if maybe the average American barkeep wouldn't seem less enthusiastic; it looked like a wild time. I know in Maine a bartender isn't allowed to serve anybody who appears intoxicated, but I had to admit as the boys came alongside us and sat down that they didn't really seem loaded.

Some nonmembers joined in the first song, and after about three songs they all did. In about fifteen minutes

Dorothy and I were full members in good standing of this club, and knew when to join in the chorus of the official club song. The grandmother adroitly circulated up and down behind the boys, urging this one to drink up, calming this one down, and showing masterful generalship all along the line. New to us, this was an old story to her, and the boys would soon finish their beers and be off to the next pub down the street. At last came the farewell song, and with *auf Wiedersehens* from everybody in the dining room the boys started for the door. Grandmother brought out her rubber stamp.

Germany is the land of the rubber stamp. Everybody has one with his name on it, and if you ask a waiter for a receipt he will scribble the price of the meal on a beer check and validate it by getting his rubber stamp and an inkpad out of his pocket. There is always one on a hotel desk to stamp bills and letterheads and bar tabs, and now the boys all wanted the rubber stamp of the Gasthof zum Stern put on their white caps — along with the others they had collected and were going to collect. Grandmother stood by the table at the door and obliged them.

Then one boy, instead of placing his hat on the table for her to stamp, gestured for her to stamp it right on his head. She did. She wound up like a baseball pitcher with the bases loaded and a three-two count on a pinch hitter, and she fetched him a wallop over the temple that would have felled an ox, and he reeled over past a couple of tables and came up groggy. He kissed her hand and went out. The next boy wanted to see if he could take it, and the next, and until the last had gone it sounded like somebody knocking on an empty icehouse door with an ax. Grandmother came back to our table, all flustered from the exercise, and her grandson brought her a wine.

The dining room was silent for a time after that, but it

soon got back into shape and there were no more inter-
ruptions. There were nightcaps, and with a chorus of
Schlaffen-Sie gut's we went up to bed. It was in Mindelheim, that very evening, that Dorothy looked out the window over the ancient rooftops, and perhaps overcome by
the long gaiety of the evening said, "Now, this is just what
it's like in Europe!"

I lugged the great, hulking featherbed up over my
shoulders and said, "Eyañ."

Art in Apfeltrach

Only because we picked the
room ourselves, we had a bathtub, and in the morning we
soaped down and decided on beauty treatments. Grandmother sat with us at breakfast, and I told Grandson
Hermann we'd like to stay another night. He said there
was nothing antique about the cowbells we'd heard along
the way, and we could buy all we wanted in the local
hardware store. So we struck out on foot, and a woman in
the hardware store sold us eight of them — jangling each
in turn to see if we liked the flavor. They were ridicu-
lously cheap, as they'd have to be for farmers to bell all
their cows, and I did some back-thinking about the price
of any kind of a bronze bell in a Portland ship-chandlery
or plain two-inch butt hinges in brass at $1.50 a pair. She

wrapped them all tidily, pushing in a wad of paper so they wouldn't clang in transit, and I staggered out with this heavy load to walk all over Mindelheim. We'd have done better to find the barber first.

By now Dorothy had the beauty shop situation under fair control. I'd lead her in and tell them to make her beautiful and ask how long it would take. It was always an hour, and that's what it always was. Then she would enjoy an hour's conversation in a language of which she knew but a half-dozen words, and two of them were tea and beer. Many a Phi Beta Kappa student who has majored in German would be hard put to keep up an hour of talk in a German beauty parlor, but she had mastered a kind of communication which can't be taught. She'd come out telling me about all the places they suggested we go, and all the things they thought we ought to do, and I'd say, "Somebody in there speaks English?" No, all they spoke was German. She came out this time with an upsweep hairdo suggestive of Saint Pauli on a busy night, and was all agog about going to Apfeltrach. She could discuss anything except how she liked her hair.

I had fun getting a haircut. The two barbers stood waiting for me to make a choice between them, and I didn't think it made much difference. So I touched my head, pointed at one, and flipped a coin. It came down heads. This proved an altogether happy way to decide, and I had offended neither. As I got the cloth adjusted my barber said, "But you are not German?"

This is encouraging. In many restaurants in Germany the waiters take pride in spotting nationalities, and they have a supply of flags on a sideboard. If they guess you are American they come waving a small Old Glory and set it in the middle of the table, and you are supposed to look pleased. Not once in all our meals in Germany did we ever get a flag. The closest was to be in the pilot's lounge in the Bremer Lagerhaus, where the steward would whip out a Canadian flag for us — but he cheated a little; he had heard us say we sailed from Montreal. So we were a little proudful that we were getting by on our own, and now the barber was trying to guess where I came from.

"France?" he asked.

"Nein."

"Netherlands?"

"England?"

"Denmark, perhaps?"

I kept mum until I came to tip him, and I said, "Amerikaner." And my barber said something that pleased me more than I can express, for it sums up this whole bit about being a typical American tourist — he said, "But this is impossible!"

It gave me a great lift. I stepped across the main street of Mindelheim, bearing my great burden of brass cowbells, and I didn't feel entirely a stranger in a strange land. I found my wife beautiful, and somewhat Germanic, and I shook hands with her gravely in the native style, and I thanked the girls who had prettied her up. We linked arms and started off, and she said the girls had told her we simply must drive over to Apfeltrach. We went back to Grandmother's and got the VW.

After we had returned to Maine I wrote to the German Tourist Information Service, asking them to tell me what they knew about the church at Apfeltrach. Promptly, a Miss Ruth Aldendorph wrote back that they couldn't tell me anything about it — that Germany is full of priceless treasures, occasionally discovered by tourists who "have the time," but it would be impossible to prepare and

108

disseminate detailed information such as I wanted. And, surprisingly, she suggested I might write directly to the mayor of Apfeltrach and ask him. I never did, because I had been in Apfeltrach and the mayor had eluded me. He was working in a beet field.

Just a short ride south of Mindelheim is Apfeltrach. It is a small village of farm homes, and when we came there nobody was in sight. The manure piles were handsome, and the urine pumps were in good shape. Since German farmers live in the villages and work fields at a distance, and since the whole family helps, a German farm town always looks as if nobody lives there. The church is on a knoll, reached up some worn stone steps, and we climbed to it and found in the doorway our one and only Apfel-tracher — an ancient female suggesting the poor, weak, churchyard thing of Keats, and she had a mop and a pail of water and she was finishing the morning *nettoyage* of the ecclesiastical property. She was sloshing water around and she went all to pieces when she saw us coming in — she clearly had made a monstrous blunder in having the portal damp at exactly the wrong time. She bowed away from us in pitiful subservience, and I suppose she was the only woman in town too old to pull beets. I tried to question her, but my stupid German and her reluctance to socialize made an unbeatable combination. All I got was the Holy Father was not at the moment in residence, and nobody else was around.

It's pretty hard to think of anything so completely suggestive of peace as that church was. I remember once I saw the sun come up over Umsaskis Lake, a scene of natural serenity to remember. Absolute silence, no stir of the air, and color and brilliance and beauty. I could have been deaf as a haddock and Umsaskis could have been no quieter. This church was the same. There just wasn't anything to hear. High in the dome, immediately over the pews, were rounded paintings depicting Biblical stories, and all about the walls as backdrop for the statues were murals. Our eyes swept around and up, and we knew we had come upon something special; we settled in and spent the rest of the day.

We stretched out on pews, looking at whichever painting in the dome was best in line from that position, and then we would change over to the other ends of the pews and look at the opposite picture. To rest our eyes we walked around and looked at murals. Neither of us knows art from a knothole in a spruce board, but we stayed there fascinated hour after hour. Nobody came in, and from the sanctity of the church we heard no traffic outside — there probably wasn't any. We came out at last knowing nothing about what we had seen — time, occasion, method, color, stroke, none of the things lovers and students of art would know about. All we knew was that there had been an intensity of peace, a very quiet moment in a world that is not quiet, with a beauty that solaced us, and a spirit over all that was comforting. Somebody asked me afterwards if these were frescoes, and I have no idea. What difference would that make? I think the big thing that got us was the lonesomeness of the place — do you suppose we were the only strangers in a thousand years who had the time to find Apfeltrach?

Up in Armstrong, just over the Maine border in Quebec, the town has a roadside sign advertising its attractions and opportunities, and one line says, "Population — 68." But Armstrong has declined, and the figure 68 is crossed out and under it is lettered a new and revised figure — 66. It is always refreshing to find this kind of rebellion against chamber-of-commerce attitudes. Apfeltrach must be even smaller than that. Too many places vie and brag, and too many cities and states promote and expand, until only the "fastest growing community" is worth visiting. Germany brags of art galleries in the hundreds and quotes figures in the millions about annual attendance, but Apfeltrach is not on the list. I'm sure the Apfeltrach church doesn't draw a Sunday attendance of even 66, and the German Tourist Information Service has no pamphlet.

When we came out of the church it was growing late, and the little old lady was puttering with bouquets on the churchyard graves. We stood aside a moment, as if in meditation at one stone for Maria Muntz, aged 78, and watched her take a few alp violets and marigolds and rearrange them from a windblown disorder into a precise display, her gnarled old hands fumbling at it, and then she poured a little mop water into the vase. We said *auf Wiedersehen* but she only bobbed her head and smiled — a good smile, but sans teeth and clearly out of courtesy and politeness, not because she felt like smiling. Whatever pain, sorrow, sadness and misery were her lot, she was nonetheless the curator of the best art gallery we saw in Europe. We saw nobody else in Apfeltrach, and we drove back to Mindelheim quiet and contemplative, for it had been a tremendous day.

In a way, Grandmother was no help — but perhaps it's just as well. Yes, she said, the paintings in the church at Apfeltrach are beautiful, and very old. How old, nobody knows. In the early days, even before the Renaissance — oh, long before that, even — wandering artists, monks of course, came up from Italy, and this was one of the ways they came. They had a good thing going. Good German stonemasons laid up the churches, and a monk who would stop by and embellish the cold stone and rock and mortar was sure of a good living as long as it took him. He could, even as house painters do in the United States, make the job last. Sometimes they never finished, but painted on and on until they died, and then another monk would come and take over. Now and then a monk would be smack in the middle of the Beatitudes when he would hear that a larger and more prosperous parish, up in the wine land, was building a church, and he would take off with the Beatitudes hardly started and they might wait for four hundred years for another monk to come through from Italy and pick up the brushes. "Nobody knows who painted the church at Apfeltrach," said Grandmother, "but he was a very famous artist."

Such is fame. For those who take the time, said Miss Aldendorph.

That evening Grandmother told all the guests in the dining room that we had been to Apfeltrach to see the paintings in the church, and some of the good Mindelheimers said they, too, planned to go someday and see them. "They are very famous," everybody said.

Grandmother kissed us goodbye when we left the Gasthof zum Stern, and handed us a little package to carry home with us. In it were the two glasses we had used when we joined the students' white-cap drinking club.

And So to Munich

The Trots, known more politely as the Tourist Complaint, occupied us somewhat during our advance on Munich, and we sent a postcard to Bill Spear, our local doctor back home, saying, "Wish you were here!" Actually, the standard professional answer to this disturbance is a big bomb that comes either blue or red, and it is meant to quiet down the alimentary situation without too much bother with diagnosis. After a time things clear up, and they did with us and we weren't bothered again.

During World War II the government urged Aroostook County to grow all the potatoes it could, and when fall came the need for harvest hands was great. Maine never has enough hands anyway, and always imports Canadian labor, but the wartime crop was the biggest in history and a national emergency was declared. A National Manpower Emergency Agency was set up, and some of the things that happened were comical. First, a shipment of West Indians came, and they landed in Presque Isle just as the thermometer dropped to a comfy Aroostook normal and water froze in the hand basins. Tropical labor is interesting to watch as you rout it out at daybreak to pick up potatoes before they freeze. The Aroostook farmers were in their shirtsleeves, remarking on what a lovely fall morning it turned out to be, and the West Indians were frozen stiff. Another work force came from Kentucky and West Virginia, but they were all farm people and they adjusted well enough and made out fine. But it was the Boy Scouts that mattered. Kind, courteous, etc., the Boy Scout officials saw a chance to perform a vast public service, and they quickly organized volunteer groups of Scouts from our leading urban centers to converge on the potato harvest and solve everything. They came in droves, each group of boys with its merit badges and flags, and under the escort of competent adult leadership. Of course, being all city people and unable to act unless something in the manual covered the matter, the Boy Scouts were more trouble than they were worth, but you don't knock a patriotic war effort, and Aroostook County went along.

Well, two days after the Boy Scouts got settled in, the entire congregation came down with the tourist complaint, and there wasn't a lad in the bunch had strength enough to lift a potato basket. In desperation the Scout leaders began flying in specialists from New York, Hartford and Philadelphia to save these boys from their terrible affliction. A great wealth of double-talk was being fed the newspapers to keep the parents back home from worrying, and Aroostook people were saying the only intelligent thing you can say about this complaint, "Oh, they'll be all right in a couple of days, as soon as they get used to the water."

Munich is one of those cities, like Ogaste, which turns out to be something else when you get there. It is called München because in the Dark Ages some monks came and set up a brewery, and because they have not yet been

114

turned out I suspect the idea was popular. If I may offer an opinion, I would suggest that the best beer in Europe is found in Copenhagen, Antwerp and Dortmund, in that order, and that while Munich produces many good beers and has an international fame, a great many local breweries scattered throughout Germany make just as good, and better, brews. We know of no domestic United States beer which compares with any of the Munich products, although we think Canada has one, and perhaps two. Temperate Americans, thrown into a foreign situation where they quickly become experts on beverages, perhaps have no right to advance any such opinions, but we subscribed to the customs of the lands we found in a methodical manner with a clinical approach.

Munich is a large city, and of course Bavarian. She has every problem common to modern metropolitan areas on any continent, yet she has that particular charm so few cities can keep as they grow — a small-town flavor through all the bustle and hullaballoo. It is a chummy place, and full appreciation comes after you have assessed the Bavarians as a whole — they still think they have their old kings and that Europe sort of fans out from them in all directions. As odious as comparisons are, Munich stacks up rather well if you think of London, Paris, Hamburg. There aren't many cities, when you come right down to it, that stand out amongst cities, but Munich will be one of the half-dozen that do.

Coming from the resort area about Starnberger See into Munich was like coming from darkness to light, and we promptly got hopelessly lost in as fine a traffic snarl as I ever saw. But in the bewilderment there was still something of charm and delight in the plain fact that we were trying to get from Maximilianstrasse onto Leopoldstrasse, which is something you can't very well do anywhere else.

The fact that now was Oktoberfest time partly caused the congestion, because Munich is in carnival and everybody comes. That was why we had prudently reserved two double rooms months before at the Pension Olive although willing to take our chances with hotels everywhere else, even in Paris. During Oktoberfest people sleep in the English Gardens — a huge park. We knew Ohmstrasse and the Olive were off Leopold, and in that section of Munich called Swabing — sometimes loosely compared to Greenwich Village in New York. Because of traffic we saw almost all of Munich, even to the airport, before we located Ohmstrasse and parked our VW up on the sidewalk in such a way that the numerous *Einfahrts* and *Ausfahrts* were not violated. We pushed the *Klingel* at No. 13 and became acquainted with Renata. Renata was the chambermaid and abigail of the establishment and when, later, I asked her how big are the English Gardens she said, "I don't know, I come from Frankfurt."

Renata spoke only German, and Frankfurt German, and as she settled us in our room she asked us when the Morrills would come. Because of our dillydallying in Mindelheim we thought the Morrills would arrive in Munich before we did, flying from London. Their trip to Europe was not at all like ours — they had signed up to "crew" on the *Yankee*, a sailing yacht that was coursing the rivers and canals of Europe under the sponsorship of the National Geographic Society, a voyage we later watched back home on television. Things worked out so they could pause in England, and then spend two weeks with us in Bavaria and Austria before going on to Paris to join the *Yankee*. Renata was not worried about the failure of George and Betty Morrill to show punctually, but she was concerned that a reserved bed might go unused while Oktoberfest customers slept in the park.

116

Next Renata brought in Frau von Itter, the proprietress of the Pension Olive, who thrust out her hand and welcomed us in magnificent English, cultured and refined, and set the mood for our wonderful stay in her establishment. No longer young, but far from old, Miss Itter, who told us the "von" was honest and not married-into, was most attractive, and in later conversations she told how she had been the friend of Mr. Olive (o-leev-a) who had, on his demise some time since, left her the pension, previous to which she had managed it for him. On an upper floor of a huge stone building just like several others on the street, the pension had a front apartment reserved for Frau von Itter, a cubicle to the rear for Renata, and the other rooms were for the public. "Mostly my friends of long time," said Miss von Itter, and although we weren't then we soon became such. Her apartment was loaded with priceless antiques and personal effects, and during the war she and Mr. Olive had moved them to safety — a good thing because the building had been badly bombed. As soon as reconstruction was done she moved everything back. In addition to a pittance Renata was supposed to be getting instruction in the operation of a pension, and ran about all day to the raucous call of "Renata!" from Frau von Itter, whose dulcet voice became a bellow when she needed her slavey. Miss von Itter (in German *Frau* and *Fräulein* are not always the equivalents of Mrs. and Miss; an unmarried lady past, say, thirty, may if she wishes assume *Frau*) also inquired about the Morrills, saying she was having many opportunities every hour to rent that room. I told her George would pay anyway, and if he didn't I would, but this wasn't the answer — a vacant bed during Oktoberfest shouldn't happen.

And it happened — George and Betty still didn't

come, and there was no call for us to meet them at the airport, and people were sleeping in the English Gardens, and it rained that night, and the bed went unused. Frau von Itter kept harping on it.

The pension differs from a hotel in many ways. It will serve breakfast, but it has no dining room. It offers the homey touch and, in Frau von Itter's pension, some of the feel of sleeping in a museum. Renata stood ready constantly to perform any and all services which a decorous household can reasonably offer.

That noon, wondering whatever became of the Morrills, we walked to a restaurant and made a unique discovery. We discovered a waitress with a bosom it is difficult to describe without extending the arms, and she fascinated us. She was a wonderful waitress and gave us every courtesy — but she protruded in front beyond belief. She was young and extremely pretty in the face, with a fine complexion, but we felt so sorry for her — it was too much. She had to walk leaning backwards. She had a wonderful smile, bright and regular teeth, and all in all it was a haunting thing. We were to see her twice again. After the Morrills arrived I naturally took George around to see her, and then several days later we took our ladies to a beauty parlor and we looked in through the curtains and saw our waitress under a drier. We waved chummily at her and she waved back, smiling from under the drier as if she were peeping over two sacks of oats. I mention this mostly to make the point that all the sights of Munich are not included in the all-expense brochures.

It was at this girl's restaurant that George later discovered the slot machine that paid off every time he played it. The ten-pfennig slot machine is common in Germany; it pays off up to a mark. It matches pears and plums, and so on, and as ten-pfennig is their smallest practical coin

118

the risk is not great. Almost any hotel has one in a bar, and often in the upstairs corridors. All in all, I doubt if I lost over 50c to the things. So while dining in the shadow of our interesting waitress George and I would get up every few minutes and slip a coin in the slot machine and yank the lever. Then George went farther, to the toilet, and on the way he found another slot machine. It took a mark, and as he played it he got his mark back — ten ten-pfennig coins. He played it again. He never won anything, but he never lost. He came back to the table exulting in his lucky chance. It was, of course, a change machine, so you could put in a mark and get coins to play the other machine. When we told our waitress why we were laughing so hard at George she went into raptures of hysterics and jiggled through the rest of our dinner in a manner that is truly memorable.

But that evening the Morrills still hadn't come, and Renata and Frau von Itter grumbled again about people sleeping in the English Gardens, and after Renata fluffed up our featherbeds we slept.

Maine Lobsters

Still waiting for the Morrills, we read in the newspaper that a big international food fair was taking place in Munich, at IKOFA. Newspapers

119

are something no tourist should neglect, and we made a practice of looking at all we could find. Throughout Europe local newspapers are hung in bars and restaurants for the customers, and if you don't understand the language you can at least be amused when Dick Tracy speaks German, or you find that Dagwood has become Dinkwart. The American family mores of the Bumsteads, of course, are completely unintelligible to a German man and wife, and the strip is far funnier there than it is here, but not for the same reasons. And in Germany the American tourists ought to study the newspapers with either national pride or national regret, because they are our baby. During the Occupation we "licensed" publishers and insisted on certain maneuvers quite at odds with good United States constitutional ideas about a free press. We created quite a few millionaires, a condition most Germans are willing to embrace, and by edict kept a great many friendly and competent editors from appearing. When we removed the license, after five years, the unlicensed publishers could again print, but their traditional circulations had been gobbled up by the millionaires. It was pretty sticky for some time, and still is here and there. In Germany, we found, it is quite proper to ask if a newspaper is Protestant or Catholic — this has no spiritual bearing, but it helps explain the political editorials.

So in the Munich *Mercury* the word "Maine" leaped out of an article, and with much frisking of the dictionary we learned that the United States had a booth at this big food fair, and among the six states taking part was Maine. Frau von Itter told us which trolley car to take on Leopoldstrasse and we headed for IKOFA. It was, by glorious coincidence, the same car that was hauling beer-thirsty Bavarians by the long ton to the Oktoberfest, which is

120

held in a park right alongside IKOFA. The juxtaposition of these two events makes for great happiness, because food and drink walk a thin line of distinction in Munich. We went to IKOFA in an Oktoberfest context — which means being jerked inside the already overcrowded streetcar by those aboard, and then in turn jerking in some more at every stop.

Munich has a subway, but the surface trolleys will go down fighting the good fight. Indeed, all over Germany the electric streetcar holds up well in public esteem. To have ridden on any one of them is a delight, but to ride on one in Munich during Oktoberfest has no equal in transportation joy. The car that came along was so completely full that nobody in Boston or New York would think of trying to get into it. But as it came to a stop the doors opened and we were actually pulled inside by the arms, with gay laughter from all. And at the next stop our waists were encircled by those behind us and we pulled in some more. How the woman conductor squirmed through the mass, taking our fares and handing us the *Quittung*, cannot be explained, but she did it and we have the receipts among our souvenirs. We shall keep them always, not just because they are souvenirs, but because the German streetcar receipt must never be thrown away or they will make you pay again, and such is the efficiency of those women conductors that we expect one to show up at the farm any minute. I can't tell you why they haven't gone to turnstiles and tokens. Most of the crowd in our car went one way to the Oktoberfest, but we bought tickets and walked onto the IKOFA grounds. It's a huge and handsome area, designed for great exhibitions, and we were already feeling a little proud that our plain and rugged homespun state, perched on a nation's edge, had made this long trip to Munich to display the lobster of which we are so proud. The Munich *Mercury* had been most explicit about the Maine *Hummer;* it had not dwelt so much on the other states.

German is a good language, and if hard is also rational and logical. And the average German is linguistically wise enough so a floundering tourist, if he makes an effort, will seldom know if he has scored or made a near-miss. If English words and ideas are given some kind of German sentence order it is fairly easy to handle most situations. I stopped a man and inquired for the *"Amerikanischeausstellung,"* and I have no idea even now how close I came to anything. Not the slightest expression came over his face, and I'm sure he was inwardly amazed and curious, but he quietly and slowly, in Bavarian German, directed me to the left, through the first, second and third buildings, and straight ahead to the far end of the fourth. We couldn't miss it. As we went along, exhibit after exhibit and building after building, the food story of the world was laid out — everything from cakes on little plates to huge stainless steel hotel kitchens, country by country the earth around. And as we were halfway through the fourth huge hall a most distressing thing happened — there was a power failure. The place was plunged into darkness. I imagine the Bavarian Ministry of Illuminations promptly went out and cut their throats in shame, for in efficient Germany this would be a public disgrace. I've seen the fog close in on the Back River at Friendship until things were just as dark, so this seemed an appropriate welcome to a Maine exhibit in Munich. Then, up ahead, there was a flicker, and then another, and over the crowd in the flickers we could see the word we were looking for, "Maine." We got to the booth, and at least two dozen Germans were holding their cigarette lighters aflame while two of our old friends from back home in Maine were frantically dipping water in a glass tank, with a snatch of good down-east lobsters crawling about on the bottom.

"What the hell's going on!" I asked, and both friends said, "Hi, John," without looking up. They recognized not only the greeting, but the voice, but this was no time to stop dipping water and shake hands. When the power went off the motor that rectified the saline tank water stopped, and until the power came back on the water had to be agitated with paper cups — two by Bob Dow and two by Hildreth Hawes. When food is in peril any German will lend a hand, and the best assistance was all the cigarette-lighter illumination that could be bunched. Dorothy and I grabbed some paper cups and went at it. We paper-cupped the crustaceans through the crisis, and when the lights came on again all over IKOFA, we shook hands and had a reunion. Bob Dow, who knows more about lobsters than any other living man, was a student with me in Bowdoin, and is now the research director for the Maine Department of Sea and Shore Fisheries. Hildreth Hawes is with our State Department of Agriculture, in charge of displays and promotions. The trip to Munich was a weird kind of publicity stunt, and cost Maine a lot of money for nothing much. Such is the perishable nature of the Maine lobster and the pixilated way airlines are run that the whole idea of building up a demand three thousand miles away was sheerest whimsy. But Maine does have a sizable trade with West Germany in poultry meats, some potatoes and some apples, and the lobsters offered a come-on window dressing that was well worth the price quite apart from any business that might come from them, if any. Bob and Hildreth had combined an excellent exhibit of numerous Maine foodstuffs, and the lobsters drew the crowd.

But they'd had a time of it getting the lobsters there. Several conferences were held with the airlines, and with good modern-day frugality with transportation truths the airlines had said, "Oh, yes — certainly; no problem." But you can't leave a crate of Maine lobsters sitting in the sun at Logan Airport while you change an engine or wait for the movie tapes to come, and the State of Maine had insisted on more than a routine yes-yes. So firm interlocking schedules had been set up and every airlines employee all along the way had been briefed and instructed. "Nothing can go wrong," they said, and with this assurance the State of Maine signed up for the IKOFA fair.

Of course, the airlines could have said no. This would have been the smart thing for them to do. It's one thing to haul passengers and freight — quite another to haul live Maine lobsters. But the airlines said yes, and nobody has yet explained why the shipment of luscious Maine lobsters plainly marked for Munich got off a plane in Vienna, where nobody knew what they were or what to do with them. The lobsters were so agitated by this unexpected turn that they became listless and uncooperative, and if they had eventually come to Munich they would not have had much fun there. But Bob and Hildreth had gone into action, and new shipments had come through all right.

It was fun to watch the Germans drool at our lobsters. Anything that can be cooked and placed hot on a plate mesmerizes a German, and the *Hummer* looked good to them. Now and then Bob and Hildreth would boil one off and pass small pieces of the meat out on good Maine birch toothpicks, and whenever a lobster began to turn red in the pot the crowd at the Maine booth grew to enormous proportions.

Only Illinois was doing any better, and they got out of

it much cheaper and more simply. They brought a popcorn machine, and passed out paper cups of hot buttered Illinois popcorn. The Germans have discovered popcorn only recently, and call it *Poofmais*. They say sailors on German ships coming to the Great Lakes fetched it home, but unlike the American style the German version has sugar on it. They like it sweet. Nobody had told Illinois about this, and perhaps it's just as well, because everybody liked it anyway. Some Germans kept coming back again and again to have their cups filled, and there was one fat fellow the Illinois marketing specialist was calling Fritz already.

In the Maine booth was a frozen-foods case, and amongst the goodies were some fat Cacklebirds from Belfast. In Europe the market bird runs small, and in Germany they don't do much oven roasting so compared to the chickens we'd been eating, these beautiful Maine capons were huge and handsome. Hildreth asked me if I knew somebody I'd like to give one to, and the idea of bringing one to Frau von Itter came up. So on the day the IKOFA exhibition ended, the little German girl who had been Maine's interpreter in the booth brought two Cacklebirds to the Pension Olive, and that's how we came to have a dinner party in Frau von Itter's apartment, and began calling her Edith.

It was late when we left the IKOFA grounds, and across the way the Oktoberfest was letting out — some who had already taken their three liters of beer felt like going home. We got jammed amidships in a trolley car and wondered all the way back how we'd ever get off at Ohmstrasse, but before many stops the car was a rollicking songfest, and you could see that with almost everybody it wasn't important to get off, anyway. "Wer soll das bezahlen!" they sang, "Wer hat soviel Geld?" Dorothy yelled, "I don't know as I dare to go to the Oktoberfest!" But wild horses couldn't hold us away, after that trolley ride. And we sang, as soon as we caught on to the words, and it's a dandy Oktoberfest song; "Who's going to pay for all this; who has so much money?" When we came to Ohmstrasse we yelled, "Aus, aus!" so convincingly that quite a few said, "Gute Nacht! Schlaffen-Sie gut!"

"Gute Nacht!" we called back as the doors shut on two or three dozen German noses, so close many of them touched the glass, and suddenly Munich was quiet. Our own heels were all we heard as we walked along Ohmstrasse and came to our VW on the sidewalk. I had the key to the pension, and we tiptoed down the corridor toward our room. Renata was standing there in the shadows and she whispered that the Morrills had not yet come. "Perhaps tomorrow," I said.

Chief Poolaw Pays Off

The arrival of George and Betty Morrill was a sensation for Renata. They came by taxi from the airport and Renata opened the pension door at their tinkle of the bell. Then Renata fled, bursting into our room in wild-eyed confusion shouting, "Herr Morrill! Herr Morrill!" You see, George is a tall, good-looking man without a hair on his head that ever was made, and baldness is rare in Germany, and George didn't have any hat on. Renata never learned to keep her eyes off his gleaming top, even though Frau von Itter would see her staring and admonish, "Renata!"

George Burnham Morrill, Jr., is the ultimate heir of the great food-packing firm of Burnham & Morrill. He is descended from both the original Burnham and the original Morrill. They started long ago with down-east fish, took on sweet corn and green beans, and over the years their most famous product has been the oven-baked bean, often imitated but never bettered. When George came into a dominant position in the company he sold it to the competing Underwood people, and the transaction left him in a position of affluence. A good part of his time is taken up with amusing himself, at which he is very good, and his pretty wife Betty is a great help to him in this department. We've known them for years, love their fine family, and from time to time have helped George with his amusements. To prepare for his voyage on the *Yankee* George had enrolled for the total-immersion French course at Berlitz, and in the beginning had no intention of coming to Germany at all. But Munich was the best place for the four of us to get together, and the Oktoberfest made the excuse. So we had our reunion in the front room of the Pension Olive, and while Renata stared Frau von Itter came from her apartment and welcomed George and Betty with all her charm and personality and then turned and cried, "Renata!"

George had three complaints. First, he was so full of tea from England he was eager to find some other beverage and had been told Munich was a fine place for that. Secondly, he was suffering from the opposite of the tourist complaint and was so bound up he couldn't tie his own shoes. And thirdly, he would like a good bath. The bath

127

was the soonest, and this is when Renata misheard and thought he said *Dusche* when he said *Tuch*. Because one usually discovers his need for a towel after he is in a bare and undraped state, the arrival of misunderstanding Renata to show him how to use the shower nozzle made a gay introduction to Germany. George said afterward it wasn't really too bad because Renata looked only at the top of his head.

We were to have an even bigger party. George and Betty knew a couple of girls from Portland who had been in the Peace Corps in Morocco, and they were taking a fling at Europe before going home. Cathy MacDonald and Nancy Langmaid. Arriving in Munich because they knew the Morrills were to be at Pension Olive, they had luckily found a room not far from it, but in a house Frau von Itter said was not exactly a pension, and she raised her eyes and said, "Tch, tch!" The girls had surmised as much when they moved in, but they couldn't find anything else. So they arrived at Pension Olive and our Oktoberfest party was now six.

But that afternoon it jumped to eight. Dr. and Frau Friedrich Bechtle of Esslingen am Neckar arrived — and for us this was a wonderful sight. Some years back they, as newlyweds, had come to America, and we had entertained them at the farm. He is one of three brothers who own the Bechtle Publishing Firm in Esslingen, with a daily newspaper called the *Esslinger Zeitung* with a circulation of about one hundred thirty thousand. Besides that, and a considerable book publishing business, they print the south German edition of the *Bild Zeitung* of Hamburg — a daily stint of five hundred thousand copies. So Fritz is something of a tycoon — a young man whose English is even better than ours, poised and knowledgeable, and at the moment eager to return the courtesies we had shown him in Maine.

When Fritz and Irene Bechtle had been in Maine we had no notion of ever going to Germany. We didn't know that they had spent their wedding night in a small inn high in the Black Forest, and that the greatest joy of their lives was to return to the scene as often as they could and walk hand in hand down the paths. Their love for "the forest" made Maine a natural, and their eyes bugged at the miles and miles of winding wilderness road we showed them. I paddled Irene around in a White canoe, and we had cookouts, and when they got home to Germany they had two loves — the Black Forest and Maine.

But the greatest thrill of their entire visit to America came when I introduced them to Chief Bruce Poolaw at the Penobscot reservation at Old Town. The Germans are Indian crazy. Some say there is a great national complex about this, and in the American Indian they see an abuse which solaces their own feeling of guilt about minorities. Maybe so, maybe not; but they do take great interest in our Wild West lore. At Bad Segeberg, a north German town, they hold an annual pageant which runs for a week, sort of on the Oberammergau Passion Play idea, but instead of a Biblical theme they tell the story of the American Indian. Thousands come to see this, and to an American some of it is more amusing than historical. The eastern Indians who greet the Pilgrims, for instance, seem more like Sioux and Paiutes. So if this effects a "proper purgation" for the national German conscience, it is all to the good, and when Fritz and Irene were at our farm in Maine they said they were looking forward to seeing New Mexico and Arizona, where they hoped to get some movies of real American Indians.

129

"Shucks," I said. "You don't have to go to the sow-west to see an Indian — tomorrow we'll go and call on the Penobscots."

Chief Bruce Poolaw and I are old friends. Once I did a dance with him at a Republican State Convention, some kind of a demonstration for Margaret Chase Smith. He isn't a Penobscot himself, but originated out in Oklahoma, and is a college man of good intelligence and culture, and a very fine business sense. He married a princess of the Penobscots, and for many years has had a "tepee" just at the end of the bridge onto Indian Island — it's a souvenir shop. He guides, gives lectures on Indian lore, and is frequently the spokesman for the tribe. So we drove up and parked in front of his tepee, and I stepped in to see if the Chief were around.

No, his wife said, he had just gone over to Old Town on an errand, but he would be right back, and why didn't I bring my friends in? We were touched at the awe with which Fritz and Irene approached the Chief's wife, and I stepped out in the back yard to wait for Bruce.

Presently he came driving in with a brand-new, white-wall Cadillac — he had just picked it up and that was his "errand." "Hello, John," he said as he got out — dressed in a smart flannel suit, with shirt and tie and shining black shoes — "good to see you again, how are you?"

"Fine, Bruce," I said. "And you?"

"Never better; never better."

So I told him we had some guests from Germany who had never met an American Indian, and this was to be the high spot in their tour of our great country, and I thought if I tipped him off beforehand he might outdo some of the tribes they'd meet later out West. "Perfect, perfect," he said. "This will be great fun. I'll give them

130

the ten-dollar treatment. You go in, and I'll make an entrance by the back door."

Chief Poolaw never put on a better show. He came in wearing a magnificent warbonnet with every eagle feather and horsehair in place, his store clothes completely hidden by a vast blanket. His moccasins alone were worth a special trip from Germany — beaded and adorned with rattlesnake buttons, they must have cost him a pretty penny from Sears Roebuck. He had even managed, in that short time, to get on some warpaint. He stood poised in the doorway for effect, and then he raised an arm in the gesture of Peace and spoke. "How!" he said. "Welcome tepee!"

Fritz and Irene were overcome. They were instantly mesmerized. They each raised an arm and answered, "How!"

Dorothy and I managed to keep straight faces, but Bruce's Penobscot wife had to retire to the dingle with her giggles. The Bruce satisfied every possible desire of the Bechtles. He did a rain dance and a war dance, and taught Irene the steps. He brought out a warbonnet for her, and while Fritz ground away with his motion-picture camera Bruce and Irene conversed in sign language. The pictures "came out good," and are a sensation back in Germany every time Fritz shows them. Whenever I see Chief Poolaw he wants to know how my German friends are doing.

But there were some other things to make the Bechtles remember Maine. Our Department of Economic Development staged a press party to open a trade fair in the Augusta armory, and we took the Bechtles to it. The cocktails were weak and the fair wasn't big enough to impress a German, but Fritz did meet all our big shots, including our governor. This was a high social accomplishment, and the only

American governor Fritz was to shake. And even better, perhaps, the German Consul from Boston was a guest at the party, and he recognized Fritz and began showing a little deference. This didn't hurt at all, and when the deference ended up in a tavern that almost rivaled any German *gemütlichness,* Fritz had good reason to remember Maine.

So, all in all, this explains why Fritz and Irene came barreling into Munich that afternoon in the big chauffeur-driven Mercedes-Benz to take us to the Oktoberfest. It also explains why we didn't ride out to the whing-ding on the wonderful Munich trolley cars, singing and laughing. We went, instead, in the air-conditioned, executive, status model with a purposeful German driver who solved every traffic problem by blowing the horn.

The Oktoberfest

With his bath over and tea forgotten George reported that his third problem was behind him, and we could hoist all flags and forge ahead. Fritz gave us a fine example of a German businessman dividing his time. He and Irene would devote two weeks to us and the Morrills, off and on, but all plans must now be adjusted to his business calendar. Day by day, hour for hour, the time was set down on a pad and shortly everything was *bestimmt* and he handed the pad to his chauf-

132

feur. The chauffeur would give it to the secretary, and she would do the rest. Now, Fritz was free as the wind and he said, "Now, let us get in the mood!" He embraced all the females and shook hands with me and George.

The Bechtles are a good-looking couple. Fritz was wearing his Swabian suit, which is not unlike the Bavarian. Irene is a stunning woman, tall and dark. Her family has a jewelry business in Pforzheim — manufacturing. Both are old enough to remember some of the war, and a good deal more is hearsay. Since the Bechtle newspaper was licensed under the Occupation Fritz came to know many American military and State Department people, socially as well as officially. By and large we avoided all political conversations throughout our whole trip, but we had several with Fritz, and we told him it's a shame he can't come to America and tell our Congress some of the things they need to know. He had what we thought were sound attitudes toward American military activities in Europe, and he was unemotionally convincing with his opinions about Russian purposes. He also was articulate about South Asia, and as a German journalist flew to Vietnam to look things over. But these talks with Fritz came later — right now we were in Oktoberfest mood!

There are pamphlets which explain the Oktoberfest. In the more genteel it is called a folk-gathering, but it would be a mistake to picture Burl Ives singing Jimmie-crack-corn. We did pick up a mimeographed sheet that told all about the Princess Theresa, and this makes a pleasant, if unlikely, story. One of the old Bavarian kings had a pretty daughter, Theresa, and it came time for her marriage. Now, right here, a tourist needs to wonder. Munich is a style center, and has many pretty women. But the word "Bavarian" suggests something with a wider bottom, hearty and husky. When you see a store window in Bavaria displaying brassieres and find that the German word is *Büstenhalter* you begin to get the idea. After you've seen a bevy of beefy Bavarian belles you naturally wonder about this fair princess. She could have been a tub.

And you doubt some more when you read that in honor of her nuptials somebody proposed that they hold a great free-for-all horse trot. This improbable wedding entertainment is given, all the same, as the basic explanation of the Oktoberfest. It seems that she was married, and that every nag in Bavaria turned out to honor her in what must have been the wildest charge since Wagner personally conducted the Valkyries. The canter took place in a section of Munich which was immediately dubbed the "Theresa-field," and ever since then, annually, a big horse race is held as the opening ding-dong of the great festival. In the Bavarian dialect the big park sounds something like "Teezieweezie." A sort of Boston Common or Central Park the rest of the year, it is given over to the Oktoberfest every September — the thing does run two weeks into October, so that's all right. After the horse race, which is now a legendary necessity and has no honest bearing on anything, they hold a parade of beer wagons — and this is much more in keeping. The event is the annual blow-off of the Munich breweries, and that's all it is. The new brew is tapped, everybody tries it, and without variation in centuries the results are pronounced superior. For this event, and for this event alone, the normal alcoholic content of Bavarian beer is pepped up eight or ten percentage notches, and here and here alone you can get "Oktoberfestbier."

Each brewery erects what is called a "tent," but it is a huge wooden beer hall with kitchens protruding from one end and toilets from the other. These tents come

134

apart in sections and are stored from year to year. The smallest appeared to be the Pschorr tent, said to seat eight thousand people; the largest was the Löwenbräu, holding up to twenty thousand. The six or eight other tents average ten thousand to fifteen thousand apiece. How do you come back to Maine and tell your friends you saw a building where twenty thousand people were seated at tables, eating, drinking and singing?

In the center of each tent is a bandstand, with musicians in Bavarian costume, and the old oompah is belted out from noon on. The tables stretch away under balconies, with other tables on the balconies. And there is a promenade area where unseated people can march around and around until they find a place to sit down. There is no dancing.

A German beer glass generally holds a quarter of a liter, but at Oktoberfest the glass stein holds a full liter. This is more than a U.S. quart. Three liters are normal for an Oktoberfest evening. In the old days the steins were really of stone, or crockeryware, but now they are of heavy glass, with the crest of the brewery concerned. No German ever contemplates stealing an Oktoberfest stein, but all tourists are expected to lift one for a souvenir. The way to steal an Oktoberfest stein is to pick it up when you leave and walk out with it. The Germans all point at you and laugh and sing, and the doorman will suggest it is more sporting to conceal it under a coat, so the whole devilishment of the theft is a little thin.

True, the only possible way to believe what goes on in an Oktoberfest tent is to walk into one and spend the evening. It is an incredible orgy of food and drink, singing and funmaking, but never rowdy and not at all the spectacle temperance lecturers promise from such goings-on. Fritz led us directly to a table, and not until later

135

did we realize he had told the headwaiter we were important American dignitaries and that a little money changed hands. He was giving us the old Bruce Poolaw routine. We picked up the menus, and Fritz made a sign for the beers.

Just then a pleasant gentleman of rotund persuasion came wobbling up to our table and told of an incredible happening. He said he had been seated at this table in jolly attitude, meditating on the great happiness that prevailed, and all at once he had found himself out in the open, behind the Ferris wheel, and it was with the greatest difficulty he managed to locate his table again — which he now found occupied by a considerable group of strangers. We all shook hands with him, marveled at such a strange story, and gave him our fullest sympathy. So he told us all about it another time. The headwaiter then came over and listened, and he said, "Do you mean like this?" and with a discreet and gentle maneuver he so handled the rotund gentleman that he found himself out behind the Ferris wheel again. We suspicioned cahoots. The fellow kept coming back again, off and on, and each time we shook hands sedately and he thanked us for so patiently giving ear to his troubles. He never got mad, and never raised his voice in complaint. I'd have been sore as hell.

Then there was a woman who wanted to join us. She kept going by in the promenade area, and finally she plucked my sleeve and asked if we had a place for her. Irene shouted, "No, no!" but afterwards she told me this wasn't really a solicitation and I shouldn't feel so pleased about it — the woman merely wanted a seat, and that's all. "Always room for one more," said Irene, but thanks to her not at our table.

The waitresses are in Bavarian dress, and are famous

for their ability to bring great numbers of the liter steins
at once. Eight steins was nowhere near a record, but it is
still a goodly heft of glass and beer, and the trick is done
by looping the fingers through the handles just so and
balancing the whole snatch on the *Büstenhalter*. When our
waitress came the rotund gentleman was telling us again
about the Ferris wheel, and she let out a wild "Vorsicht!"
and caught him a clip in the tail with one knee. It set him
over about five feet, and in the same moment she slid the
eight steins off her bosom in such a way they slid along
the table and came to a stop right where they were supposed to be. I think a brain operation may require less
skill.

Then a woman came by with a great board of souvenir
postcards. We picked out a good supply all around, and
the woman sold us postage stamps and carried them away
to be mailed. The postcard theme of the Oktoberfest is
mainly the tipsy Bavarian farmer who blows his blast and
then catches hell from the Frau when he gets home. Back-
house humor is even better portrayed than in the English
music hall. The signs in Munich that point to the "00,"
or the public toilet, are a golden cupid sitting on a pottie,
his arrow showing the direction, and the whole thing up
on a lamppost. By the time we finished addressing the
cards the waitress fetched our second liters of beer.

From another souvenir board Fritz bought the girls
some funny carnival hats, and I picked down a paper
envelope of very black festival cigars. Just then a man
going by on the promenade smiled at me, no doubt want-
ing a seat, and I shook his hand over the railing and gave
him a cigar. He thanked me and moved along. But a
half hour later he was back, picking at my sleeve, and
bubbling all over the place with friendly elation. He said
when I gave him the cigar he thought it was a joke, and

probably made of rubber, but when he had located a table and had a chance to sit down he looked at it — and it was real! So he had come all the way back, and probably lost his place, to thank me! I scratched a match and lit him up, and gave him the rest of the envelope. He was puffing away and waving back as he slipped into the stream and disappeared from my life.

Both George and I led the band. According to tradition anybody can lead the band if he buys a round of drinks for the musicians. With Fritz squiring us it probably didn't work that way, but we don't know. A man came and got George first, and we could see his bare head moving through the throng toward the bandstand. But just before they took him up the steps they clapped a great Bavarian hat on him with sweeping ostrich plumes and he stepped before the band looking more Oktoberfesty than anybody. In full dignity he raised the baton, and on the downbeat the whole beer tent shook with the wild brass and boom of an ancient Bavarian march, and George was in a frenzy of stick-waving which threw the crowd into an ecstasy. They all believed, of course, that George had bought the round of drinks, and this would run into a figure any Bavarian would respect. When he finished the tumult went on and on, and he took his well-earned bows with the ostrich plumes sweeping the atmosphere. When he returned to our table we all rose, bowed, and clapped, and this was picked up throughout the tent and he had another rousing ovation. He made a great success.

When the man came a little later to get me, I learned that what George had just done wasn't easy. We didn't know the tunes, to begin with, and when you get up on a bandstand a band doesn't sound very much like a band. They didn't put the hat on me, perhaps because I have hair, but I improved on George somewhat by instituting a few pregame maneuvers. I shook hands with the real conductor and gave him a courtly bow. Then I bowed in all directions about the tent, and finally bowed at my musicians. They rose and bowed back. This had gone so well I did it all over again. When I finally brought down the baton I caused the wildest squawking and tooting and honking and pounding I ever heard in my life, and for a split second I thought they were having fun with me by producing discord. I couldn't hear any tune at all. But that's the way a band sounds to a leader, and after a few booming bars I had things under control. It was another march, and a dandy, and from the drummers I could foresee the beat. Since the march had considerable repetition I could do better each time it went around. Out of the corner of my eye I saw some trumpets getting ready to blow, and with a shrewd guess I turned and brought them in perfectly. I did the same for the glockenspiel solo. I was now so intent on suiting my movements to the music that I even saw the real director give me a motion to turn and face the crowd behind me. I did, precisely on the right note, and everybody in the hall stood up and began marching around two by two and singing. You'd have sworn I'd directed this a thousand times before. I looked down and saw Dorothy and Fritz march by, arm in arm, with Fritz singing as if the top of his head would fly off and Dorothy with her funny hat and a bunch of violets.

At the conclusion I bowed through the amenities again, shook hands with the real director, and acknowledged the tumultuous applause. It is my only musical triumph — I who cannot sing and cannot play an instrument, or tell "Dixie" from "The Last Rose of Summer."

Three days later George and I went into a hardware store on the far side of Munich and a clerk stopped short in his tracks when he saw us come in. "I know you!" he said, sticking out his hand. "You led the band at the Teezieweezie!" Betwixt us, George and I have had many happinesses in our lives, and we plan to tackle a few more, but nothing will ever quite equal that moment. To be recognized as celebrated artists in storied Munich must top all else. That next Christmas George and I had wonderful ideas for presents. We gave each other a baton.

Far into the night we caroused with the Bavarians, and now and then we would eat supper again. The specialty of the Oktoberfest is half a barbecued chicken, but there are other dishes. I remember one supper of sausages and sauerkraut. We rode the roller coaster and I took Irene in the tunnel of love. We shot air rifles in a gallery, but nobody could hit anything. Somebody came up with a plush rabbit by tossing rings. Then we'd go to another tent and start all over again. Of all the memories, perhaps the strongest is of thousands of Germans with linked arms rocking back and forth to the band music, singing and having just the best time in the world. That night, too, we learned the rest of the words to that song we'd heard on the trolley car:

> *Who's going to pay for all this;*
> *Who has that much money?*
> *Who's got so much change?*
> *Who ordered all this?*

They sing it over and over, with varying inflections and changing tempo, and at Oktoberfest those are good questions.

The statistics on Oktoberfest are astronomical — so many millions of people, so many hectoliters of beer, so many chickens and sausages, and so much kraut and potato salad. But there is no statistical way to compute the

140

complete and uninhibited, if otherwise proper, conviviality of the Bavarian people when they break out and sample the new brew. And they do not leave this autumnal decision solely to the palates of the populace — they have an official test of the beer's quality. Twelve good men and true, wearing the *Lederhosen* of the region and the velvet green with the staghorn buttons, parade on stage and receive the plaudits of the crowd. The Lord Mayor of Munich makes a speech, and the band plays fanfares. Then a long, hardwood bench is brought in — just long enough to accommodate twelve broad Bavarian backsides. The top of this bench is now covered with the new beer, poured from tankards by costumed *Fräuleins*. When the top of the bench is thoroughly wet the Twelve Good Men and True sit down on it. A table is pushed before them, and there they sit before the crowd until each man has consumed the last of his traditional three liters of beer. When the final stein is empty the table is pulled away, and now the beer hall is silent as a tomb. The new brew is about to receive the acid test. The men, upon a fanfare from the band, stand up, and the great plank bench sticks to their leather pants and comes right up with them!

This proves the beer is good. Such is the nature of beer, plank, *Lederhosen* and the Bavarian anatomy that the bench always comes up. It has never failed in centuries of trial.

If you didn't know what to expect it remains forever as a memorable sight. But the Bavarians do know what to expect, and they always act as if it were a great surprise. They yell and whoop and link arms and sing and the band plays on. The twelve men and the Lord Mayor leave the stage, and Bavaria is safe for another year.

141

Our Roast Chicken

The next morning was amazingly serene. Fritz and Irene had been chauffeured back to Esslingen by Autobahn, and Renata had our breakfast ready when we woke up. Frau von Itter asked us what we thought of the Oktoberfest. We said it was fun, and she said it was disgraceful. She said the stupid people who went to it were no worse than the brewers who encouraged it, but it was a waste of time and a shame on the cultural escutcheon of Munich and she, for one, would never go near the place. She seemed to feel we ought to have big heads and bloodshot eyes and not care too much for breakfast, and we could see she had an erroneous idea of just what the Oktoberfest really was. Then the door bell rang, and it was our interpreter friend from IKOFA and she had brought two frozen Cacklebirds. She said Bob and Hildreth got on the plane all right, and the Maine exhibit had been crated and shipped. Frau von Itter clasped the huge birds to her bosom, and she must have had a chill before she got them to the kitchen, and then we heard Renata exclaim over them. Frau von Itter pulled a German hen from her refrigerator, and it looked like a pigeon alongside two geese. Then Frau von Itter asked how they should be cooked.

142

Dorothy and Betty said, "We'll show you." So Frau von Itter invited us to a chicken dinner in her apartment for the following evening, because the bird — one was enough — had to thaw first. Dorothy, who is about as good a cook as they come, had already done enough poking into kitchens in Europe to know there might be some of the standard New England items that would be hard to find, and this proved correct when they made a quick rundown with Frau Itter and Renata. Our kind of stale bread for the stuffing, and our kind of seasoning. And a roasting pan big enough.

So while we nosed around Munich that day and the next we kept looking. George, with his interest in food-stuffs, wanted to go through a big new supermarket, and this was fun. No matter what label a can bore, he knew who packed it, and the prices kept him interested. We found a sale on champagne, which Germany calls Sekt, and I bought four bottles for a dollar. France claims to be the true champagne country, but in the old days some of the original champagnes were perfected in France by German vintners, and afterwards the cuttings and the skills were taken back to Germany. Anyway, at 25c a bottle one embraces a sale. George attracted a lot of attention going up and down the aisles bareheaded and scrutinizing everything — the manager thought he was a spy from the competition. And Dorothy and Betty went to the big Loden-Frey department store and bought twin Bavarian suits — handsome things with lace shirts and all. At noon we found an out-of-the-way restaurant and we had to divide up for seats, so we all had table companions who practiced their English on us. And that evening we took George to dinner to see the waitress with the big bosom, and while she greeted us as if we were old friends she stared at George's head as if it were an oddity. Munich can be a wearisome day, so when Renata fluffed the featherbeds we turned in and slept like lumberjacks.

The next morning, after Renata finished the breakfast things, the kitchen went into action, and with Frau von Itter and Renata looking on like student nurses Dot and Betty began preparing the bird. They had found about everything they needed, although George and I were sent out for a couple of things, and pretty soon the kitchen looked and smelled pretty much like our own farm kitchen back in Maine on any good Thanksgiving morning.

George went out and bought a vast bouquet of standard bronze chrysanthemums, paying about a dollar for what would cost ten back home, and I said I would buy the wine — did Frau von Itter have any suggestions as to kind and place? She would do better than that — she would personally go and select the wine, and she knew a place where excellent wines are very cheap. We had been buying picnic wines all over the place for little or nothing, and George looked at his bouquet of posies and wondered what cheap meant. But in the afternoon, with the bird in the oven, she took my money and climbed on her bicycle and rode clear across Munich to save twenty pfennig, or about a nickel. She did bring an incredibly delicious white wine — German red wines come and go and you don't get excited, but a German white wine is worthy. Frau von Itter said she was sure her choice would please us.

The aroma of the Pension Olive, that day, must have puzzled the other guests. They came and went, sniffing, but restrained their curiosity. Renata trotted around all day, not only doing her regular work but helping with the party. She got out some priceless silver from Frau von Itter's treasures and shined it. She shined china. She spread out a white tablecloth that would make the Ajax knight quit his job, and Frau von Itter said it came from the time of the Czars, and thus and so had come into Mr. Olive's hands and hence into hers. The water heater at the Pension Olive has a slow recovery, so we spaced our baths, and this gave Renata time to scour down the tub each using. Betty and Dot got into their new Bavarian suits, and they looked like two million dollars on the hoof, and George and I got into the best we had. Renata gave our shoes an extra polish. And during all this, somehow, Frau von Itter managed to bathe and dress, and she appeared for dinner in considerable magnificence — a very pretty woman indeed, and we felt — as she probably did — that it would be nice if Mr. Olive might join us.

She led us into her apartment and the girls began exclaiming about the antiques. She showed us a photograph of Mr. Olive, and another of his wife and children. She apologized because she couldn't offer us an American mixed drink, but we assured her we frequently managed to get along without them at home, and we had not come to Europe to inculcate Americanisms. Simple schnapps would suffice. Renata lighted the candles and hovered to attend us, and we belied our own intent and inculcated the Americanism of hot roast chicken with all the fixin's right into the very heart of Bavaria. Mashed potatoes, carrots, onions, turnips, beets, and even a bit of squash — although it was not much like a good Hubbard and Frau von Itter said she didn't care much for it. And neither did I.

"George," I said. "I would like to propose the toast!"

George said, "If you don't, I will."

"All right, and I want to include everything. First, to all the American schoolmarms who buy quick-trip tickets to Munich and then come home to tell what they saw. Then, to us — who will go home and nobody will believe us. To Frau von Itter, her charm and her memories. To Renata. To friendship abroad, health in München, and reunion sometime."

Renata didn't understand a word, but Frau von Itter tensed a little, and Betty and Dorothy swallowed hard on such small sips of wine. George said, "Hear, hear!"

Renata thought he said, "Hier, hier," and she came running to see what he wanted.

It was a gay, festive, gastronomical success. Frau von Itter became reminiscent, and we listened as she told of the old days before the war. Her floodgates of memory let go, and she told of chalets in the Alps, villas in Italy, and things that happened once upon a time. About the coming of the war, the frantic flight with valuables, the bombing and the restoration of her home, and the happy day when she could open her rooms once again to her friends — many of them no longer living, of course, but enough to give her security. Finally Renata brought the Asbachs, and after fervent farewells and lingering goodnights we went to our rooms, where Renata had fluffed our beds.

Certainly the Cacklebird Industries of Belfast, Maine, had never, in their wildest corporate fancies, imagined this ultimate consumption of their finest product, and George said he couldn't think of any way he could explain to the Maine Department of Economic Development just exactly what had happened.

The next day we planned to look at the Bavarian Alps and go to Salzburg.

Fritz Goes Hunting

With the Morrills we had wonder and delight. We inspected the Alps and found them beautiful, awesome and magnificent — and evidently durable. No matter how much they use them, I think the Alps will last a long time. From the south German side they look about as well as anywhere, and most of the resort and recreation appurtenances look expensive. We came out of Munich on the throughway, but soon left it and hunted for side roads, and late one forenoon came to Bad Reichenhall and almost missed lunch.

We never really grew accustomed to the noontime closing of the shops. We'd lose track of time, and come to buy our picnic things after the shutters had been drawn. In Bad Reichenhall we actually bought lunch between the first and last strokes of twelve, and in the excitement each of us grabbed up about everything, and we had quite a selection when we came to a green field and parked to eat. George had a camera, and the pictures he took with the mountains behind our picnic are the only photographic record of our trip abroad.

We flashed our Green Sheet and thus came to Austria, and in Salzburg we paid homage to Mozart, who is a

147

patron of the pigeons, and also got involved in the archeological excavations before the cathedral. Just as we arrived a momentous discovery had been made and a carved stone dating from early times had been scientifically revealed. The excavations into the debris of Salzburg seemed to be a continuing tourist attraction, and I suspect the work is on a calculated economic schedule that permits them to find only so many relics per season. We were fortunate to arrive just as one turned up, and a television crew was set up with a formidable group of historians, professors, and archeologists moistening their lips and practicing cheese.

Of course, the whole thing was one of these "reenactments." There was a time news was reported as it happened, but today you have to do everything once more for the photographers. They had dug this stone out some time before, but had covered it again until the cameramen could come. The whole church square in Salzburg is being methodically sifted. Here is a crossroads of Europe, made important by the salt, and every tribe and every nation crossed and crisscrossed. Men who looked more like mason's helpers than archeologists were pushing wheelbarrows up out of the hole over planks, and each load was tagged and piled by itself for expert analysis. We stood by the railing, in a throng, and looked down as this stone was carefully uncovered again. All the scientists feigned astonishment when it came to light. They shook hands with one another all around until the cameras got just what they wanted. I said, "After me cometh a builder; tell him I, too, have known," and I turned to see if George appreciated my apt poetic allusion. He was nowhere in sight; neither were Betty and Dot. They had wandered off, and a sad, bewhiskered beatnik with a sack over his shoulder stood beside me

148

and smiled, and said, "Giblin!" Thinking it would be simpler for three to find one than for one to find three, I retreated with the beatnik to a bar and we had pleasant communion. Afterwards I went in and looked at the church, noting its antiquity, and then George and Betty and Dot came running up out of breath and said I had wandered off.

So we did what tourists do, and we eventually came back to Munich for one more night with Renata and Frau von Itter, and then we packed the VW for our trip to Swabia and a few days with Fritz and Irene — this time we would not return to Munich so we had to take everything. The VW had quite a load, with the luggage carrier on top piled high, and once on a hairpin turn in the Swabian Alps we thought we were tipping over. But we made it to Esslingen, and we found one of the most charming communities in all Europe. Esslingen is very old, and at one time owned Stuttgart just down the river. In one place the ancient city wall hangs right over the marketplace, and publicly owned vineyards come down almost to the street. We were to meet Fritz and Irene at the Jägerhaus for lunch, and this is an inn high on the heights above the Neckar River, so you can see off for miles. Directly below was old Esslingen, and far to the south were the Swabian Alps. Downriver, to the right, were the tall buildings of Stuttgart, and across the valley we could see the great television tower that sticks up close to the airport. That would be the airport George and Betty would use when they left us to fly to Paris and pick up the *Yankee* cruise. Fritz and Irene were waiting for us, and the waiter had laid out "something Swabian." *Jägerhaus* means a hunting lodge, sort of, and besides being a public inn it is the hangout for the sporty nimrods of Esslingen, and the place is adorned with staghorns

149

until there is a gamey tone. Fritz turned out to be a member in good standing of the local deer-hunting gentry, and as we admired the trophies he said he had applied for a permit to shoot a deer and it should come through any moment now.

It did come through, and our visit with Fritz had to allow for time out while he hunted. I showed my Maine Guide's License all around, but it didn't impress anybody and I couldn't seem to get myself invited to attend. Chasing the wild deer and following the roe is a select status matter in Germany, and I think few Maine hunters would admire the sport. Fritz rose at 4:00 A.M. to don a handsome green Swabian hunting costume that nobody in his right mind would dare to wear in the Maine woods, and he took down a German-made over-and-under shotgun-rifle and stepped out to the sidewalk just as his chauffeur arrived with the MB. They came at the right time to the rendezvous out in the Alps, and here they found a farmer, a guide and a game warden. The guide was to chase out the deer; the game warden was to decide if it were the right one; and if it were, the farmer was to take the meat. The trophy, which is the head if you want it but at least the horns, would belong to Fritz. Fritz came home about nine o'clock, changed to his business suit and spent the rest of the day at his office.

He told us that evening that the guide had chased out several deer, but they were not the right ones. Fritz would lift his gun to shoot but the game warden would cry no-no. The permit was for a particular deer, selected by the ministry of conservation for harvest, and Fritz could shoot only that one. It was, of course, only a matter of time — one day the guide would chase out the right one, and then Fritz would shoot him. He got up every morning while we were there and went out, but he had a lousy guide — which I've heard before. After we'd returned to Maine he wrote and said he never did get his deer.

Irene said she prayed every night that he wouldn't get one. She said it made things terribly complicated. He got one once, she said, and everything was in a turmoil for weeks. First, it took forever to fill out all the government forms, and then there was the celebration at the Jägerhaus. Fritz had to buy drinks and meals for all his hunting cronies, and the feasting and carousing had no end, and he got tired and surly, and if he ever shot another deer she'd consider leaving him.

One day Fritz and Irene had a meeting in Hamburg, so the four of us struck out to see Ludwigsburg Castle. It was to be an outstanding day. First, we wound over the hills from Esslingen to Waiblingen, through a vineyard valley that proved to be our best view of grapes — even though we later did the famous wine roads, the Moselle and even the Côte-d'Or of Burgundy. The road came over the rim of a great cup, wound down through grapevines to the floor of the valley, and climbed out again. All the way we saw people working in their vines, and we chuckled to find one oddball farmer had an apple orchard. The Ludwigsburg Castle fascinated us; we had seen the bigger, better and more touristy Nymphenburg Castle in Munich, but this one delighted us more. Napoleon gave some Swabian collaborator a freehold here, and the estate is said to be patterned on the Palace of Versailles. It has parks and gardens on end, and interminable Germans sitting on benches to watch swans and eat their lunches. And, of course, miles of castle corridors with galleries and collections. Off to one side so the noise doesn't intrude into the formal flower gardens is a snack bar, and we repaired to it and contributed liberally to the cause, whatever it may have been. A little orchestra

151

played American Western music for us and for the many others attending, and it was all very fine.

But it was on our way back to Esslingen that we made a real discovery. We came to the old post office square in Waiblingen, and happy fate ordained that we would enter the Hotel Stern and throw ourselves upon the good fortune of their hospitality. Like so many of the European hotels, this one looked vacant and in disuse from the street, and the heavy door needed quite a push. But there was instantly a fine brown-gravy smell, and the four of us came in to find the place well filled and a large evening in progress. Over the door was carved, in old-style German letters, an admonishment that we heeded: "Nur mit humor dein Sach bestellt; dann lacht dir froh die ganze Welt!" In such mood we introduced George and Betty Morrill to the people who live between airports.

They had come to Europe on the *France*, the plush liner with every amenity promptly scheduled, and until Munich had lived by one or another kind of timetable. The whirl of Oktoberfest had been something, and our visit to Austria somewhat revealing. But this was their first German brown-gravy inn, and our easy entrance was something they couldn't readily imitate. George instantly found that his elaborate Berlitz French stood him in no stead when a very pretty and black-haired waitress looked his head over and asked him what he'd drink. He asked me what the motto over the door meant. I said, "Order with a smile or you'll get kicked out." This will never get an A in a freshman German exam, but it's really not a bad rendition.

We had a wonderful meal, and some of the company moved in on us. Two tables away a young couple, a boy and girl too young to have beers in Maine, was having beers, and we envied their budding ardor as they held hands on the table. A couple of school youngsters. Suddenly the girl arose and came directly to us.

"I zink I hear you speak English!" she said, slowly sorting the words.

We all shook hands.

"You are English?" she asked.

"No — Americans."

"So! How do you do?"

Then she was done. The lessons hadn't gone any farther. The interview so bravely begun ended dismally and she stood flustered and embarrassed. "Anschliessen?" I asked, not too sure what it meant or how it should be construed, but it was close enough and she and her boyfriend moved over.

Then we heard a rumbling, and the old man at the very next table, who had been ramming food home for an hour, was heard saying to his plate in a gruff monotone that could have been intended for anybody or nobody, "I learn it in school! I learn it in school! They have some small lessons and they can say how-do-you-do and I-speak-English, and they think they have become masters of another tongue, and then they insult our universities by saying I-learn-it-in-school. She was a brave girl, but inadvised. She should not make such efforts until she has completed her examinations."

"Won't you join us, too?" George said, and now we were seven. The old man had learned it in school too, but for purely academic reasons, and was himself a teacher. The girl couldn't understand his English at all, and her boyfriend didn't understand anybody's. The drawing of beers behind the bar was being done by a yellow-haired woman who was plump and short without being dumpy, and as the evening progressed she found chances to come and ask if we were happy, and later she came and sat with us a time. She was the landlady, widowed by the war but remarried, and there was a latter-day son just starting school. She had no English, but Dorothy managed to communicate and I could see that before long there would be a visit to the kitchen, a handshake with the cook, and a recipe swap. While she was sitting with us she had a cognac, and George insisted that it be put on our bill. I'm sure it would have been on our bill anyway — didn't we invite her to take a place? As the dining room thinned out many came to shake hands, and the gruff old gentleman stood and made quite a recitation before he pulled down his cap and shuffled out. The black-haired waitress hoisted her apron, let down the flap on her leather wallet and made change. The landlady held the door as we went out, and made us promise to come again. George and Betty, of course, didn't; but we did, and we had Thanksgiving Dinner with her. By the time we got back to Esslingen Fritz and Irene had returned from Hamburg, and we told them what a wonderful day we had enjoyed.

Who Was Nordman?

Fritz had cleared his calendar and the next day was all ours. I have never spent a more meticulously divided time — everything was on a split-second schedule, and I said he was so good at this that he ought to run a tourist bureau. "Our company does own a tourist bureau in Stuttgart," he said. First we toured the new Bechtle publishing house. And I felt a little silly because when Fritz was in Maine I took him to see the new printing plant of the Kennebec *Journal*. The Kennebec *Journal* may print fifteen thousand copies a day, and in Maine is defined as "the official state paper." Fritz had toured the plant and was most polite. The only thing he said was, "It is very fine, but small." Now I could see why he thought it was small. We stood and gazed up at his presses, one of which does over a half million *Bild Zeitung*s a day.

There is one conversation that takes place every time an American visits a German printing plant — and it is not about Johann Gutenberg. The German will point at a Linotype machine and say, "And, of course, you know it was invented by a German."

Then the American says, "Yes, but he had to go to the United States to get it in production and to make any money."

To which the German always replies, "Ah, yes — that's what drove him crazy!"

It is pretty much so. Mergenthaler was a jeweler's assistant, and he used to sit at his bench and look across a little river into the windows of a print shop. He wasn't a printer, himself, and as he sat there watching the compositors tediously picking up hand-set type, and then as tediously distributing it again, he thought there must be a better way. So he invented the Linotype machine, but the old Germans who believed in the old ways wouldn't have anything to do with him, and he did have to market his invention in the United States. Afterwards the Germans acclaimed him, and perhaps it's no wonder he went crazy — or as we say, etaoin shrdlu.

Next we went to the excavations under the church, and of all the history we saw in Europe this was definitely it. Fritz had arranged to have the Herr Doktor Professor in charge of the excavations show us around, and just as we got to the church he showed up, punctual as a bullet. Esslingen is very old, and its situation in the Neckar Valley made it a crossing-point for the earliest wanderings of the tribes. Nobody knows when the prehistoric peoples began passing this way, where they were from or where they were going, but they did leave records which have just lately been dug into. Legend says there were two small streams that came down, with a spring close by and high land for camping. The Neckar Valley was beautiful and attractive, as it still is, and somebody came to stay. The Esslingen church sits on the site of previous churches, and in the ground under it are the archeological secrets now being delved. It is a big church, although not the biggest, and its great areas of beautiful stained glass are interrupted by one towering corner where the glass is plain and tells no story. Yes, Fritz said, long ago there was a famine and the town needed money, and some of the glass was sold to the English — the Esslingen glass can be seen today somewhere in the British Isles, but he didn't know where. Fortunately prosperity returned soon after, and Esslingen has never had to sell any more of its precious glass.

The engineering that went into this archeological study makes you shudder. The vast, stupendous masonry of the church stood on the buried past, and somehow they had gone in under the foundations and dug everything out — basket by basket and barrow by barrow. The church never budged, never buckled. There was no strain on a single pane of glass high up in the towers. The church was so shored as it was undermined that services con-

156

tinued regularly, and nobody above needed to know that everything underneath had been shoveled out. I thought it was exciting that a fine modern heating plant had been installed in one part of the archeological excavations, sort of killing two birds with one stone and also smashing the European notion that because Christianity entails suffering all communicants must freeze to death in church. Electric lights had also been wired all through the diggings.

This was a "first." Nobody except the workmen and the professional experts had ever gazed upon the discoveries. At that time, no announcements had been made of the findings. We were cautioned not to touch anything — in particular any fossils found protruding from the dirt. That a great many people had lived in old Esslingen seemed a justified conclusion after we saw how many had died there. In places almost the entire side walls were bones — a great common grave of prehistoric people. They had found some sort of temple in one place, and scholars had not yet agreed on all its mysteries. Some sooty, smoky, greasy spots on stones had been identified as from candles — perhaps for illumination but more likely of religious significance. There was an altar, presumed to be sacrificial, but still in dispute on this score. Era after era could be read in the sliced-off earth, down as far as they had gone in the search for the beginnings. Our professor told how ultraviolet rays were used to assess age, and explained how methodically and systematically every ounce of excavation was examined. Then he brought us to the most important of all their discoveries — the stone of "Nordman."

Again, experts were still cogitating, but this stone put a completely unexpected date on Christianity. Presuming it was a gravestone for Nordman, whoever he was, it bore Roman letters, a date in the 600's, and before the date it said, "anno domini." No question about it. The "A.D." touch eliminated all paganism from the digging to that point. The stone was soft, some kind of sandstone, and the workmen, sadly, had broken it as they lifted it from the dirt. But it had been cemented and placed in a permanent setting approximately where it had been found. Nobody had ever imagined, according to the Herr Doktor, that Christianity had moved into the Neckar Valley at that early time, and the discovery of this stone forced a good many presumptions to be changed. "You are the first to see this," said Fritz. "Except, of course, for the scholars."

We walked the ancient battlements of the Esslingen city wall, toured the town's very old buildings, inspected the municipal grape crop, and looked at the oldest champagne cellar in Germany — right under the city hall. And then in the early evening we had the sad task of driving George and Betty Morrill through Stuttgart and to the airport — for it was time that they head out to meet the *Yankee* in France. We left them sitting on suitcases waiting for the flight, and as we climbed the long flight of stairs up towards the parking lot we looked back, and they seemed a little sad. At this farewell-to-Esslingen I think a National Geographic Society boat trip appealed to them most slightly. So we made the *auf Wiedersehen* as abrupt as we could, and Fritz and Irene said we would have supper at their home tonight.

It was, of course, our first evening alone with the Bechtles. Their house sits high on the hill above Esslingen, with great plate glass windows giving on the valley, and as it was now dark we could see only lights. It was a beautiful sight, until Fritz drew the drapes. It is the European way. Close everything out; yourself in. The way the hill slopes, a man would have to be eighty feet tall to look in Fritz's windows, but every evening after the sun sets the drapes are drawn. Doors are to be closed; everybody lives behind walls. Then, because he had been listening, Fritz suddenly threw open the big door onto his balcony and called us out. "Come wave goodbye to George and Betty!" he cried, "Come, come quickly!" From across the valley, where the lights of the Stuttgart airport were brightest of all the lights we could see, a jet was coming directly at us, lifting as it came. It banked to the left, made a great circle over us, and howled around toward Stuttgart, and then toward Paris. "The Paris plane always goes right over here," said Fritz, and he waved at the plane with just as much fervor as if George and Betty, up there, had known he was doing it and were waving back. We all waved. "Auf Wiedersehen!" we called.

That evening Fritz ran off his pictures of America, and we sat in his Swabian living room supported by Dinkelackers and watched the long sequence with Chief Bruce Poolaw of the Penobscots and Irene — making their hands go in friendly Indian gestures of peace and brotherly love. She is by far the prettiest Indian squaw I ever saw.

At bedtime Fritz said, "Now, dear Dorothy and dear John, I have a conference tomorrow in Munich, but Irene shall have the chauffeur, and she will take you to see the Black Forest. I shall be home by the time you return."

And Rothenburg, a. d. Tauber

We had already fallen under
the magic spell of the Black Forest, but that was nothing
to the spell Irene wove as she guided us. I sat up front
with the chauffeur, and conducted occasional prayers
as he took some of the turns. For our special benefit he
tuned the car radio to the American armed forces network, and for about fifteen kilometers we had the worst
razzle-dazzle of stomach-turning music, so called, that I
ever heard. It is the sort of thing we turn off at home, and
if a station plays it we don't listen to that station. So I
mulled over my words enough so I could ask him would
he please find some German concert, and I never saw a
man so happy in my life. He was willing to go along listening to that crud as part of the occupational penalty
for being Fritz's chauffeur, and a burden to be borne
patiently while entertaining Americans. He flipped to the
Süddeutscherundfunk, and we rolled up into the hills to
beautiful music.

But first we had to see Pforzheim — Irene's hometown. She showed us her early neighborhood, although
things have changed, and the factory of her family. And
the mountain of debris. After the war all the bombed-out

mess that was Pforzheim was taken, truckload by truckload, and piled up in one great mountain — a memorial. When I was a boy we used to take a lunch and climb Hedgehog Mountain, spending the day clambering over the ledges, and we thought it was quite a hill. Today Pforzheimers can take a lunch and climb the much larger cairn of their wartime debris, and I suppose look off with their thoughts.

Time and again we were struck by the unemotion with which Europeans speak of war. War is a consequence of affairs and it kills people and destroys things — but one day it is over and affairs begin again. The intense friendship developed 'twixt us and the Bechtles has no overtones of national enmity, and any reference to strife has been matter-of-fact. It seemed to us that something ought to be said, one way or the other, and perhaps with some emotion, about the mound in Pforzheim — but Irene merely showed it to us, and we looked at it, and the chauffeur drove along.

Irene was sad that Fritz wasn't with us, for the two of them consider the Black Forest their own special private place — as does every German — and she was extra sad when we came at last to an inn high in the hills where she and Fritz often come. It was "Zuflucht," and the people knew her and inquired for Fritz. We admired the small glass cups in which our Kirschwasser was served, and Irene got a half-dozen of them for us and we have them at home — but without any Black Forest Kirschwasser to adorn them as they were adorned that day. Possibly I made a boo-boo by asking if the chauffeur mightn't sit with us at table, but Irene said, "Of course," and he had a "small beer" because he was driving. The menu included *Hirsch*, and as this is venison anybody from Maine is bound to have it. In Maine it is illegal to serve any game or game fish in a public eating place, but the German law permits both. It was delicious, and no doubt field-foraged so it had none of the gaminess you get from a cedar-fed rauncher along the Machias River. And then we took our walk.

All walking is done on paths, and they run all through the Black Forest. And all walking is purposeful in Germany. We met couples and parties, bounding along as if they had miles to go before they slept, red-faced and hearty, intent on getting every last bit of enjoyment from their outing. And none of them spoke to us — they just kept on bounding. I told Irene that in Maine, on the trail, you stopped and had a visit with anybody you met, but she said this was not the custom in the Black Forest. Everybody is as alone as he wants to be. I think she is right; I think anybody could hang by his thumbs from a lamppost in Germany all day and everybody would consider it a private matter not to be inquired into. That is, until everybody had finished whatever he was about and decided it was now time to get concerned over people hanging by their thumbs. Then he would give it his all. He would plunge himself into it. But the Black Forest was never more beautiful, and Irene communicated her love for it until we felt quite German, ourselves, under the trees. I noticed that every tree we went past had a tag on it, so efficient and thorough is the forestry program, and I wondered what Forester Bun Bartley, back in Millinocket, would say if the Great Northern woodlands department told him he had to tag every tree north of Ambajejus Lake.

Late in the afternoon we stopped off at Baden-Baden in time for the concert in the shell before the casino, and here Irene had a most painful embarrassment. The gambling casino may be entered only upon full identification,

162

and Irene had forgotten to bring her travel papers. We, as outlanders, had only to show our passport and we could go in. But Irene, our hostess and a German, was told politely but firmly by the man on the desk that she couldn't accompany us. She made a valiant try, and she said, "But I have been here many times!" It was no good. "But you know me, and you know my husband — we come often!" she pleaded. I did the gentlemanly thing — if they wouldn't let her in, I wouldn't go either. So we bought a ticket for Dorothy, and as she disappeared through the great doors into the magnificence of the inner dens of iniquity Irene and I found a couple of comfortable seats and waited. So I have never been in the fabulous gaming salons of Baden-Baden, and all I know about them is what my wife tells me — and she has never told me how much she won or how much she lost — or even if she played. But Irene was terribly embarrassed, and nothing I could say helped assuage the loss of face she felt. "Stupid German," she kept saying.

Before we left Fritz and Irene, and the Stuttgart area, we had one other errand — to call on Hermann Heistermann. Back around 1914 two brothers had come from Germany to our town, Karl and Fritz Heistermann, and for long years had operated a grocery and meat market. We began trading with them when we were first married, and continued until the chain stores froze them out. Both were now dead, but Karl's wife Annie still lives in town, and she asked us to call on Cousin Hermann in Stuttgart. We found him, the proprietor of a printing and advertising business, and evidently in most prosperous and comfortable circumstances. He had great trouble with our German, but shortly understood, and he called into a back room for his very pretty wife to come out. As soon as she found out why we were there she retreated and came at once with plates of cookies and some beer. This is a commercial and industrial nicety I think American firms might embrace. Some American companies have cafeterias, and some know how to send out for goodies, but in the German manner the fortified conference is different. I would certainly make more calls on local industry if they would receive me the way German businessmen do. We had much difficulty with the Swabian dialect, but we conveyed the love and greetings of "Aunt Annie," and we brought back to her the tidings of her cousins in Stuttgart. They write, but have never met.

So we said goodbye to the Bechtles.

Everybody has to see Rothenburg, and we went to Rothenburg. It is a compact walled city kept about as it always was, and is devoted to tourism 167 percent. On the Tauber River, which isn't very much of a river at that point, it remains a memorial to the ancient *Bürgermeister* who once swilled three liters of wine at a draft. All over the place you can see these three-liter mugs, and you've got to admit the old Lord Mayor did a remarkable thing. It seems the King of Sweden took the place, and in merry mood he promised to spare the city if the mayor would down the potion. History doesn't say what he did for an encore, or for an Alka-Seltzer, but he must have been laid away stoned for a month. Anyway, the King of Sweden kept his word, and Rothenburg remains a fairyland town which, I suppose, a good many American tourists will say reminds them of Disneyland. We had fun there, and found we could mingle with a group of tourists and listen to the guide, and then wander off and fall in with another group of tourists. The place is full of groups. Rothenburg is a nice town, but I would not want to be its Lord Mayor.

Odds and Ends Northerly

With the Scandinavian coun-
tries in mind we meandered northerly, and Dorothy
kept the map on her lap so we wouldn't hit any major
routes. We stopped at any place we pleased, for as long as
we wished. And there was no lack of interesting things.
At one point she misplaced our plastic wine cups, so we
had nothing to drink from at picnic time, and she said,
"We'd better stop the first chance we have to buy some
new cups." She had hardly said it when we rounded a turn
and came upon a glassblowing factory. We parked, and a
sign said the salesroom was upstairs, but through the
open end of the building we could see the men and boys
with their tubes puffing out wineglasses. We bought two.

We found Mittenberg, on the Main River, charming.
We heard the oldest inn in Europe is there, but we don't
know if we found it or not. We did find the Hotel Rose,
with one WC for twenty-five rooms, and it was dated
1622, WC and all, so we saw no reason to carp over a
century or two. It was fun to watch the river traffic, and
to walk the narrow cobbled streets. We went by a church
and heard a choir rehearsing, so we stepped in and enjoyed a concert.

165

The farming country was as interesting as anything to us. When I saw milch cows being worked as draft animals it made me think of Bill Nye and his comments on the Tarheel Cow. He said if the farmers of Carolina would work their cows less and their butter more they would confer a favor on the consumers of both. The primitiveness of much German farming is nicely balanced off by complete modernity and sophistication in some of their machinery. Sometimes, I would say, to a point of absurdity. For instance, after we'd been watching dairy cows hauling carts of beets, we came to a place where five men were sawing firewood. With good German love for precision machinery, they had a rig that Rube Goldberg would love. It was a bandsaw driven by a complicated overhead shafting that ran to an electric motor. Meantime, a handsome diesel farm tractor was standing by idle, with which one man could saw as fast alone. Another time we saw a crew mowing grass along the shoulder of a road, and they had some kind of flexible-shaft power with a rotary cutter. The machine must have cost a great deal, and while it functioned beautifully it was not really cutting much grass. With my little farm tractor and a cutter bar I could do a mile of German highway shoulders while this great machine and its crew were doing a hundred feet. Then, of course, we'd see women yanking and trimming beets in one field, looking like the old paintings of peasants, and in the next field we'd see a handsome machine doing the same job at fifteen miles per hour.

I felt sorry for the cows. Down in the Mindelheim area we'd seen the sleek Brown Swiss with their heavy udders, and these cows pulling carts didn't belong to the same race. Their teats flopped back and forth as they walked along, suggesting low lacteal content. When you look at

166

the strong hands of a German farm woman you become dismal at thoughts of milking time. It must be very painful for the cow, and tears must course her cheeks. No man, of course, ever chores a cow in Europe, except the Swiss. For some reason Swiss men don't feel it is beneath their station to milk a cow, and in olden times landed gentry would import Swiss farm workers to handle their dairies. In fact, any man in Germany who handles dairy cattle is called, in German, a "Swiss" — whether he is a Swiss by nationality or not. I learned that it was comical to the German cow-women to have me show any interest in the cattle — my sex was wrong.

We came to Bad Neustadt. Germany has many Neustadts, but only one Bad Neustadt, and this is where the artist Willi Lemm, who came over with us on the *Wolfgang Russ*, lives. We didn't have his street and number, so we headed for the city hall. Bad Neustadt is another ancient walled city, and has kept much of its antiquity, but the new new-city with beautiful homes and apartments sprawls outside the old fortress walls to make quite a complex. We came through the modern part to enter the old through the stone gate, and it is easy to find such a town's marketplace, and having found the marketplace it is easy to locate the town hall. Finding Willi Lemm turned out to be easy, too.

The Germans respect the cultural arts, and are proud to line up with them. In the United States I would expect to find the home of a baseball player a familiar local item, but not so much that of the dabster — "He doesn't do anything; he paints pictures!" At the city hall we found five people behind a counter, and I said, "We're strangers, and we're looking for an artist named Willi Lemm." Five faces looked up from five desks and five voices recited the Lemm address in concert. Willi was certainly honored in his own home, and with directions we came quickly to his house — a fine new home in a development. A truck was maneuvering in the street and we had to wait to park, and the commotion brought Willi to his studio window and he saw us getting out. He rushed into the street to embrace us and hurried us into the house where his wife did the same. So we had a chance to see the landscapes of Canada in finished state, and they were magnificent. Willi also showed us many portraits he had done, and then Frau Lemm brought the kuchen and coffee, and we had a grand reunion. They wanted us to spend the night, and we nearly did, but Willi had to deliver a painting before dinnertime and we took that as an excuse to be off.

A priest in a small mountain village nearby was very old, and his parishioners had taken up a collection and wanted to buy him a gift. They had brought the money to Willi Lemm and asked if he would paint a canvas of the little village church where the priest had spent his lifetime. I am sure the collection was a mere pittance, because Willi Lemm had been artist enough so somebody had paid his way to Canada to do a portrait, but Willi had said yes and set about the job. The villagers would make some excuse to get the priest away from his church, and then Willi would erect his easel and paint. Soon somebody would come running to say the priest was returning, and Willi would pack up hurriedly and wait for the next excuse. He had made many trips up to the mountain village before he had finished the picture, but now it was done and tonight the parishioners were giving the priest a birthday banquet and were going to make the presentation. Willi and his wife were to be honored guests, so he had to pack the painting into the back of his VW-bug and be off. He waited, to spend as much time with us as possible, and at the very last moment he got into the back seat holding the frame and Frau Lemm gunned the automobile off. In the best German traffic manner she clipped the curb at the corner and blew her horn because some children were in the way. The last we saw of Artist Willi Lemm he was waving through the back window, a church spire in view over his shoulder. It was the fastest moving church I ever saw.

Then we left Bad Neustadt and went as far as Seiferts-Rhön. Castles were by now a dime a dozen, and we got so we looked at every tenth one. We found the Weser River, which is sometimes deep and sometimes wide, and scenery enough for everybody. Once again it came home to us that Europe has more open country than we had anticipated. We saw so many Hotel Eagles, Crowns, Posts and Suns that we suspected a chain, but there are no chains.

Highway signs are fun — we saw one that said, "Dangerous Curve" and somebody had taken a can of paint and added one word, "Very." The use of picture signs in Europe is good. Canada has picked them up, but the United States should, too. There need be no question as to what they mean. A picture of a bicycle with a line drawn through it means no bicycles. A "P" meaning parking becomes no parking when a line crosses it out. And in Germany all directional signs give the mileage — you not only know you are on the right road to Hannover, but how far it is, kilometer by kilometer. The famous Hitlerian autobahns didn't see much of us, but we found all lesser roads good. Detours may wind for miles and in devious places, but they are well marked. We found out how to maneuver in the narrow places — it is not considered bad manners to get around a parked truck by hopping your auto up onto a sidewalk and going around

169

it. And for anybody from Maine, where our highway program is an excessive burden and no job is worth tackling unless it runs to millions, it was comforting to see German road crews carefully relaying old cobblestones across country. And these were cobblestones, not paving blocks. The "Zimmer frei" signs amused us — it means a room is available, not that it is gratis. And we grew adept at distinguishing the *Gasthof,* the *Gasthaus,* the *Hotel,* the *Stube,* the *Fremdenhaus* with *Fremdenzimmer,* the *Gaststätte,* and the other variations of hospitality. We found but one common denominator — they all have beer.

We had about ten minutes before the inexorable stroke of nünne, in a town called Hümme, to get some checks cashed, and I ran the automobile up onto the sidewalk and leaped out, headed for the bank, when a young fellow stepped up and grabbed my hand as if I were his long-lost scoutmaster. I've never seen anybody so glad to see me. He was an exchange student from California, and had spotted us as touring Yankees. He was living on a farm in Hümme with a boy who had, the year before, exchanged in Louisiana. He introduced me to the boy, who spoke English with a German inflection and a Louisiana accent. "Hold everything until I get a check cashed," I said, "and we'll drink lunch!"

When we came to Paris I went to the American Express office and cashed three hundred dollars worth of checks in about fifteen seconds, but getting a ten-dollar check cashed in a German bank is worse than trying to get your subscription out of the *Time* magazine computers in July when it doesn't come up until November. You must show your passport, and they fill out eighteen dollars' worth of papers. They have state banks, land banks, savings banks, cooperative banks, credit unions, and anything we've got, and we tried them all and it was always the same. They exact a small service charge, which can't begin to pay for their time and trouble, and when the transaction is at last completed and you have the money the manager comes around front and shakes hands like a doctor congratulating a new father, and he holds the door open as you go out. Here in Hümme, with but minutes before the noon closing hour, I wondered if they would hurry things along. They didn't. The entire staff stood at attention and accorded me every long-drawn-out courtesy. And the manager took notice that my passport showed no place of residence. This is true — the United States passport shows where you were born, but not where you live. Could I, please, show him some proof of my residence? I fished out my Maine driver's license, and he nodded. Then he noticed that my Maine driver's license wasn't numbered. For some reason our statehouse minds hadn't got to that, and until 1968 a Maine operator's license had no serial number. All this time the two boys visited on the sidewalk with Dorothy, and I came out and said, "How do I tell the banker that in Maine we don't number motor vehicle operator's licenses?"

We had a fine visit with the boys, and I asked the Californian if he were old enough to drink a legal beer in a taproom back home and he said, "Gee, no." The German boy's mother came in then, having driven to town to pick them up after classes, and she shook hands in such a manner that I knew she could milk one of those sad-faced German cows until it would cringe at her approach.

The Piper Pigs of Springe

I can repeat almost all of "The Pied Piper of Hamelin," and there was a time I could run through it without a hitch. When we began to hit the roadside signs that said "Hameln" I began on the poem, and as we rode along the mood was set for a happy visit to the scene of the old legend. I'd come to a line I couldn't quite hit and we'd think on it as we went along, and sometimes we'd remember it and sometimes we wouldn't. Before we came to Hamelin I'd got the most of it in hand, and we'd practically conjured ourselves into the nursery days of yore. We'd been following the Weser River, and now we began to wonder if we'd recognize Koppelberg Hill when we got first sight of it.

So, of course, we came to Hamelin and found it is about as fanciful a place as Bridgeport, Connecticut, and with one of those dull, swooshing thuds we fell from the beddy-bye mood smack into the full hustle of modern German industrialization. Somebody had told us the city still keeps a Pied Piper on the payroll, and that with a clarinet he may be seen and heard piping the youngsters home from school every day. If so, we didn't see him, and after one look at Hamelin we decided we didn't want to hang

172

around for him to show up. Piping a batch of children through Hamelin Town today would be like trying to hold a Maybasket party on Storrow Drive at rush hour. True, a man's reach should exceed his grasp, but this was no eagle's feather on the moor. The Pied Piper story tells us if we've promised aught, to keep our promise — but Hamelin Town has let the story go by the boards. It's all gone. "Two marshmallows by the fire —Browning!" said Dorothy, and my reply was, "Rats!"

We circled Hamelin several times, in thick traffic, and then we drove on to Springe — and here we found everything we had expected to find in Hamelin. The old inn on the corner had a room for us that looked out on the fountain in the square, and the beam-and-stone house across the way had great meandering adages and Biblical quotations carved into the timbers. Some carpenter had labored long to do this, and I labored almost as long trying to translate them. Some I never quite got. The village street could well have accommodated a piper and his trooping children. Indeed, as we stood in our window entranced we saw a chimney sweep come riding along on a bicycle. The *Schornsteinfeger* of Germany is a sign of high good luck, and I believe in this one because I put ten pfennig in the slot machine in the hall and got eighty pfennig for it. The dining room that evening became gay, and when the landlord said the oxtail soup and the fillet steaks were good, he spoke unvarnished truth such as Hamelin had not. There was a fireplace in the dining room, and we asked him why he didn't touch off a blaze in it and he said he didn't have any wood. I thought that was an excellent reason. We saw a lot of fireplaces throughout Europe, but only one ever had a fire in it — in France. The featherbeds were wonderful, and we awoke next morning to a joyful sound.

173

At first, in my sleep, I thought it was the Pied Piper, fingering his way up the street with thousands of children laughing and dancing along, but as I came to full wakefulness I knew better. It was the noise of a truckload of pigs being unloaded for the abattoir behind the hotel. I have never known of an American hotel that provides this for its guests. And the squeal of a pig, either in an aria or the toot-ensemble, is a prosperous noise, and sweet music to a farmer. When, in preprandial exercises, a farmer steps into the barn and swirls the big paddle in the barrel of skim milk, cornmeal and with-its, the way a hungry pig announces his desires is just as good as money in the bank. The more a pig eats and the bigger he gets the more he brings on the hoof. And when, in mortal extremity, the fattened porker is brought at last to fruition, his cry, although piercing, is not a mournful sound. On the farm it is, rather, a glad promise of a nourishing winter, and when all is salted and smoked and cured and tried out the squeal is the only thing we didn't know how to hang up and eat. That morning in Springe, I leaped from beneath the featherbed and thought it was daylight on the old farm. Dorothy said, "It's real!"

Assisting in the funeral services for a batch of German pigs is not, I'm sure, included in the brochures of the Ideal Tours. The reason German sausage is better than ours, they told me, is because the entire animal goes into the making, whereas we go for the scraps. We market roasts, hams, shoulders and chops, and whatever is left over goes into the weenies. But they just make sausages.

This may explain the big puzzle to me about ham. The slice of cured, smoked ham, fried, is seldom seen in Germany, except you ask for it specifically. Then you don't always get it. The famous Westphalian ham is delicious, but it is not, by our definitions, ham. It looks

174

like the "SOS" dried beef. The gin called Urquell is always advertised *mit dem Schinkenbild* — "With the picture of a ham." And the picture, not only on the label of the stone bottle but on billboards, shows a beautiful Virginia-style ham. But when you order plain ham-and-eggs you generally get some meat that is rather like our cold sliced sandwich ham. I didn't find out just what I wanted to know about ham, but the processing of pigs in Springe was an exciting prelude to a farmer's breakfast, and we decided things were so nice we'd stay another day.

While we were lingering over breakfast the front door opened and two trashmen came in. I suppose the English would call them dustmen. They were not young, and they wore tattered and patched clothes. They looked like unprosperous dump pickers. They seemed a little unsteady on their feet, and as they began carrying out the hotel's trash they had a little trouble negotiating the door. Out on the street they had an ancient wagon already well piled with odds and ends, and a doddering old horse who leaned against the atmosphere and looked as if he couldn't pull a hat off. The two men were quite gay and grinned and laughed with everybody in the dining room as they went back and forth with the baskets and boxes. When they had all the trash on their wagon they came back in and stood up at the bar.

The landlord poured them two Steinhagers, drew them two beers, and handed each a cigar. In great solemnity they lifted their glasses to one and all, and quaffed. I got up and went to the window to see them get on their wagon, urge the poor old horse off down the street with robust language and a great deal of hilarity, and I saw them pull up in front of another hotel. It seemed to me they had a good thing going, and labored in a profession with admirable traditions. After we got back to Maine I went to the dump one morning, and when I came home my wife greeted me at the door with a glass — but no Steinhager. She was just trying to be funny.

When we left Springe I went to bring the VW around, while Dorothy stood by the hotel door with the bags. The landlord came to her and with all the dignity of a Congressional Medal of Honor award he handed her a chocolate bar. It was his going-away gift. We had paid his bill, left some tips, and had behaved pleasantly in his house, and he sincerely hoped we would come again to honor his hotel with our presence. We like to think he doesn't thus speed every departing guest, and that we deserved his special gift. It was not, of course, very much like our American chocolate bars with almonds, but the rich, good German kind with hazelnuts. We ate it as we drove along.

Then we ran into rain. The drizzly north German wet. We dug out our weather gear, and saw Lüneburg, and again Lübeck, through thick, overcast fog and rain, and although we continued on into Denmark, we began to think of Sunny Italy and the Midi and how we could get warm and dry when we turned to the south'ard.

Along with the Zugspitze and the rock of the Lorelei, the old city gate of Lübeck is a favorite German photographic subject. Again, there is no connection 'twixt Lübeck in Germany and Lubec in Maine — although we dug out our greetings from our governor and made a little presentation in the old city hall. Lübeck is "the Queen of the Hanseatics" and dates from A.D. 1000 or so. They told us a good many American tourists look up at the old church, built in something like 1160, and ask if it was Protestant or Catholic. And they told us how red wines from Burgundy were traditionally shipped to Lübeck for storage — that the sea voyage and a long rest in the

176

Lübeck climate improved the quality and they were much better when they got back to France. During the war the British bombed Lübeck and one night dropped a great many incendiaries. Almost everything was on fire, and the town water system failed. So they broke open the casks in the city's wine cellars and put the fire out with good Burgundy.

One time Gus Garcelon and I had been fishing at Rangeley Lakes and on the way home we came upon a truck that was afire. Gus grabbed a bottle of soft drink from our supplies, ripped off the cap, shook it, and the carbonation made such a good squirt that the thing was an excellent fire extinguisher. It happened to be a bottle of strawberry soda, and when it hit the flames a delicious aroma of ripe strawberries wafted over the scene, and it was easily the most fragrant fire I ever attended. I was sorry for Lübeck and sorry for the Burgundy, but I stood there in the city square and imagined what the place smelled like after that bombing. Otherwise, Lübeck is a city worth some few minutes in the history books — she was an original cosigner with Hamburg back when the Hanseatic League commenced. Modern politics have erased much of the importance, but Hamburg, Lüneburg, Bremen and Lübeck still make a great deal of it, and some knowledge of the lore adds much to visiting these cities.

It was in Lübeck we decided to skip Jutland and go to Copenhagen, so we took the "crow-flight" route to Puttgarten and ate our way to Denmark on the *Kong Frederick IX.*

We Love the Danes

Eating your way to Denmark is no idle remark. As you drive your automobile on the fine ferry at Puttgarten and step out to the deck you notice a sign that says, "To Restaurant." You go up the steps, and on the next deck you see signs that say, "To Other Restaurants." The *Kong Frederick IX* is a floating dining room, and serving a meal coincides perfectly with the passage across.

"Turn slowly," I said to Dorothy, "and you will see your first Danish woman lighting a cigar." I'm sure Dorothy thought it would be a ladylike little cigarette-size cigar, but it was the kind our horse jockeys chew for three heats in the 2:10 pace and then light. Soon almost all the women had their cigars going, but as with *ausfahrt* signs and the second washbowl, you soon don't notice any more.

All countries come up with their own flavors soon after you have crossed the borders. No country in Europe does it sooner than Denmark. It is a kingdom, and its history has much to do with the shaping up of the continent. There is hardly anything in Denmark big enough to be called a hill, and there are no large rivers and lakes. You soon notice you are northerly, by the way the sun goes up and comes down. The woodlands run heavily to beech trees, from which the Danes make a beautiful and distinctive furniture. The cattle are fat and productive, a fine discovery after you have been looking at the cart-pullers of the German farm women, and a glass of cold milk for breakfast is a national custom. The grain fields have a different look, and I suppose it's the more northern climate. But at once you notice the people — the Danes tend to be tall and lithe, good looking, and at once nationally characteristic. We loved every minute in Denmark, but our initial sally was not propitious.

I made the unspeakable error of going into a hotel and asking for a room in German. Well, I didn't know any Danish, and since Danish and German have common derivations I fancied this was the closest I could come. It worked in Holland and Belgium. So I asked for a *doppelzimmer*. The man was civil, and we got a fine room, but nobody stood up and cheered and the transaction had about the same warmth as getting a stick of gum from a coin machine. We tidied up, because we had been told Danish food is worth dressing for, and when we came down to the dining room the man asked me, in German, if I would come and sign the register. "Ja, gleich," I said, and as an address I put down, "U.S.A."

The instant he saw it the whole tone changed. "You are American!" he said in better English than our President uses. He stepped to the head-boy and said, "Mr. Gould is American!" The word ran around — I'm telling you, everybody was overjoyed to learn we were not German! And, of course, the Danes hate the Germans, with good cause. The next morning this man took me up the street a piece and showed me where their priest had been

179

brought out and, with the townspeople forced to watch, had been mowed down by machine guns just to assert German authority. "I come here often," he said. "I do not intend to let myself forget it."

Our first evening in Denmark is unforgettable, but every evening was the same. The Danny Kaye complexion of Copenhagen is quickly dispelled — it is a large, busy city of great charm and orderly, if profuse, traffic. The Mermaid is abundantly lovely and any eye must mist at the sight, but we found the great fountain statue of the sea-oxen with its mossy-green patina far more exciting and wondered why it gets less publicity. And as we moved north along the Baltic Sea we found it suggestive of our own coast of Maine — not so colorful in one respect, because our ocean water is a deeper blue-green and the Baltic paler. But the resort area along the beaches had to be tried out for comparisons, and we kept an eye peeled and finally chose a hotel.

"Welkommen til Skotterup Kro!" said a man as I came in the front door, and although I had no idea what he said, I knew well enough what he meant. He shook my hand and gained that we spoke English, and told me we were fortunate to arrive on the Wednesday — that on Wednesdays they serve a great buffet of everything from the sea. Lobsters, shrimps, caviar, salmon, smoked eel, everything! I said we were from Maine and Denmark would find it hard to impress us with this menu, and he knew something of our geography and nodded. He rushed and brought a folder describing the inn, and pointed out that it was in two languages — Danish and English. Their English is no tribute to the U.S.A., but derives from associations with England. He took us up two flights to a dream room with sloping wall and a balcony that looked out upon Sweden and the Isle of

Hveen. On the near shore fishermen were mending nets and fixing a boat and a small raft of mallards was just beyond. It could have been Maine, almost.

The dining room at the Skotterup Kro makes the NBC peacock look like a wet Dominique hen. A rich, thick pile carpet in deep red, not quite maroon, was wall-to-wall, and the beamed ceiling was toned the same color — with the beams on the purple. The walls were light, but caught up some of the red, and even the window glass, looking at Sweden, had a pinkish tinge from the interior. The tablecloths were bright red, and the chairs were heavily upholstered with a striped material of red, green and yellow. The dinner china had a light green pattern, and the napkins were white linen. A part of the dining room was given over to a fishing motif, with an arrangement of nets, boat models and gear. Somebody with an absolute command of color had done all this — it could otherwise have come off rather badly. But it hadn't, and it is the prettiest dining room we ever saw.

The American version of Danish pastry is an insult. And in Denmark we smiled at restaurants at home which give you a choice of whipped, baked and F. F. Pots. Here we would get five kinds of potatoes, whether we ordered them or not, surrounding the meat on a great half-acre silver platter, and the other vegetables between. Every waiter in Denmark made us think of the little Belgian in tails at the Klokkenhof Bredebaan, and although I think none exceeded him they all gave him a hard time. And everybody who goes to Denmark must report on the Akvavit. It is used as the Germans use Steinhager and Kirschwasser, but has a delicately lingering flavor I attribute to caraway. It is not to be lightly regarded, and it favors the tongue as prelude to a Danish beer — of which there are two: Tuborg and Carlsberg. Here, as in all

Europe, the temperate visitor will courteously adjust and think nothing of it, and many a pleasant relationship begins with a nice word about Akvavit and Danish brews. We had a farmer from Maine who went off on one of these exchange junkets to Russia, intended to cement relations and promote good feeling, and he went all through the Soviet Union holding his hand over glasses and saying, "Not for me, please — I never touch the stuff!" No doubt he felt himself true to his convictions and a strong, moral citizen — but we did sample the Akvavit, and we learned to respect it, but we weren't about to offend the Danes by denouncing their national shrines.

We saw another attractive resort inn farther along toward Elsinore and thought we'd stop at it. I went in and couldn't find anybody. The dining room was set, and a radio was playing on a stand. I looked in the kitchen and called upstairs. Nobody was around. Just by the front door was a toilet, and I used it, and then I went out to the automobile and told Dorothy, "I can't raise anybody, but there is a toilet just inside the door." So she went in to use the toilet, and she looked in the kitchen and called upstairs, and she couldn't raise anybody either. So we drove along, pleased with Danish hospitality.

I wanted to give Elsinore the full treatment. In college I had done a major paper on the Hamlet theme, leading up to Shakespeare's play, and I had more than common tourist interest in visiting the castle. My very first observation was that some streets in Elsinore are named for characters in the play and that there is an "Ophelia Way." That's about the way we approached our whole trip, feeling our way along, and I liked that. We saved the castle for the next morning, and got up bright and early to walk to it, arriving at 8:00 A.M. all ready to go. We

182

walked past a shipyard where winches and jackhammers were hard at it, and the prow of a Great Laker sticking up with the name *Wisconsin* painted on it. I naturally quoted about the impress of shipwrights, whose sore task does not divide the Sunday from the week, and causes this posthaste and romage in the land. It was good prologue to the platform scene, but when we got to the castle a sign said it wouldn't open until ten o'clock. The swans in the moat seemed ready, and the big gate was open, so we went in and decided the sign was for other people. We had the whole place to ourselves for two wonderful hours.

The ancient castle, actual seat of Danish royalty and preserved beautifully, is far from small and sits on an eastern shore. Shakespeare, of course, never saw it. Here, so many miles from the *Globe*, or any English theater, was the scene and theme of the greatest triumph of England's greatest poet. With the flush touch of his Elizabethan enthusiasms, he caught up the sordid family tragedy and gave it ultimate stature. So you don't go there to see Danish history at all — you go to quote the Bard, look to see where Polonius was stabbed in the arras, and catch the ghost walking on the platform. That Shakespeare never saw the place is immediately evident from its situation — if Horatio saw the morn in russet mantle clad walk o'er the dew of yon high eastern hill he could have reference only to a low-slung beet field across the way in Sweden. We could just make it out in the morning mist over the water, and obviously the poetry stemmed from Stratford and not from Elsinore.

Up on the platform we found a Danish soldier on guard, and some sixteen ancient guns of our Civil War cannon kind pointed threateningly at Sweden. The soldier came out of his box, executed a few quicksteps as if trying to get warm — for he probably was as cold as the cannon after his early watch. He said nothing to us about the place being closed; neither did several other guards we found here and there. We ran through all the acts, and I threw in a few Osric things with lace at the cuffs, and we came at last to "Good night, sweet prince" and the play was done. I pointed up toward the rampart where the cannon were leveled at Sweden and like old Fortinbras himself I said to Dorothy, "Go, bid the soldiers shoot!"

When we came out a whole line of tourist buses was drawn up in the castle's new parking lot, and it was ten o'clock and the Hamlet morning was beginning. The stench of so much diesel fuel intruded on the magic we had created for ourselves, and we quickly returned to our own time. A Japanese was in the forefront of one guided tour. He had thick eyeglasses, and a half-dozen cameras were hanging on straps around his neck. He gave every evidence of bounden intent. I stepped in his way and smiled for him. He broke stride, and in bewilderment looked closely at me, instantly suspicious of something that was not included in his tour. I struck my very best Sir Henry Irving style, with mournful melancholy sticking out a yard in all directions, and I soliloquized:

"Tuborg, oder nicht Tuborg — das ist die Frage!"

Then we walked away and he went in to call on Gertrude.

We went as far up the Island as we could, and at the northernmost town, Gilleleje, I found the post office and went in to mail our cards and letters. I was glad I did. I found the postal clerk one of God's most beautiful creations — a fair-haired young lady equal to any role in Hollywood or any pose at Atlantic City, and as I was now well aware of Danish talents I said good morning in English. She weighed my mail and took my money, and we entered into a delightful conversation that promised to leave Dorothy sitting alone in the VW for some time. She was the prettiest and most personable girl I saw in Europe, and I wanted to write some more letters so I could go in again. Incidentally: of all the uniforms man has devised to garb himself for fancy appearance, even including that of the Royal Canadian Northwest Mounted Police, the most beautiful is that of a Danish letter carrier. Crimson, it is rich and magnificent, and you can see one ten miles down the road.

And, incidentally again, I repeat the glass of milk for breakfast. The dairy products of Denmark are excellent, and any American is foolish if he listens to the warnings about unsafe milk in foreign lands. We didn't invent pasteurization, you know. The glass of cold milk in Denmark is the nearest to our own farm-fresh milk at home, and far above the quality of anything off a truck in the States.

We spent our last night in Denmark at Mirabo, driving under an arcade to park behind the Ebsens Hotel. A man to get our bags was with us before I shut off the ignition. There was a wedding party that night in the main dining room, so the hotel guests were fed in the pub, and we were a cozy group — all Danes except us. A young man alone at a table soon moved over to join us, and then six men over beyond asked us to join them. The couple who own the place brought cognacs and sat with us. Long after the wedding party had given up and gone we stayed and stayed. This was to be our last night in Denmark, and since we had no place to go except upstairs we were not permitted to say good night. I remember the young man, who was Bent Gregersen from Aarhus, insisted that we go over to Jutland, since we were so close, and let him entertain us at his home, for he was a salesman and was just finishing his calls and would be there when we arrived. I don't remember if we promised to go or not, but we never did, and I remember how he was still insisting as he shook our hands good night at the door of our room.

I had two glasses of milk for breakfast.

Luckyville Toward Joytown

We had as fine a time in Bremen as we had in any European city, including Paris. We came there anticipating nothing in particular, and found the place in thrall of the Brothers Grimm — exactly the thing we had not found about Hamelin and Browning, Copenhagen and Andersen. Bremen is a big, busy modern city with magic casements opening on the foam and people who still believe in fairy tales. To get to Bremen from Denmark we ate our way back on the boat, and hugged the old Kaiser Wilhelm ship canal from Kiel over toward the Elbe River. This allowed us to avoid Hamburg again, and brought us to Glückstadt. We had our wedding anniversary coming up and we wanted to spend it at Freudenstadt in the Black Forest, and to journey to Freudenstadt from Glückstadt seemed a most well-named course — luck and happiness.

The orchard country we came through was interesting, and we loved the little field railways the farmers use to

186

haul out their crops — narrow-gauge jobs that look like toys. The canal was also well worth exploring — this is the way the old German navy got its vessels from the Baltic to the North, and about halfway its length the city of Rendsburg is quite a place. Here the railroad trestle climbs high over the canal, so the biggest warship could sail under, and it looks from a distance just like something a smart boy has built from his Erector set to handle his Lionel. At Glückstadt a ferry would take us across the Elbe to Wischhafen, and then we'd have a short run into Bremen — another of the ancient Hanseatic cities.

We had a checkup for the VW at Glückstadt, and once again the authorized agent proved a good travel adviser. He fixed us up with a pension right alongside the ferry slip, so in the morning we had only to drive aboard and be off, and we wandered about the old town while he changed oil. The pension was a great rambling house seemingly operated all alone by a young woman who either understood my German or graciously made believe she did. She would give us breakfast, because that goes with the room, but otherwise she ran no dining room and she suggested the Rathouse for dinner. The German word *Rat* is unfortunate to an English ear, but it actually means counsel or advice. It also means the town council — the board of aldermen — and the building in which the town council meets is thus known as the *Rathaus*. The *Hotel de ville,* or the city hall. It does sound odd when you are directed to the Rathouse for supper, but some of the best restaurants in Germany are municipally operated in the cellars of the town halls — the renowned *Ratskeller.*

To folks from Maine and New England, where the Puritan faith was superimposed on local government and still wields traditional influence, the idea of the town's

187

EUROPE ON SATURDAY NIGHT

running a restaurant at all is unthinkable, but to have it serving beers and wines is worse. The German philosophy was that each community should have a comfortable dining room where citizens and visitors could get good food at reasonable prices, and they were never fettered either by pious notions or by devotion to private enterprise. Today the operation of such municipal restaurants is farmed out, and some good cook and manager will have the concession. Without exception, you can go into a *Ratskeller* with confidence. The Glückstadt *Ratskeller* was excellent, and we had the *schnitzel*. The onion soup was one of the half-dozen best we had — the best being in Tübingen and the second best being in Beaune. Anybody who thinks onion soup is best only in France has a lot to learn. We found that *Ratskeller*, in general, never warmed up as do the hotel dining rooms of Germany, and you eat in a relaxed, dignified atmosphere rather than in the *gemütlich*. We found that the huge key the girl had given us did fit the front door, and long after the pension was dark and silent we came in, pressed the minute-light, and tippy-toed up to our featherbeds.

These minute-lights are a lot of fun. After hours everybody goes to bed and all the lights are doused, so if you come in late or have to get up betimes you push the minute-light and a whole circuit of corridor and stairway lights comes on and stays on for just about a minute. It's long enough to get you up to your room, or out to the WC. It is not always long enough, however, to get you back to your room from the WC, and you have to learn to push the button again to reset it if you plan to linger. Some hotels and pensions protect their light bills by having a minimum of reset buttons, but usually they are frequent and strategically placed. We found it wise to locate all buttons immediately.

Crossing the Elbe was in a pea-soup fog as good as anything I've ever seen settle in over Matinicus, and any hope we had that we might see some of the Hamburg ships coming and going was lost. The approach to Wischhafen is up a long tidal estuary, narrow, and I was curious about the rise and fall of the tide in those parts. The deckhand on the ferry understood me, and in kind deference attempted to convert meters to feet, which proved to be too great a demand on his arithmetic, and he said they had a tide there of 187 feet. I nodded in amazement, as well I might, because the highest tides in the world are in our down-east Bay of Fundy and they never exceed fifty feet. The deckhand was pleased that he had communicated so well.

So we came to Bremen. We were received well at the Bremer Hospiz, which is pronounced just as you surmise, and since this was a new hotel built after 1945 we had a bathroom and all equipment. The Hospiz is just around a corner from the main railroad square but in the heart of the city, keeps much of the charm of the German country hotels, and has an excellent dining room. Because Bremen is an international trading port we expected to find a desk clerk who could answer any language we might throw at him, and we did. He was a young fellow with very thick eyeglasses, and he knocked himself out giving us every care. And he also handed me one of the old-style registration forms, now so seldom used in German hotels, with its little line where I could write my occupation — peat farmer. The fellow held it close to his lenses and laughed heartily.

Our first dinner in Bremen, at the Hospiz, proved a lucky stab. Our waitress was a bottle-blonde of pleasing size and shape, and after she had us comfortably disposed she brought in another couple and put them at the next

table. We bowed as they came in, but there was no immediate sociability. They were an interesting couple — he
was tall, distinguished looking, perhaps ascetic. She was
what my mother would call a hearty woman, well fed. So
we kept on eating, and all at once I looked up and our
waitress was bringing this couple a huge bar of Such-
ard — a chocolate bar — on a plate. When our waitress
put it on the table the woman covered her eyes with her
hands as if she didn't want to look, and the man said,
"Mon dieu!" They were French.

The waitress, positive she could not have erred, retreated, and the woman began thumbing a dictionary. It
seemed to me the hour was at hand to advance on all
fronts, so I stepped to their table as if I had just trotted
my *jarrets-noirs* out of St. Georges de Beauce, P.Q., and
I asked if I might be of assistance.

There immediately flowed from the woman a torrent
of rich and fluid French such as St. Georges de Beauce
has never heard, and she said they spoke no German but
had tried to order two cups of hot chocolate by finding
words in the dictionary. I crooked my finger at our
blonde, and in German I said, "You don't speak French?"

She turned her nose up as if the very idea made her
nauseous clear back to her Prussian grandfather, and
said, "Naturally, no." So I said this gentleman and his
lady would like two cups of hot chocolate to drink.

"So!" she said, and she trotted out to return almost immediately with two cups of hot chocolate — and in
Germany they have better chocolate than they do in
France. So everybody was happy, particularly the waitress, and we interpreted the couple pleasantly through the
rest of the meal.

He turned out to be the present world's best authority
on stained glass, with a business in Chartres where,

190

everybody knows, the blues of Chartres in the Church of Our Lady are unique in all the history of sacred glass. As a consultant, he was in Bremen at the invitation of the city government to inspect the great windows in St. Peter's, to see what must be done to protect them. He would be in Bremen some time, and might get a contract for a job. So we had a pleasant evening in Bremen, and we laid by much that we would recall later in Chartres.

In our room we found a maid had made everything ready for retiring, and beside each bed, where our feet would touch, was spread a clean linen towel that said, "Bremer Hospiz." We set our shoes in the corridor to be shined, and hoped we would find Bremen as fine tomorrow as it had been tonight.

With a Red Rose

After the war Bremen was in shards. Hit early by the British and after by the blockbusters, the city had been a prime target, and like those in Hamburg the harbor installations were tangles. But if war has benefits, here they may be seen — as Breman rebuilt she came up with the finest harbor in the world. There is one salient and important difference between the rebuilding of Hamburg and Bremen — in Hamburg the city owns the port; in Bremen half the stock is owned by the businessmen and merchants of the city. The profit motive at work.

Nobody knows just when fishermen along the sand dunes of the outer Weser River began to sail farther and commerce began, but since that time Bremen has been a city where the goods of the world meet and pass and pay their dividends. You can walk along the docks today and see the flags of forty-seven countries from mastheads — everything from the liner *United States* out of New York down to tiny river barges that move far up the river and into canals. The vast complex stretches from the outer Bremerhaven sixty miles downriver to the heart of Bremen itself. Ships and cargoes come and go, and the dock-side facilities tick like a watch. All this was planned and projected by the Bremen Port Authority, which operates from a building on the waterfront called the Lagerhaus. This is the best place to begin looking at Bremen, and up on the top floor we found Mr. Johann Schröder who was sitting at a desk with his jacket off, and he hurriedly slipped it on and came with his hand out. His English was fine, and he quickly told us he had been a prisoner of war in Medicine Hat, Canada, and had put his time to good use. He reminisced a moment, telling how he worked on a farm for an Alberta farmer who was good to him, and he was put to doing something any German knows much about — pulling sugar beets. Because of the war even those who grew beets were without sugar, but this farmer kept his POW's sweetened up with honey, and they could have all they wanted because he kept bees. Mr. Schröder had come home to Bremen to find his city almost flat, and he had joined the restoration job with enthusiasm. Part of his work now is to publicize and promote, and he was ready to give us all the time we wanted. Did we know, he asked, that Bremen would be

192

the first seaport in the world to be completely ready for container cargoes?

At the time we didn't know anything about containers, but before Mr. Schröder got through we knew all about them. They are the big metal boxes, as big as a truck body or boxcar, that are loaded at the factory and sealed, and proceed intact to their destination. It does away with loose freight and many stevedore problems, almost eliminates damage and theft, and on shore the container rides a flatcar or a flatbed truck. "We saw containers coming, and made ready," he said.

He quoted tonnage and values until our heads whirled, but all this was something we more or less knew about Bremen. The old Hansa city, free, and Germany's smallest state. We had heard that Bremers are *stur*, which means about what dour means to the Scots, and that above all else they attend to business. Mr. Schröder himself was fast proving that this isn't true, and it isn't, and after we listened to his harangue a decent time I said, "We'd like to see the model room."

He did a double take. "How do you know about the model room?" he asked. I said I'd heard of it somehow, and I understood it was a fine place to get the feeling of Bremen. "But it is not open to the public!" he said.

I'd heard this, too. I said, "Yes, but we are not the public." The model room is probably the world's finest mechanical toy, and it is a complete working scale model of the entire Bremen waterfront. Everything moves through cycles started by push buttons — ships and trains come and go, derricks hoist and lower, all in miniature. That it is not open to the public makes sense — they keep this as a special attraction for important guests of the city and the Lagerhaus, and here the mayor holds receptions for visiting VIP's who may enhance Bremen's trade position. To have visited the model room is a rare privilege, and you just can't have everybody running in and out. Mr. Schröder smiled and walked us through some Bremen harbor traffic to the separate building where the model harbor is housed.

Some part of this model was originally made for the New York fair that was interrupted by the war. When the German Pavilion closed suddenly the exhibit, or part of it, was somehow returned to Germany, but nobody knows just how or if he knows he doesn't say. Another portion was made for a later fair in Chicago, and some other exhibitions. But none of it was turned out by the famous toymakers of Germany; rather, the work is done by modelmakers employed by the Lagerhaus for that purpose, and they have an envy-provoking workshop on the floor below. Their job is to keep the model up-to-date, and as fast as the Bremen Port Authority expands the real facilities these men duplicate it in miniature. The whole show is in a fairly large room, with effective lighting, so plenty of honored guests can mill around and play. Mr. Schröder was just like a little boy with Christmas all to himself as he pushed buttons and ran through his publicity spiels. I liked best the activity around the huge Bremen grain elevator, where suction tubes load and unload carriers, but everybody likes trains and I suppose the real attraction is the way freight cars are shunted around and their contents lowered into vessels. In one panel, depicting Bremerhaven, an American passenger liner leaves Columbus Key, or Quay, and puts to sea over a vast pool of water, and she is no sooner out of sight than a German liner arrives and docks. A helicopter flies across, and tiny tugboats maneuver the ships to and from the wharf. I suppose Mr. Schröder has pushed that button a thousand times, but something of the mesmerism that prevails with toys was tipped off when he said, "You don't see the passengers, of course — they are getting off on the other side!" I remember Dorothy, delighted, said, "Of course!"

We were there a long time, and I said to Mr. Schröder, "I have heard that this model room is a key to the true Bremen spirit, and that with all its hurry and hustle the city is really pixillated — do you know what I mean by that?"

I think he answered me very well. He said, "Yes, and now let us go this way, please."

In the social strata of cities like Bremen and Hamburg the topmost rung is inhabited by the pilots. They are the cream. When a ship comes or goes, the skipper is obliged, no matter how great his ability, to turn his wheel over to the pilot. The pilot alone has all the responsibility, and with it goes pride and status. And of all the pilots in all the world, the pilots of Bremen acknowledge themselves the best, and I guess they are. In deference to their select situation, the Bremer Lagerhaus has thoughtfully arranged a nautical lounge just off the model room, and here a dedicated steward is ready at all hours to answer their slightest whim. Mr. Schröder led us into that lounge, and that steward was the one who put a Canadian flag on the table.

So many have said to us, "Ah," or words to that effect, "Ah, but the ordinary tourist can't do these things!" This is absolutely untrue. We walked in on Herr Schröder as cold as a Cod Cove clam in January, and only by approaching him tactfully and in pleasing fashion we persuaded him to oblige us. He owed us nothing, had never heard of us, and was a very busy man with plenty else to do. I can add that we have since had correspondence, and when he returns to America he will visit us. But getting to

195

see the model room and the pilots' lounge in Bremen is precisely something that anybody can do if he wishes — because we did it.

Mr. Schröder said the liqueur we were about to enjoy was made exclusively for the pilots of Bremen, and there was no other place in the world to taste it. Except for a bottle later in France's beautiful Burgundy, this was our outstanding alcoholic experience of the trip. There is no way to describe the liqueur of the Bremen pilots, because unless you have tasted it you couldn't know. The label said it was a Kurfurstenlikkor Magan, produced in Danzig since 1598, and now supplied by the widow of Isaac Hekker and one Eydam Dirck Hekker. When you see it in print it is so, and I believe it. A small, delicate glass was all we had, with assorted cookies and a Canadian flag, and I believe the pilots of Bremen will find Heaven dull and unexciting. I understand they also have good salaries.

And Mr. Schröder told us they have a bit of a racket going with cigars. Bremen is a big tobacco port, and every time a ship comes in bringing leaf the import officials size up the cargo and by ancient tradition well kept the finest is adroitly diverted, and it finds its way to a local cigar-rolling factory where they, and they alone, are competent to roll the particular cigars the Bremen pilots admire. Mr. Schröder had the steward bring a box, and I was permitted to select a cigar for my very own. I never smoke a cigar, but you can be sure I took one. It was not a handsome thing — certainly it was hand rolled, but the tobacco was black, and on the mouth end was a curlicue like a pig's tail. Mr. Schröder said this was the trademark of the Bremerlotsescigar, it would be known and instantly recognized, and admired, in any seaport the globe around.

We left Mr. Schröder shortly, but not until I had repeated my opinion that there was a fairy-tale side to Bremen which he had nicely introduced — the forty-seven flags of all nations, the electric trains, the Magan and the cigar, and his own evident willingness to forego a morning's pressing work to visit with two crazy Americans he might never see again. He answered me well again; he said, "Yes."

And he was right. Before the city hall of Bremen, 1405, which is an ancient gingerbread fabrication that either holds up the statues or is held up by them, stands the best evidence of Bremen's adoration of the whimsical. This is the statue of the Bremen City Musicians — the Bremerstadtmusikanten. Once upon a time — and you find it in the Brothers Grimm.

Once upon a time the donkey, grown old, decided to break from the whip, and he started out for Bremen where he had heard there was an opening as a city musician. As he went along, telling of his plans, he was joined by a dog, a cat and a rooster. What fun they would all have when they arrived and got jobs as city musicians in Bremen! So they came on a house in the forest where some robbers were hiding out, and the animals decided to serenade them. The donkey stood on the ground under a window, the dog on his back, the cat on the dog, and the rooster on top. When they began to sing the unholy noise frightened the robbers and they ran away, leaving the house in the forest to the animals who "lived happily ever after." So while Paris has the Eiffel Tower, and New York the Statue of Liberty, Bremen has this silly community monument to their official city musicians — directly before the old town hall in the most important spot.

But there is more. Just across from the town hall, smack in the middle of the old marketplace, is the statue of Roland. Roland the knight of Charlemagne; Roland the protector of Bremen. His statue makes Roland look silly-simple, and he appears to be meditating on why in Heaven's name he didn't blow his horn that day. His good sword Durandal is in his hand, and his shield before him. The statue runs up high enough so you have to crook your neck to inspect it. Well, the legend is that if the statue of Roland falls Bremen will fall, and during the war the good citizens left their precious docks and warehouses to be blasted to bits, but they carefully laid sandbags all up around their statue of Roland until they had him safely covered. Bombs hit all around him, but after the war they removed the sandbags and Roland hadn't been hurt a bit. There he stands to this very day, and so does Bremen.

And still more. Right in the middle of Bremen's new chrome and concrete stands the municipal windmill. An air photograph of the city shows you how splendidly the piles of bomb rubble were replaced by modern construction, and also shows you the vanes of this ancient windmill. Carefully kept in working order, it could be used again, and again it is a testimonial of Bremen's whimsical fairy-tale standards. Long ago this mill was provided so the citizens could grind grain if they were besieged, and when enemies came and bottled them up they were all right so long as the wind blew. It's a good thing to have, of course, and Dorothy and I stood looking at it and thought of all the priceless old ship captain's homes we've torn down back in Maine to put up filling stations.

And not far from the statue of Roland is a walk-through called Böttcherstrasse, a place of souvenir shops, restaurants and galleries. This is Bremen's most obvious bid for tourist attention, and the click of camera shutters proves they have a good thing going. But here, if often missed by many, are Bremen's statues to the Seven Sluggards. By now you believe Bremen to be the last place in the world where laziness would be memorialized — but here they are, lolling about, sleeping, symbolizing inertia in perpetual stone, and not one of them ever looking up in busy Bremen to see if there is anything to do. Once upon a time, of course, an old Bremen farmer had seven sons and he worked hard from morning to night to fetch them up to be good citizens. But they were ungrateful and they all ran away. Years later they all came back, and now their father was old and couldn't work as he once did, and the boys pitched in to run the farm. But they used their heads instead of their backs, and they began ditching the fields so they wouldn't have to haul water, and they thought up many a labor-saving scheme. Soon they were doing more farming then anybody else around, but they had things figured out and were able to spend a good part of every day sitting in the sun and taking life easy. So the Seven Sluggards of Bremen are not really a memorial to laziness at all, but a symbol of Bremen's way of doing things — use your head as well as your hands.

We went twice to the St. Peter's Cathedral, dating from 1043, an edifice the Pope lost to the north German Protestants some time back. First to church, then to an organ concert. We paid special attention to the glass, and wondered how our chocolate-drinking Frenchman was doing. At church the sermon was beyond us, even though the minister spoke with crystal-clear diction and we heard every word he said. The organ concert was on a Tuesday, and I found it a disappointment. On Sunday the great organ had made the old pile vibrate, and the voices of both choir and congregation had added to the effect. Now we came in to listen to some Herr Doktor Professor of Musik run the scales all evening in some finger exercises Bach had left for his students, and the program had about as much music in it as the thrumming of a dozen buckets. The audience was attentive, but more polite than appreciative. I believe the organist was a sadist.

In the famous Bremer Ratskeller no beer is served, but they have the best selection of German — and only German — wines. Many German wines are appreciated out of patriotism and not quality, but some are excellent, and if you want to become an authority on the subject this is the place. The male waiters are in white ties, and dining there is a great pleasure. Above the Ratskeller is the ornate reception hall where the Lord Mayor conducts state parties, and here will be seen another bronze statue of the City Musicians — this one including the frightened robbers. Indeed, you bump into the theme all over the city, and stores sell all manner of items with the musicians stamped, stained, cut, marked, and so on. The first night we went to the Ratskeller we happened to get a waiter who has a sister living in Minneapolis on Park Street, but he couldn't remember the number. He wondered if we might know her. I asked him if he would show us the Apostle Cellar, and just as Herr Schröder had done about the model room, he did a double take. But the Apostle Cellar is not so well-kept a secret as the model room, and some of the Bremen pamphlets describe it. Our waiter said he would be glad to, and he held back our food so there was a hiatus, and he asked another waiter to see that nobody took our table.

There are no electric lights in the Apostle Cellar, so he conducted us in with a flashlight. There are twelve huge wine casks in this vault, each bearing the name of an apostle. I imagine many a good Baptist and Methodist back home would think this profane, but it seemed more mirthful to me. I like the idea of the Twelve meditating there in the dark for centuries on end while the wine ages. Unfortunately, the wine in the casks is so very old that it has lost all quality, and today the Apostle Cellar is merely another of the delightful old items that Bremen has kept. If, and this is purely fanciful, these wines were still potable they would have market values of war-debt proportions. Our waiter pulled the bung on one cask and dripped a single drop of its aged wine onto our fingers, and we tasted it. It was musty and of no particular flavor, but it was not, as I had expected, vinegar. He said that single drop, if wine that old had quality, would be worth $23,000. At that price I would think one drop enough. We promised to look up his sister in Minneapolis.

But for the Baptists and Methodists who may sense an indelicacy when the apostles are associated with a German wine cellar, I have more news. I guess it is the final, super-duper moodsetter for Bremen. Since this Apostle Cellar is without lights, and visitors see only what ranges within a flashlight area, many people must come and go without ever seeing the painting up on the plaster of the arched wall. Our waiter, since we would be good enough to look up his sister, concluded our tour by whipping his flashlight into the air and revealing this final touch. In the Middle Ages, he said, a wandering artist came to Bremen, and for food in the Ratskeller he agreed to do a mural. In the dark Apostle Cellar, with candles burning at both ends, he had fulfilled his agreement. There was the painting high on the wall over the twelve casks — a lovely nude with smooth, white, marbly limbs and other agreeable feminine particulars, posed in such a way that the long-stemmed red rose in her hand seemed to distract from the main theme. Our waiter permitted a discreet inspection and then snapped off his light. We went back to our table and he brought our chicken.

201

So we came to leave Bremen with a happy regard for their wholesome combination of fact and fancy, legend and commerce, past and present. The wharves and the ships and the mystery and magic of the sea, the musicians and the sluggards, the mighty Roland, and the Twelve Apostles down cellar with a naked woman.

Even Paris wasn't going to top that.

The Bremen Cigar

There will be a short passage through the industrial Ruhr. Any American tourist who wants to see it should go to a psychiatrist instead of a travel bureau, and a week in Pittsburgh is a good substitute. We kept off the through routes when we could, but we got to Osnabrück, Münster, Dortmund and so on, and to Düsseldorf which is a gay, sophisticated city that keeps busy day and night. We drove over to Solingen to see where they made all the *Fahrtenmessers* we were taking home to our hunting and fishing pals, and we came back to Cologne to see the big cathedral, as everyone must.

Unlike the wide-open doors at Amiens and the hospitality of the *Dom* at Bremen, the situation at Cologne is rather commercialized. The first sour note came from an officious nobody who thought he knew more about parking my VW than I did, and he was laboring under a foolish notion I was going to give him some money. You run into this now and then, but it doesn't mean anything. Somebody, sometimes under the ruse of being a war veteran, takes over a public parking lot and makes believe he's in business. He waves his arms around as if he owns the place, and will take a mark if you hand it to him. It seemed to us the great cathedral at Cologne ought to be able to stand a few more centuries without this kind of padding, so I told the fellow to go fly a kite. He set out to find a policeman and we inspected the masonry. The souvenir business seemed good, and the guides taking the hordes of people from item to item seemed proficient and glib. There is, if you search your own inner faith, a faint and light-scented flavor of religion present, and at times you detect it, but a great deal goes on to minimize this. When we came out the parking man had forgotten us and was away down at the other end assisting an Indiana station wagon into a select spot. We drove along to Bonn.

When Bonn was made the capital of West Germany the place was a quiet university town at a scenic spot on the Rhine, and to most Germans the idea was something of a joke. Berlin was the only true capital in the minds and hearts of the Germans, and in those days reunification was believed close at hand and the arrangement was purely temporary. But time has run on and Bonn is no longer a quiet little place. You can see somebody there from every nation in the world and the city is geared to high-level diplomacy, intrigue and profits. Bonn is not a friendly place, and in the protocol-minded atmosphere a stranger is a nuisance and intrusion. Bad Godesberg, a suburb just up the river, was HQ for the American Occupation, although the big building where our postwar efforts were seated was actually in the next community, Mehlem. All this area is now busy-busy being the heartthrob of Germany, and any old books that describe the scenic charm and the quiet Rhenish atmosphere can be hove out. We soon caught on, and we went along past Mehlem up the river and got far enough away from Bonn to find a congenial inn where we felt less like spies and would not be mistaken for consular agents. The main railroad line up the Rhine had to be crossed in order to reach the hotel, and the trains run so frequently that the crossing tender is one of the busiest men in Europe. These are fast trains going and coming from about everywhere, but the roadbed is so smooth and the equipment so efficient that hardly any noise of this traffic came into the hotel — there was a sort of swoosh that told you a train had just gone by, and that's about all. Near our hotel a chairlift went up to a mountain crag, and after dark they lighted the thing.

When we came into the dining room that evening we politely spoke to everybody. You mustn't do this with a Hello-Bill Elks approach just off the Rotary-Kiwanis-Lions circuit, because if you do you are dead. We merely shook hands with the man at the door, and then bowed as we passed tables — saying *Guten Abend* here, *Mahlzeit* there, and *Guten Apetit* again. Everybody responded. Some gentlemen stood and bowed, and one man shook hands. We shook hands with our waitress, and I'm sure many of the other guests noticed with approval that she brought us Steinhagers — the right way to commence a proper evening. When we raised our glasses the man at the next table lifted his in our direction and wished us health. "Danke," we said, and the evening had begun.

I don't recall how it ended. The final contenders for the championship were ourselves and a couple from Hamburg named Herbert and Thea Rehders. They were on holiday and like us had found Bonn cool and unreceptive, so they had moved up the Rhine looking for something more congenial. I think they came over to our table, but we may have gone to theirs instead. There was some Asbach. It was one of the pleasantest associations of our whole trip, and as train after train swooshed by we sat there in joyful mood — they murdered English with the same merciless attack we used on German, and every syllable in both languages came through clear and distinct. As our bilingual skills increased we found our diction enhanced, and we soon became the greatest conversationalists in the world. And we grew wiser and more profound. I vividly remember Thea emphasizing the difference between *reisen* and *abreisen,* obligato to a learned dissertation by Herbert on the ninety-five theses that prove Hamburg the greatest seaport in the world.

This made me think of my Bremen pilot's cigar in the suitcase upstairs, and after I found the minute-light I brought it down and offered it to Herbert. He took one look at it and, as Herr Schröder had said, it was instantly recognized for what it was — it topped anything he had been saying about Hamburg. "Ein Bremerlotsescigar!" he said.

Thea said, "Where to hell you get it?"

It was a supreme rebuke to anybody from Hamburg. Hamburg and Bremen are sister cities, and each thinks itself the prettier girl. Only a Hamburger could possibly appreciate the high honor, and consequent deflation, of being offered a Bremen pilot's cigar with its curious, curly tail. Even the pilots of Hamburg don't get these.

I offered to light it, holding a match, and Herbert said, "No! I must take this home and show it to the beepul of Hamburg. I shall act superior. In Hamburg this will be famous. It is not to smoke, ever — but shall be kept always as a souvenir of our happy meeting!"

The Rehders made us promise to visit at their home when we returned to Hamburg to sail for America — but the shipping company changed to a sailing from Bremen so we never did return to Hamburg. We wrote them a note, sending very real regrets, as soon as we learned of the change. Not until the night we bought the wallpaper were we to have such a rousing evening — passing the time so pleasantly amongst the folks between airports.

Toward the Wine Route

The Rhine is like Thaddy Kneeland's daughter, the redheaded one who had the bedroom over the woodshed — everybody went to see her. Its varied vistas need examination, but all at once the song of the Lorelei was lost in the tumult of barge engines churning the water and the traffic of highways and railroads along both banks. We began looking for byways instead, and just above Koblenz we turned aside and left the Rhine to its business. In this way we discovered another river — the Lahn.

There is a dreamland town called Bad Ems. Coming over the hills, moving up from the Rhineland, we found it hard to believe the Lahn River was flowing in the direction it was taking — an illusion is created by the frequent locks and consequent deadwater. But it does flow toward the Rhine, and riverboats can navigate all the way to Giessen, which is north of Frankfurt. At Bad Ems the Lahn seems to be a contrived community beautification, like a duck pond in a park. The highway comes over the hills so your first sight of the town is from above, and because you have just left the frantic Rhineland the peace and beauty deserves at least a ten-minute stop to sit and look. *Bad*, of course, is the German word for bath, and the ancient spas have their charm. This one in particular. An old Russian church suggests historical uses of the resort, and the plush chrome and aluminum hotels perched on the overlooking mountains prove the place is still used. Some of them surpass the wildest expectations. All, of course, arranged to take advantage of the hills, valley and river. And it was in Bed Ems that I got my crude American English corrected.

The Germans have a pipe tobacco, made in Virginia, marketed under the brand name Lincoln. True, Lincoln is English, even though Maine had a Lincoln County before anybody ever heard of Honest Abe. I would consider Lincoln a word I could toss off as my own. Here in Bad Ems I stepped into a tobacco shop and asked for a package of Lincoln. The old lady behind the counter had some, and I could see it on the shelf, but she couldn't understand me. I finally had to point it out to her, and in mock disgust she blamed me for mispronouncing it. "Link-Koll'n!" she said.

We paused in Bad Ems some time, because it was so charming. We pursued the Lahn upstream, and stopped several times at locks to see them lift and lower the boats. We wondered if George and Betty Morrill, on their expensive cruise aboard the *Yankee*, would get to see anything better than this. The boats here are smaller than those on the Rhine, because the river and locks are smaller, but the people live on them the same way. Washings are hung out to dry, potted geraniums line the wheelhouse windows, and up from one boat came a magnificent aroma of something being cooked with a generosity of onions. It interested me that the lock-tenders always seemed to know if the next boat would be coming upstream or downstream, and they would have the water level ready for whichever it was. The telephone is the answer, and there is a dispatching system.

So we came along the Lahn until it was time to turn off for the Taunus Mountains, a rural area not far from Frankfurt, and in a busy little town called Oberursel we found a traveling carnival set up in the marketplace and so surrounded by children of all ages that it scarce needed our business. But we donated happily.

Here in Oberursel we hunted up Dr. Georg Dietrich, the editor of the local paper. He had been in America for a month one time, on one of the exchange programs, and with massive Germanic erudition had come home to write a book called *Das Ist Amerika*. His doctorate, of course, is not in medicine. I was interested in talking to a man who had thus comprehensively "covered" his topic, and it turned out to be a most enjoyable visit. Some of these international experiments really seem to work. Frau Dietrich's family had owned this newspaper, and Dr. Dietrich had given it a fairly liberal tone after the war. At one time he had collaborated with some United States information officers in Frankfurt, and with their help had brought out an edition patterned on an American small-town newspaper. The ordinary personal item of commerce so important to our hometown press, saying that Mr. and Mrs. So-and-so spent Tuesday in Bangor, is impossible in

208

a dignified German newspaper. It invades privacy. The great American axiom that names are news has no standing in Germany. But egged on by the information officers Dr. Dietrich tried it, and although the stories were all in German they had the style and content of local American publications. Most other German editors laughed at the idea, but Dr. Dietrich felt his community rather liked it, and as a consequence has kept his stories more lively and his typography more daring.

And this condescension to Americanization won him the exchange visit to the States, and influenced his older son to go to America to study. Then there was a young lady from Kentucky who came to Germany as a Fulbright Scholar, and there she met this same son. He courted her in both countries, they live in Oberursel and have two small daughters. So it made quite a combination to look at. Frau Dietrich speaks no English, and the Doctor very little. The son, who presumably will one day inherit this extremely prosperous newspaper, speaks excellent English, and his American wife handles German with very little Kentucky overtones. She has, of course, given up her whole American background, and will someday enjoy the full status that belongs in a German community to the wife of the publisher. Meantime the two small daughters are being brought up in this household to speak only English.

The Kentucky mother said she felt this was the best way. When they began going to school they would have to use German, but by that time they would have English well in hand and they would never lose it. Grandparents Dietrich agreed, she said, although this arrangement was hardest on them. They couldn't always respond to the children, but they restrained themselves and didn't impose German so the plan could be undermined.

It seemed to be working fine. The two youngsters were happy, intelligent and easy to meet. I went out in the dooryard with them to look at their playthings, and all at once they ran over to a basement window of the publishing plant next door and tapped on it. The window opened, and a jolly German printer thrust his head out and began talking to the girls. He spoke German entirely. They answered him, and some banter ran on until he held out a small paper sack and they helped themselves to some candy. They knew as much German as he did! It's a wise parent who knows his own child, in any language.

Sheila Dietrich, the Kentucky girl, told us many amusing things came from this overseas alliance. Her mother-in-law had never been to America, but developed a great interest, and when President Kennedy was assassinated she was most horrified, and very frightened. Sheila said she tried to explain, unemotionally, the mechanics of American constitutional succession, but to Frau Dietrich none of this was comforting. She brought Sheila a wad of marks and told her to hurry to the shops and lay in a supply of dried peas, flour, beans and long-lasting staples to help tide them through the war that must surely now commence. Sheila asked what war, and Frau Dietrich tearfully revealed her belief that this tragedy promised total world destruction.

Sheila said, "It took a lot of explaining — not only to her, but to me. I had no way of knowing what war meant in her mind — she had seen war and I never had. To her it meant, first, food. When my husband was small and there was no food, she had to walk up into the hills and gather mushrooms, and for a long time they had nothing to eat except mushrooms. I was completely frustrated in trying to tell her that the United States would survive this

210

tragedy, but they have been frustrated when I don't understand them. It seemed amusing at first that she translated the death of a President into beans and flour, but not after I realized the stark terror in her memories that made her do it."

So we visited this uncommon German family in the hills of Taunus, which in many ways remind of the hills of Maine, and after we left them we saw Frankfurt, Wiesbaden, Darmstadt, Mannheim and Heidelberg — taking our time and lingering when we wished, and often wondering how many mushrooms it would take to feed a family for a month. Heidelberg, of course, occupied us for some time, and halfway up the steep hill to the rim-wracked old castle Dorothy got chicken and insisted I drive the VW the rest of the way. It's quite a climb, but as Vergil says of Hell, the descent is easy. Next we would cross the Rhine again, toward the west, and we had in mind to follow the long *deutsche Weinstrasse* its whole distance down to the border of France. It was just in the vintage, and we would roam the ancient Palatinate, the Rheinland-Pfalz, cask by cask. Somebody told us the wine road is well marked — by roadside signs bearing a bunch of grapes.

A Touch of Ivanhoe

We looked up many things before we began our trip, and brushed out some history — which is a wise thing to do. I chanced, in this preparation, to read the issue of the German news magazine *Der Spiegel* for July 19, 1961, which had an article called "Water in Wine?" The big controversy over adulterating German wines didn't excite me, but the article was a wonderful explanation of the European system of growing, making, marking and marketing wines. It would be foolish to tour the long length of the German *Weinstrasse,* or to visit any grape region, without some prior knowledge of this. The wine labels of Europe, once you get the hang of the wording, will tell you almost down to the grape what is in each bottle — or even more important, what is not. Not that the tourist needs to become an expert but that he needs to know enough to appreciate what is there to be seen and tasted.

There are many "wine routes" in Europe, and we didn't confine our close study of this subject to Germany, but we did drive the entire length of two of them — the *deutsche* and the *badische*. The books by the experts don't rate too many of these wines in the top categories, but there are many good wines, and there is a tumultuous production. Mile after mile of vineyards stretch back from the winding series of roads that make up the marked route, and although the terrain is completely different the effect is much like that you get from crossing the Iowa corn country. Spaced fairly close together are the small villages, all of them hiding winepresses behind their high stone walls, and sitting on caverns where the precious juices are aged, blended, bottled, and tasted. After you have driven by vineyards and come into a village, you see a grapevine running up in front of the post office, and bunches of grapes hanging down from a telephone wire over the street. Viticulture is the word, and Europe cultures a vast viti.

Midway of the German wine route is the ancient city of Neustadt an der Weinstrasse, thus easily distinguishing from all the other German Neustadts, and even if it costs Paris or Munich, the quick-hopping tourist should come here to get the feel of the grape business. Here, something which never happened elsewhere, we found the first three hotels we approached full-up, and each suggested we apply to the Hotel Löwenbräu. The influx of about everybody interested in the vintage put a strain on accommodations, and since the emphasis is on wines we thought it odd to be hunting for a hotel with a definite malt beverage flavor. Whether on not wine people purposely avoid Neustadt's beer-hotel we didn't learn, but the Hotel Löwenbräu did have a nice room for us, and it was unquestionably connected with the Munich brewery of the same name. The table cloths had the great lion for a design, huge Löwenbräu steins adorned the walls, and the draft from the bar was the certified product. The torrential flow of beer in the heart of the wine country was magnificent to behold, and we got the idea this hotel was headquarters for the dissenters.

We did stop in one small town and attempt to assist in the pressing, but the proprietor had gone to Frankfurt for a buyers' conference and in his absence the underlings weren't sure if we should be obliged. They were kindly and apologetic, but they were very busy. I've had people drop in at the farm and want to stand around and talk while I had some bees to swarm, and I appreciated the situation and we didn't intrude too far. We watched the gathering of grapes, and I did a little poking around in the soil from a farmer's curiosity. And we made ample investigation of the taste-and-buy opportunities, learning from seasoned experts how to swizzle around and spit. This seems, at first, like a great waste, but the *Weinstrasse* is long and prudence dictates restraint. You could get crocked in two kilometers if you tasted unwisely. In three days Dorothy and I spit out more wine than we ever consumed in our lives back home.

It was just off the *Weinstrasse* we found Trifels. This is another snatch of the old lore, for here on a peak is the castle where Richard of the Lion's Heart was imprisoned while Isaac the Jew raised the shekels to buy him back. All the history books I could remember said that Richard was held for ransom in Austria, and this castle high in the Palatinate is a far piece from anything that today is called Austria. Since the local historians are most definite on this subject, we assumed the history books are wrong, as usual, and that Trifels is the place. We found the three peaks that give the place its name, and came to the highest and the dungeon-castle where poor Dick languished. We looked down through the hole and could see why he stayed there. One of Hitler's early work projects began the restoration of this castle, and workmen have continued to

214

repair it ever since. You can see where a new-cut stone has been fitted in to replace one that was cracked or weathered, and the stone cutters do this work by hand just as it was done in the beginning. Dorothy said, "Be interesting to see somebody from Williamsburg give this job a gander," and I think it would.

Down in a dining hall of one of the hotels in the nearest village is a flock of murals depicting the Crusade story and the ransom of King Richard. For a mark or two one of the waiters will conduct you about and recite the patented narrative that goes with the pictures. This is all in German. Thus the tale of Ivanhoe comes through in a deep guttural, making it sound all most Teutonic and purely local, whereas any good professor of English literature will tell you *Ivanhoe* was the first novel in which Scott used a wholly English theme. We like to laugh, back home, about the Russian's inventing the electric light bulb in the tenth century (they had no place to plug it in!) but you've got to go some to beat a German when he decides to take credit for everything. Honus Wagner was a German, and he invented baseball. Thomas Nast was a German, and he invented Uncle Sam.

It is pretty hard to beat the Germans when it comes to lunchtime, too, so after our vigorous research into the true history of John and Richard we found an inn with a tasting department, and we had the farmer's omelet. Our wedding anniversary was coming on apace and we were due in Freudenstadt. From the Pfalzerwald we would go again to the Schwarzwald, and we would take with us a great bottle of *Weinstrasse* champagne which we had selected carefully.

We had been told there is a revered German custom of taking champagne for breakfast on a wedding anniversary.

215

We Cast Our Ballots

The magnum of champagne cost 62c and I got it in a grocery store that gives trading stamps. The lady asked if I wanted stamps and I said "Just one." We pasted it on our passport and got a good laugh from a customs man going into Austria. It was about a quarter of the size of green stamps back home, and they told us the idea had lately come to Germany and was going through the same merchandising squabbles common back home. We came to Ettlingen, which is not to be confused with Esslingen, or any other *ingen,* and as this was a reasonable run from Freudenstadt and our anniversary party the next night we took a room.

I gave the good-looking landlady the bottle of champagne, telling her it was for our anniversary breakfast the next morning, and it wasn't long before everybody in the place was coming over to congratulate us. They had a bowling alley off the dining room where the local Tuesday night bowling club was eating and drinking a match, and one by one the members came in to shake our hands and wish us health and happiness.

Breakfast with champagne proved a momentous occasion. Most of the tables in the dining room were taken, and our landlady ushered us to one in the middle. She served us, and after she laid on a plate of cold meats and two boiled eggs she came with the champagne in a copper ice bucket and two beautiful pieces of cut-glass stemware. She maneuvered so nobody in the dining room could mistake the reason, and the cork went to the ceiling with a mighty pop. She poured.

"Bring another glass," I said, and as this could be construed in only one way she fetched a third with alacrity. She pledged us happiness, we all touched glasses, and we sipped. I reached across and squeezed Dorothy's hand, and she winked at me, and the landlady pledged us again. We sipped again.

This may indeed be a glorious German tradition, but champagne for breakfast is not something that throws me into wild ecstasies. We didn't begin to finish our glasses, but went at the eggs and meat. Our landlady went to serving others, and as she stopped at this table and that the guests would look over at us, bow, and wish us happy *Hochzeit*. She came back to our table now and then for more sips, and I kept her glass full. She was pretty gay by the time we got up.

So Dorothy wanted a hairdo and I wanted a haircut for the big celebration we planned that coming evening in Freudenstadt, and we went out to find the shops, and did. About an hour later we came back to the hotel, and we found the dining room in festive mood. Our landlady was stewed to a wild haw-haw, and we concluded she was a laugher. The other waitress was giddy as a popper of corn, and all the guests were jolly. Copper buckets of ice and bottles of champagne stood by most of the tables, and we had triggered a wonderful hilarity. The gentlemen all tried to rise and toast us as we came through the door from the street, but some of them found this too much and resigned their enthusiasm to a sitting posture. They had a far bigger celebration that morning in Ettlingen than we had that evening in Freudenstadt.

We did swing over to Tübingen on our way, and in the old tavern off the Bahnhofplatz, right by the tracks, we had the best onion soup we found in Europe. Tübingen is the old university city, but modernity has changed the tone and you don't get much feel of antiquity until you wander up and down the old stone steps and the ancient walls cut off the noise of traffic. There is a dungeon where fractious students used to be thrown until they'd cooled off, and the thought does occur that some of our American colleges might embrace this idea with great benefit to all. The two cramped vaults have slits through the masonry so nobody ever stifled, but not much daylight comes in. Long centuries ago the poor devils tossed in here amused themselves by scrawling on the walls, seemingly with charcoal. Some of them had artistic talent. High in the rounded top of one vault some naughty student, no doubt working from tiptoe, had executed a reasonably personable likeness of a female, one whose ample breasts naturally catch your eye so you squint in the dim light for full appreciation. The bearded youth who is caressing her is, I hope, a self-portrait. But the flavor comes not from the drawing, but in the ancient German script charcoaled around it in a circle, so you have to walk about with your head cocked on one side to read it. It says, "Our dear, Mother University has enough for us all."

Then we went to Freudenstadt, which also has enough for everybody. We were to stay there a week for the happiest anniversary in thirty-five years, the great Black Forest all about us to cast its spell and the staff of the

218

Hotel Post working every minute to give us a good time.

Freudenstadt, since the first German trod the Schwarz-wald, has been a resort town. I suppose more cuckoo clocks have been sold in Freudenstadt than any other place. The quadrangle of the village left the market-place and the city hall ample area in the middle, and the town had a charm and atmosphere coming down untouched from long, long ago. But in the last days of the war, when everybody knew the fighting would end at once, the French came in one last burst of animosity and blasted Freudenstadt to bits. Demolition was complete and the carnage was horrible. Freudenstadt could never have been considered, by any stretch of definitions, a military target, and the incident has never been construed by the people of the Black Forest as a pleasantry. But it happened, and *c'est la guerre*, and Freudenstadt rebuilt methodically with every effort to restore what once had been. Thus Freudenstadt is a new town that looks like an old one. An arcade runs all about the quadrangle, so you can walk past all the shops under cover. And on a Sunday while some Germans walk the forest paths others walk the arcade of Freudenstadt, admiring the window displays without any temptation to buy, because on Sunday all stores are closed.

The Hotel Post, likewise, is new, but it has the brown-gravy smell. The young lady on the desk, who was named Giselle Günther, from Kiel, and who was studying hotel management, welcomed us by handing over a great wad of mail from home — the first connection we'd made in over a month — and she said, in her version of English, "If you please, may I have the stamps?"

I told her our children in America were going to telephone to us at midnight and she said, "That will be very expensive." But we knew how German hotels button up after hours, and we wanted no hitch in this call. She said she would arrange everything.

We had a rousing supper that night worthy of the event being celebrated. Nothing could be finer. The owner himself approached our table and inquired if we were pleased. Many a glass was lifted in our direction, and at a proper hour we retired to our room, set the telephone in the middle of the table, and waited for the dingaling to round out a perfect day.

Almost at once a pounding came at our door and we opened to find the night watchman there — a feeble, crippled old veteran of Kaiser Wilhelm's war, and if the hotel had been on fire he wouldn't have made more touse. He said the telephone had sounded, and it took him some time to find out which button to push, but he had successfully made a connection, and the operator in Stuttgart had told him there was to be a call from America and everybody should get ready for it. We gathered that Giselle had neglected to mention this to him. I thanked him and pointed to the telephone on our table, assuring him all was *fertig*, and he said, "No, no — come down with me, I don't know how to work the switchboard!"

So, appropriately enough perhaps for a wedding anniversary, in nightgown and pajamas we descended to the lobby with him, and while he hobbled around in wild excitement we patiently waited for the bell. The call came on schedule, transmission was excellent, the children were well, they wished us happiness, and everything was fine. The night watchman was weak as a dishrag after all this joyfulness, and sat exhausted. I insisted he open the closet and have himself a drop to equalize himself, and he considered this a splendid suggestion. He brought out three

220

glasses and we joined him in the German version of a nightcap. We left him asleep on his chair, pleasantly mulled, and if the hotel really had caught fire he'd have been no help in rescuing the two honored guests.

Amongst our mail had been our absentee ballots from home. We had signed the applications before we left and had told our town clerk to try to find us. It was one of the pleasantest political campaigns. We were away all during the speeches and commercials, and we didn't know who was running for what or how many bond issues and referenda had been cooked up. The two heavy envelopes looked official enough to impress any German, and Giselle had been properly impressed. We began our exploration of Freudenstadt by hunting for a lawyer. This proved to be our best gimmick. What we wanted, of course, was not a lawyer but a notary, and I foolishly supposed that since all lawyers at home were notaries public, all lawyers in Germany would be, too. The easiest way to process absentee ballots is to head for a United States consulate, and in the military they have simple ways of handling the required jurat. But we were visiting betwixt, and we wanted to do it the German, or hard, way. A lawyer is a *Rechtsanwalt,* and we found a shingle on a door and went in. The office girl appeared to be doing what a lot of American office girls do, nothing, and she started up when we breezed in to make it look as if we had surprised her in the middle of intense industry. "May we visit the Herr Lawyer?" I asked, and she motioned us through an inner door.

Here we found a man in his shirt-sleeves, smoking a cigarette and reading whatever is the equivalent of the Racing Form, and he didn't look as if business was brisk. He looked up at us, gulped, and all hell broke loose. He larruped around us and out the door, giving the office girl merry-to-do for letting us come in and catch him in-decent, grabbed up a jacket and yanked it on, and tight-ened his tie. Then he returned, bowed and shook hands, motioned us to chairs, and apologized until we thought he was going to cry. "Mox nix," I said, and explained that we needed a *notar*. He dismissed us curtly. He had an-ticipated a client, and this was a disappointment. No, he said, he was not a *notar,* and if we needed a *notar* we should apply to the *notar* at the courthouse. Good day.

We found the courthouse, and we climbed stairs to the third floor, which is really the fourth floor, and here we found what any stupid American should have known in the first place — that the *notar* has his own little racket and he doesn't spread the profits amongst the lawyers. And again, with American crudity, we made a bad ap-proach. The big man behind the desk said if we would step out in the hall for a moment he would oblige us pres-ently. You've got to do these things right. Soon a young lady came out and inquired if she could be of assistance and we told her what she already knew — that we needed a *notar*. "One moment," she said, and she went in and told the big man behind the desk that two people were waiting to see him. He said for us to come in, and when we did he asked what we wanted. We said we wanted a *notar*. He said he was a *notar* and invited us to be seated. Now that we knew the correct way to approach a *notar* he inquired as to the nature of our business and we showed him the big envelopes from Maine.

I don't know how other states make out, but in Maine a ballot can run like wall-to-wall carpeting. You get the state ballot for public officials, and folded inside it are all the local option questions, and anything else they can dream up. The highway and educational departments al-ways have a dozen or so bond issues, and very often they are reduced to ballot form in some such language as this: "Shall an act to create fiduciary tenure, in some counties, become law?" It helps if you've been around home during the campaign, but not always. I pulled the bundle of ballots, one in white, one in pink, one in buff, and so on, from the envelope, and the *notar's* jaw dropped open as he saw the volume. I'm sure he'd never seen any kind of absentee ballot before, much less the impressive ones from Maine. He pawed them over on his desk, holding some of them right-side-up, and after a minute he excused himself and took the whole bale with him out of the room.

There's a wild difference between touring Germany and ordering pork chops with potato salad and explaining about an absentee ballot. I was shuddering as I anticipated the demands that would be put on my language, but I was spared because the *notar* was too proud to ask. He intended to carry the thing off. Now he had gone through the building to show the ballots to all the judges, bailiffs, commissioners, lawyers and jurymen so he could find out what was going on and come back informed. But I guess nobody could help him much. While he was gone all manner of men and women opened back doors and peeped in at us, and some of them wagged their heads. When he came back I showed him our passport, thinking it a good place to start, and he understood from it that we had just been married and he wished us a long and happy life.

Anybody who thinks Latin is a dead language should have heard things come to life when I pointed at the spot and said, "Hier, machen-Sie bitte ein jurat." This did it, until after we had marked our choices and he wanted to see how we had voted. I fished around for words, and told him this was a secret ballot, and he was not privileged to know that. He then said he could not honestly perform the jurat unless we could prove to him that we had properly marked them. So, you see, we had a decision. We could have stood there another hour expounding the Australian ballot and its purposes, insisting it is illegal to show it around, and proved ourselves honest, upright, democratic citizens dedicated to obeying the law. Or we could very simply show him how we voted, and although this would make us criminals it would speed the affair. We showed him how we voted.

He looked to see where we had made each cross, nodding approval, and although I doubt if he had the faintest idea what an on-premises-tavern would be he seemed pleased that we were for it. He surely did carry the thing off. Then he got out a big book about a yard square and in it he wrote our names, addresses, professions, and laboriously carried each line faithfully across from left to right. The fee, he looked up from his writing and said, would be six marks each — three dollars for this outlandish display of suffrage. I paid it over.

He wrote his name where I pointed. Now some states have wisely modified the ancient requirement of a notarial seal, but Maine still holds to this anachronism, and the jurat on our ballots calls for a seal. I wondered if our precise-minded election officials back home would understand about the German and his rubber stamp, and I certainly hoped so when our *notar* reached in his desk drawer and brought out his rubber stamp and whacked it up and down on our papers. In Germany this is as good as gold, but in Maine it might seem informal. After we got home I inquired about this, and Glenys Thompson, our town clerk, said she did have a moment's wonder about it, but decided it must be all right. Then we shook hands warmly with our *notar* and the exercises drew to a close. It had taken us one hour and forty-eight

224

minutes to vote. As we went out our *notar* called, "Auf Wiedersehen! Eine gute Fahrt!"

There was a perfect finish to this absentee vote. We walked across the ancient Freudenstadt marketplace to the post office and asked for air mail postage on these whopping great envelopes. No German uses anything but tissue for any letter, air mail or regular, and to buy air postage for 9 × 11 manila bundles was an affront to the national thrift. The postal clerk was thunderstruck. And when we got home we found that every issue we had voted for was defeated, and every candidate we had approved had lost.

In such merry wise we had fun in Joytown, and then one day Dorothy said, "But we've got to go to Italy," and so we set out for Italy.

The Wallpaper

So far we had not retraced our route, but we had crossed it several times. We crossed it now again to get into that beautiful region called the Allgäu, on our way to Innsbruck. We saw some more of the Bodensee and heard Alpine cowbells jingling again from the fields along the road. And it was just outside a place called Wangen that we came upon a fairly new hotel, which looked attractive, and we stopped off for the great wallpaper scene. The place was at ebbtide when we went in, just two boys having beers and a waitress talking with them. The landlord, a young man, came out of the kitchen and said his best room was available, but there was no toilet on that floor. Translated, this means you get a room under the roof, and it is warmer and cozier, but you have to negotiate an extra stairway. Our room had sloping walls, and windows that looked for miles up the road and took in some pleasant scenery.

We wondered again why a new stone and mortar building, put up specifically for a hotel, wasn't laid out more thoughtfully, and just what it would have cost to run the flushbowl pipes up another landing, because our room did have a washbowl, and plenty of hot water; everything was spanking clean and the featherbeds were fluffy. But for the cost of one hopper that landlord was spending the rest of his life explaining that he had no toilet for his best room.

There was a plastic mug by the washbowl that showed we were amongst cultured and enlightened people. On it, in German, it said:

> *Twice daily brush the teeth,*
> *Twice yearly, to the dentist.*

We added this to our growing collection of glasses, steins and mugs. We could have taken it, stolen it — but we never did that. We'd express a desire and ask how much. Usually they would give us the item as a souvenir when we paid our bill. Now and then the price was added to our bills, but it never amounted to much. The plastic toothbrush cup became ours with the gracious good wishes of the management.

When we came down to dinner the dining room had many guests, including some boys at the football table.

Over in another corner a card game was going on. We were the only overnight guests, and a table for two was waiting for us — a big round party-size table where the two setups seemed lonely and by themselves. This was the best table in the place, of course, and we knew the landlord had been steering others away from it until we'd come down. When we did come down, the built-up curiosity about who-the-hell was so big and important caused us a good looking-over, and we bowed here and there. The meal proceeded with the usual good success, and in due time I excused myself and withdrew behind a door in the corner that said *Herren*.

I wasn't gone too long, but when I returned the whole complexion of the dining room had changed. Dorothy had become queen! Everybody was at our table, including the owner and one of the waitresses, and somebody had provided a new bottle of Asbach which Dorothy was distributing with lavish hand. The card game had ended, the football table was empty. Helping Dorothy, and with one arm about her shoulders, was an extremely handsome fair-haired man of about thirty who was telling her in plaintive lament that she reminded him of his poor, dear, dead wife who left him with two small children three years since. Hearing this the landlord burst into laughter and continued hysterically until his waitress beat him on the back. Everybody stood up and shook hands all the way around as I came back, and I could see the hospitality of Wangen was likely to set a new record.

It was, in all truth, a delightful dining room. A wainscoting in dark wood was topped by a shelf, and all around it were steins, old copper, potted plants, and odd pieces of lovely china. Above the wainscoting was about as attractive a wallpaper as I've ever seen — it was a hunting motif in a light green and sepia, showing mallards, pheasants, stags, and the appurtenances of the chase, including bottles. The paper had, actually, caught our eyes when we first stepped into the place, and all during our meal we had admired it. Not only was the decor nicely done, but the tables were thoughtfully placed, and the linen and china were in keeping. So, as the Asbach flowed, surrounded by all the friends we had in town, the congeniality and conviviality increasing, we made the most of everything, and all at once I heard Dorothy say, in whatever language was then being used, "Love that wallpaper!"

Then followed a lively discussion of wallpaper in general, and this pattern in particular. It was pleasantly brought out that Germany makes the finest wallpapers in the world, although as everybody knows there are other areas in which excellence prevails, and that this present design and texture was far and away the best of them all.

"I can see that," said Dorothy.

Shortly Dorothy was explaining about our own living room at home — white pine panels and beamed ceiling, fireplace, and a striking wallpaper. It was, she told them, a large room, thirty-five feet long and fifteen feet wide. She said this wallpaper in Wangen would certainly be a fine pattern for us to have if we ever decided to change.

It was now that the landlord arose and said, "You are very lucky — it so happens that my decorator is at this moment in the kitchen, making with some paint, and I will bring him in!"

So this meek little man came in, wearing the white coveralls of his trade and wiping his hands on a cloth, and after the introductions and a polite hesitation he decided one small Asbach would not materially hinder the business in which he was engaged, so he sat down. He was employed by a firm in Wangen, but was moonlighting after hours. He had yellow eyes, but from lead poisoning or kidney complaint I know not. He proved most friendly, and not a bit afraid of Asbach. Yes, he said as he turned and swept the wall with his gaze, this is indeed a beautiful paper and always much admired by all who see it. He told us which factory had produced it, and said his company had bought the entire run. Nobody else had any — just his company. I distinctly remember that Dorothy said, "So if I want any, I must buy it from you?"

"My poor, dear wife would also have liked this wallpaper," said the man with his arm around her shoulder.

I don't mean to say that all we did was talk about wallpaper. I remember one brisk discussion about de Gaulle and the British effort to penetrate the European Economic Community, and considerable conversation about football. I remember, too, how we bade everybody a fond good-night, promising to write frequently, and I remember how the minute-light went out before we got all the way up to our cozy room. And, dimly, I have some recollection of the exercise in higher mathematics when everybody around the table was helping the paperhanger convert thirty-five feet and fifteen feet to meters.

As we were arranging the featherbeds I said, "I suppose you know you just bought fourteen rolls of wallpaper."

"Ha, ha!" said Dorothy. "That's a good one!"

"Ha, ha — nothing," I said. "That paperhanging Hitler sized our living room, took out two doors and four windows, and tomorrow morning he's bringing you fourteen rolls of wallpaper."

"Ha, ha," she said. "That's a good one!"

"I figure a forty-dollar good one," I said.

"Don't be silly. All I said was that it would look good in our room."

"No fight about that — it's a beautiful paper. But to-

morrow morning as you are dipping your pumpernickel
into the juicy yolk of a soft-boiled egg that yellow-eyed
painter is going to come in with your wallpaper."

"Ha, ha."

So the next morning as she was dipping her pumpernickel into the juicy yolk of her soft-boiled egg the door
from the kitchen opened and in came the painter with a
big bundle under his arm and a bill for DM136.20, or
something, around thirty-four dollars.

We brought it home, and it is truly a beautiful pattern
and an excellent paper. We are not soon to forget our
wonderful evening in Wangen.

And as we drove along through the Allgäu she said,
more than once, "I keep thinking about that poor man
who lost his wife." I said, "I suspect he keeps thinking of
you, too."

But this is the land of mad kings and rescued prin-
cesses, and turrets and towers of ancient castles, and we
soaked up legends and lore. One citizen, his values a
trifle askew, told us one castle was famous above all the
others — Walt Disney, he said, had made a film there.

The Other Ammergau

When the tourist buses ap-
proach Oberammergau they go right through a small
town just up the river without stopping — this is Unter-

ammergau. On our kind of tour we could stop, and we did. We found Unterammergau a delightful place. Everybody knows about Oberammergau and the Passion Play, but we got the idea we were the first people who ever pulled up in Unterammergau and asked what's to see there. I guess we didn't cause any huge upset by this difference, and it was a little sad, in a way, to have them tell us we had made a mistake and must be looking for someplace else. It must be frustrating to live in Unterammergau and spend all your time directing tourists to Oberammergau. The two towns are not far apart — each may be seen up or down the valley from the other — and they are both named Ammergau, one upper and one lower.

But they are nothing alike. Unterammergau is an undiscovered town with red tile roofs and a few shops surrounded by homes and farms. The magnificent scenery of the region, with the Alps hanging aloft, is the same from either place. But Unterammergau remains quiet, industrious, undisturbed, and Oberammergau is one of the world's greatest tourist traps, where a legendary religious experience has been parlayed into an attraction of unequaled fame. Even Shakespeare, whose festivals beckon, cannot offer what Oberammergau owns as built-in stagecraft — the divine touch. You can line up all the Ophelias and Falstaffs and Romeos and shake them together in a bag, but only Oberammergau has a play where Jesus takes the lead. True, the whole thing is passionately devout, and the sincerity of the play makes any carping bad taste. But that's what it amounts to, and Oberammergau sits serene under a community halo, and Unterammergau plays a very soft second fiddle.

As we roamed about Oberammergau, bumping shoulders with tourists from everywhere, we couldn't help recalling our recent visit with the Twelve Apostles back in

231

Bremen. We had left these worthies in the dark solitude of their meditations, seemingly quite content to be abstractions in the mysticism of their theology. Why isn't this a good way to have them? Symbols, ideas and concepts. But here in Oberammergau the Apostles live their roles, and run gift shops.

We picked up one little-known story about the Passion Play. It seems after the war, when it came the tenth year and the play had to be staged again, there was a sticky little moment when everybody realized known Nazis would appear in a definitely Hebraic context, and there was a nicety here which demanded pondering. True, in postwar Germany many an adjustment of this nature went on, but not in precisely the same frame of reference. They told us a reporter happened to stumble on the thing while it was mootest, and he recognized it as an angle and shipped it off to his publication. But the nuances were so touchy that the paper decided not to print it. After that the reporter tried to get any number of other papers and magazines to take the story, but he never did find a publisher. Out of deference to the spiritual magnitude of the Oberammergau Passion Play the whole world went deaf to this consequence of conflict. It seems only Judas had been faithful. And this is all right, because in Oberammergau the tone is good. In spite of our amusement at finding our Savior gainfully employed, we had at the same time a deep impression of a spiritual experience — and we were there in a year when the play itself was dormant. What Oberammergau is like when the play is on we can only imagine, but it must be terrific. But we do know what Oberammergau was like before 1633 when the play began — it was like Unterammergau.

At Zirl, in Austria, we found an inn worth extolling. If some American with money and a great desire to become famous as an innkeeper wants to put up the finest hotel in America, I can give him the name and address of the architect in Innsbruck who designed the Zirler Wein-hof, but such a benefactor will have a time of it finding such a pretty location. The inn sits back from the main road, and we drove past the entrance and had to back up. Behind the inn a vineyard stands against the hills, and the design of the building perfectly suits the spot. Before the hotel is the wide valley of the Inn River, and above and beyond that the whole skyline is the Alps. It may well be the perfect spot for a perfect hotel.

But the carpenter work in the building makes you go around rubbing your hands on the woodwork and feeling the joints. I don't believe we've got a carpenter in Maine, and Maine has some good carpenters, who is qualified to set about doing such work. Huge hardwood beams and timbers are mortised and fitted like the stones of the Parthenon, in flawless fashion, and the finish is by fire With some kind of huge blowtorch they passed along the timbers and boards, scorching the face of the lumber un-til it has a surface no oil, plastic or varnish could ever achieve. Part of the effect, I'm sure, is gained from the type of wood used, which I would think to be oak or ash or some variety thereof, with the alternate hard and softer grains. The young man on the desk, watching me give the woodwork admiring scrutiny, came over and ex-plained the whole job and told me who designed and who built the inn.

The rooms facing the broad expanse of the Alps have balconies and we sat on ours and watched the sun set. Even the West Kennebago Range couldn't begin to touch this spectacle. After dinner we came up to find a moon on the night shift, and we had a third gorgeous spectacle in the morning when the sun came up and the entire southern rim from east to west was blood-red snow on the peaks. The valley, which was warm and still in full summertime bloom, was still dark, and didn't begin to get light from the sun until the morning was well along.

In the dining room a great screw-gear winepress had been set up for decor, and all else was in harmony. Unlike so many places that go to great expense to establish atmosphere and then serve institutional food, the Zirler Weinhof gave us as good a supper as we had on the whole trip. The Austrians consider themselves much better innkeepers than the Germans, and certainly are better than the Swiss, and nothing but the best would suit the particular location and architecture of this hotel. Our room had every convenience we would find in any American hotel, and more than we would find in any American motel. The price for our double room, with bath and balcony and breakfast, came to less than eight American dollars. We easily had fifty dollars' worth of sight and scenery, and I learned more about cabinetwork than I'd get in a course at a technical school. I know of nothing in the United States to compare with this hostelry, and in tourist-minded Maine we don't even come close.

On the balcony in the moonlight, before we turned in, we assessed the morrow. Beyond those Alps lies Italy, and we would wend the Olympic Route over them, across the highest bridge on the continent and through the great Brenner Pass. Then we would descend leisurely into Italy and pay our appreciative respects to all the art and history and charm and poetry and beauty that was awaiting us there. When the sun did strike the snowy peaks with his crimson good-morning we jumped up willingly — for today was to be the day of days and we were going to Italy.

"And No Birds Sing"

Nobody ever came over the Brenner Pass into Italy with such expectation, such anticipation, such unbridled enthusiasm as we did. "Sweeter than France, but not so sweet as Italy," I quoted a dozen times. Nobody was ever so ready to love the country, so eager to see it and partake of its storied charm, beauty, history, magnificence — and food.

Consequently nobody was ever more disappointed.

Italy is for the birds, except that they don't have any birds.

Someday, I would like to study Italian at the Berlitz School and then go back to Italy and find out if my presumption is correct — that lack of language was our trouble. We came into Italy supposing we would wander about and get to know people and see things just as we had in all the other countries. We expected to mingle and sing gay *funiculis* far into the night. True, we spoke no Italian, but neither had we spoken Danish in Denmark, Flemish in Belgium, and English in Britain, and we had made out fine. We instantly, of course, found out the essential difference in linguistic attitude — a Dane or a

235

Belgian will fish around, and take an interest, and help you out. If they can't get to you in one tongue they'll try another. But we found that the Italian has no such interest, or ability — we never ran into any disposition to give us a helping hand, and never encountered any curiosity about us that engendered interest.

We saw a great deal of Italy, but there came a day when we were only forty miles from Rome and I said, "Now, do you want to enter the Eternal City this afternoon, or wait and tackle it fresh in the morning?"

Dorothy said, "I can tell you what I'd rather do."

"What?"

"Get to hell out of Italy."

At the time those were the sweetest words she ever spoke to me, and we turned around and headed for France.

There is plus and minus, the first minus being the Italian driver. He is the world's worst. He drives, at top speed, with his horn, and has no sense whatever of highway courtesy. His law says he must peep-peep before he overtakes another car, and this has been construed into a great national policy. The peep-peep is in lieu of all normal safety measures. After a couple of them have peep-peeped you into a marble quarry you begin to think a country with this idiocy must have other faults. In all the driving we did before we came to Italy we never saw a highway accident, but in the first four days in Italy we saw five, one of them a multiple fatality that sent a wheeler truck a hundred yards into a field to tip over. Highway police in Italy always travel in pairs on motorcycles, because this doubles the chances that one will arrive without an accident, and along the major roads at one-kilometer distances they have radio panels with two push

236

buttons — one to call the police and the other to summon an ambulance.

We used to have that horn rule in Maine. When a motorist was about to overtake a vehicle he sounded his horn, and the other fellow was required to "yield the right of way." But this was back in the Model T days when roads were unpaved and thirty miles an hour was aggravated speed. When somebody came up behind you and blew, you looked for a place to let him get by, and it might take a mile or more. It didn't mean you were expected to climb a tree. But in Maine we long ago gave up that rule, and now we operate on "the last clear chance." The motorist with the last clear chance to avoid an accident is considered at fault, and while lawyers can fight about it all day it promotes more caution than the Italian peep-peep law. I could save thousands of lives annually in Italy if they'd give me some pliers and the authority to cut the wires on horn buttons.

Another minus was the food. Except for the celebrated French cuisine we hadn't been prepared for the excellent food we found everywhere. But we had been told about the wonderful Italian dishes. Our first Italian meal was a warmed-up lasagne with mold on it, a sour wine, and bread that had neither texture nor flavor. The most lavish meal we had on the entire trip was in Italy, as I shall tell, but we waded through a lot of poor food to come to it.

The very first minus was the dead cat. Coming down from the Brenner we could see that Italy was to outdo our fondest hopes. The mighty Alps were conquered, and the breathtaking drive keyed us up. We thought it would be smart to find a pleasant hotel and hole up for a few days so we could get the feel of the country, perhaps pick up a few needed words, and inquire about routes and accommodations. We came into a smallish place and I saw an inn with a sign that said, "German spoken here." This is to oblige the great many German-speaking people who have begun to tour and like to head for the Mediterranean. I pulled up in front of the post office, across the street, so I could walk over and inquire for a *camera*. We had been studying roadside signs, and I had mastered that word. When I stepped out of the VW a peaceful and serene pussycat, long silent in the great democracy of death, lay on the pavement beside me in a condition I would not describe as rugged, and I stepped over him mournfully to make my way across.

I was met in the bar by a beautiful young woman wearing black — stretch pants and tight sweater. She could not have revealed her magnificent anatomy better if she had strode forth naked, and along with the Danish post office clerk she was the best I saw while away. Ja, she had a room. I went back, stepped over the cat, drove the VW into the hotel's parking lot, and we stayed there three days. At the end of three days, as we were leaving, I went to the post office to mail our cards, and the cat was still there.

The girl in black was cordial as long as her German held out, but her vocabulary was limited to hotel terms. She wore the same sweater and the same stretch pants all the time we were there, and appeared to do all the hotel work including the bar and dining room. Every so often a busload of touring Germans would stop and she would dash about serving them a meal and pointing to the *abort,* and after they were gone the place would quiet down. She had the quick-lunch technique, and tried to serve us that first evening with the same speed she used for the bus passengers, who had twenty minutes. "Wir haben Zeit," I told her, but this was not in her vocabulary.

She insisted we dine, and we didn't want to rush it. I finally used a good Providence, Rhode Island, Italian on her, and it worked. I said, "Look-a no push-a!" After that we had gracious leisure, and she'd come from the bar only when we called. A poor, blind violinist came in one night and made a horrible squeaking at the bar, and she told him to come in and play us a tune. He came into the dining room and played us "O Sole Mio," rancidly.

Italy is dirty. Generalities are unkind, and there is plenty of evidence of personal cleanliness and knowledge of soap and water, but as we moved about we were aware of a general filth, stench and indifference — and if somebody tells me that cat is still there I will believe it. That Italy is "sunny" was to us a mirthful myth. We saw the sun once, and it was shining in splendor on distant Assisi, and you couldn't ask for anything more lovely. The way these stone cities sit back, the particular kind of rock giving off the ancient appearance you've seen in pictures all your life, makes you well up inside when you see the sun shining on Assisi. We never saw the sun shining on any other place in Italy. But pretty as Assisi was in the sunlight, it was less than lovely when we came to it, and here we found out about St. Francis and the birds.

All over Europe we had bird-watched. Except for mallards we didn't see many birds we recognized, but we guessed at what the different birds might be, and even in far-up Denmark, where the late season comes early, we had seen many birds. But when we came down into Italy we didn't see any. They didn't sing under our windows in the morning, or fly up from the fields, groves and vineyards. And in Assisi where bird-loving St. Francis used to stand around and talk to the birds and you can walk the very streets where his feet once trod, we found out why Italy has no birds. They eat the things. In the meat stalls of the marketplace, where St. Francis must often have come, you can see the sweet-singing, feathered friends hanging up in plump strings, their pink little tummies exposed to the haggling housewives. You can decide if you want beef liver or robins.

But then the momentary minus would become a momentary plus. We came one day to Mantua, and stood looking up at the statue of Vergil — he has one finger up as if gesticulating a spondee. "Arms and the man," I sang, and I quoted, "Wielder of the stateliest measure . . ." There wasn't any great surge and thunder in the *Aeneid*, but I waded through it in high school, and it was a big thrill to meet Vergil at last. The escape from Troy and the founding of Rome. I forgave Italy a few random imperfections for the sake of Vergil.

And then after that we would come to something like Venice. Nobody should ever go to Venice unless he is drugged or drunk, or a newlywed with something else on his mind. A vivid imagination with superoctane isn't quite enough. The place stinks, the gondolas have outboards, and the whole thing is miles out in a cesspool sea of sewage. In Florence you gaze on the treasures in an ecstasy, and you can't help it — here you find so many things you have read about from the time you were old enough to read. But a dead cat is a distracting feature. Once we saw a farmer run over a dog. He came barreling along on his tractor and the puppydog ran out of a yard. He could have stopped, but he didn't even try to. And he didn't stop after he ran over the dog, either. Two youngsters came running out of the yard crying and picked up their puppy and shook their little fists at the farmer, and he shrugged his shoulders and kept on going. It is one of our more vivid memories of Italy.

In Vicenza we met a French lady who tried valiantly to

"explain" Italy to us. She rode in our VW with us and we went around all day looking at things. She did her best to cheer us up, but never, at any time, did we strike up such an acquaintance with any Italian people. We just never did, but this kind of association was commonplace everywhere else. And it was in Vicenza that I got on the telephone and put in a call to Carlo Urbani in Scheggino and made a date to hunt truffles — a happy chance, because it gave Italy one great, resounding opportunity to redeem, and to prove to us that all is not lost. And Italy and the Urbani family came through magnificently to do just that.

I Catch a Trout

Years ago my wife and I had lunch at the Plaza in New York, and when I decided on the eggs Benedict the waiter confidentially whispered, "I'm sorry, sir, but the Plaza has no truffles." I had no idea what a truffle might be, but I said, "See that it doesn't happen again." Afterwards I looked in the book, and a truffle is an edible mushroom that grows underground and is the most highly prized of all fungi. They come in black and in white, and are used as flavoring for other foods, their pungent taste being a gourmet's delight. I also had met Paul Urbani of Trenton, New Jersey, whose uncle, Carlo Urbani, in ancient Umbria, is one of the

241

world's leading truffle growers. Nobody is supposed to know any more about truffles than Uncle Carlo. When I telephoned he said they would expect us for dinner on the Sunday, and this invitation led to a mammoth and joyful occasion which dissipates all other complaints about things Italian.

A good many truffles come from France, but nationality isn't important. The Italian and the French truffles can be compared either by the tongue or by the microscope and there is no difference. And while many people snootily proclaim that they eat only the French, or only the Italian, the truth is that you can't always be sure. Carlo Urbani, as a shipper and packer of truffles, sometimes buys from France and sometimes sells to France, and the important thing is not the truffle, but the fact that Carlo Urbani has learned in his business to speak French. So for once, in Italy, we had no language problem, and I give credit to this for the wonderful afternoon in Scheggino.

Scheggino is a small place in central Umbria, and Umbria is in central Italy. The town snuggles beside a small stream and the Apennines lift overhead so only the sun at its meridian height, if the sun ever shines there, can penetrate the valley. A sundial would be of small use in Scheggino. From Perugia, if you move southerly, you can come to Terni, and from Terni you can drive up the valley to Scheggino. We went the other way. From Perugia we climbed over and through the Apennines, and came down the valley. It was a foggy morning, but such a fog as I have never seen in Maine, where we have fogs. It didn't close in on us to spoil the scenery, and it didn't seem to be wet. But it gave an eeriness to the mountains, and it did something wonderful to the church bells. All the way we had an accompaniment as towns down in the valleys and towns up on the hills clanged the Sunday sum-

242

mons. At one point we abruptly came to a barrier in the road with a sign that said, "Alt." We alted. There was nowhere to go. Across a great gaping ravine we could see the highway continuation, but nobody had built a bridge yet. "I think they peep-peep, and jump it," said Dorothy. There were no directional signs, and as far as we knew our only solution was to go back to Perugia and start again. But we found a kind of goat track, no doubt the same that was used by the Etruscans when they overran Umbria B.C., and seldom used since. It went down the face of a cliff, and seemed to be favoring our general direction. I started down in low gear, in fear and trembling and with seat belts securely locked. "This can't be a road," she said.

But suddenly, behind us, there was a peep-peep, and an Italian driver went past us on an outside curve at 120 kilometers an hour, lighting a cigarette as he went. "This is the road," I said. At the very foot of this path we found the stream, a highway, and a sign pointing to Scheggino. Scheggino has a filling station, some shops, a pile of excellently ancient stonework which turns out to be a cluster of homes, and a huge masonry house that looks profanely new. It is new, and it is the Urbani home — the best in town. There is money in truffles.

Being complete strangers to the Urbani family we were instantly disturbed at the cordiality of our reception. It was far more effusive than we could have expected. Nephew Paul in Trenton had courteously announced us. We found ourselves in the living room, received first by the elder and younger Urbani wives, but immediately Carlo Urbani came in with his "Vous parlez français?" and established rapport. The elder Urbanis have two sons; one of them is married to a most beautiful girl named Danielle, and I gather she made the grand error of producing a girl child. The child is darling, just of school age, and although her sex is a near-miss she is obviously loved and spoiled, but neither to excess. The valley of the Urbani family was an ancient rusticating spot of the Romans, where the blue bloods came for sport, climate, scenery and social status. As Rome declined the Urbanis waxed fat, and today they hold something like one thousand acres of mountainside and the nobility that goes with them.

In France truffles are located by pigs, who are then pulled away and the precious product carefully lifted by hand. But in Italy they use dogs, and their keen noses are said to out-find any pig's. Mr. Urbani owns one thousand truffle hounds, or about one to the acre. Did *you* ever know anybody who owns one thousand dogs? When the truffles mature along about September the entire valley turns out, a dog apiece, and combs the oaken mountainsides, and it is a good deal like holding a coon hunt up the façade of the Empire State Building. Local women clean, grade and prepare the truffles for market, a job they do sitting around in a circle, by hand. Some truffles proceed to market fresh; others are tinned. The dogs seem to have no special family tree, and nobody cares what breed they are so long as they can smell truffles. I had never heard French spoken with an Italian accent, and Carlo Urbani had never heard it with a down-east twang, so we made out fine. He said, "We will have a dinner in honor of truffles — you will see the many ways they may be used."

Danielle, who held herself reserved in the presence of her mother-in-law, asked if I would like to see the fish while dinner was being prepared. I had no idea what this could mean, but we got in her automobile and with a great peep-peeping she throttled amongst the old homes

244

of the village, along narrow alleys, and through the gate of a high wall. This wall enclosed a series of pools and continued up the mountain along a small stream. It was a hatchery and rearing station, and here the Urbani family had another business — they grew trout for the hotel and restaurant trade. We learned later that they have other interests, too — they sell farm machinery, run a bank, handle insurance, make wine, press olive oil, and generally keep busy in numerous profitable directions. In the first pool I could see good-sized fish — they were the European trout. We have introduced them into Maine in some warmer waters, and usually call them the German Brown. They are the Loch Leven trout of Izaak Walton. In our Maine waters they grow to considerable size, but lose their color. Here in the pale green mountain waters of Italy they keep their color, and are quite a beautiful trout, although by no means as handsome as our Eastern Brook. We wandered up along the pools, finding that the higher we went the smaller the fish. Danielle introduced us to the fishkeeper, a young man who nurtured these trout from the eggs, and at regular occasions dipped the mature fish from the lowest pool and packed them for market. "Would you like to catch one?" asked Danielle.

Would I? We'd left Maine by way of Flatiron Pond and a panful of trout, and wouldn't it be fun to come home and tell everybody I had trouted in ancient Umbria — where maybe Caesar Augustus himself had stood in his golden sandals and pursued the contemplative man's recreation? The fishkeeper ran to his shack and brought me a long bamboo pole such as they used to roll up a rug when I was a boy, and it had a snatch of string tied to one end and a hook we'd use for harbor pollock. The rig was about fifteen feet long, and there was no reel. There was a sinker on the string. The fishkeeper jabbed a chunk of goat meat on the hook and motioned for me to have at it. I am not above dangling a worm if the fish are coming hard, but it's been years since I have, and I consider myself the best of the world's ten greatest fly anglers. My idea of nothing at all is to insult the vibrant breeds of the char family with bait, more particularly if it is a captive fish in a rearing pool. What I was about to do would look as sporting, back home, as dynamiting the glass tank at a sportsmen's show. But from what Danielle could tell me in our mismatched French nobody around Scheggino had ever heard of a flyrod or a Silver Doctor. And then I noticed that the fishkeeper was laughing.

Danielle said, "He says you won't catch one; he just fed the fish and they won't eat again for two days."

I plunked the goat meat into the pool and had the fun of watching some raunchers swim up to it, nose it, and then swim away. They could care less. I guessed these fish were edging three pounds, some more, and it was tantalizing. I'd have given many lire, right then, for my Thomas rod and a handful of George Fletcher's flies, and even if I might hook one on this foolish Italian rug-stick it would be about as much fun as connecting a gropie on a cod line. But all in vain — these Umbrian trout weren't hungry.

But, you know, every animal kind does, sooner or later, play. And even with his gorge so full he can hardly swim a trout will now and then kick up his heels and disport. And just now one did. There was a huge sploosh on the far side of the pool, and some crazy trout had made a lunge at some crazier Scheggino fly who had thoughtlessly fallen on the water. I dropped the goat meat on the boil, a maneuver somebody should have caught on film for it wasn't easy to cast with that rig, and quicker than instantly I had my trout. There is always an odd one. He

246

threw that pale green Italian water into the sky, and hugged down to the bottom as I set the hook. The fishkeeper stopped laughing and ran to my side. He called at Danielle and she said, "He says you must have fished before!"

I got the idea that in Italy the sport is over when you have hooked the trout. I gathered I was now supposed to hand my rod to the fishkeeper, and he would bring the trout in. It wasn't, really, much fun to play this fish on this rod, but I motioned the fishkeeper away and I did bring him in. I reached into the cold mountain water and tipped up the hook, and away went my trout to give his life to commerce instead. He was a beauty and I would say over three pounds.

When we returned to the Urbani marble halls dinner was ready. We were nine in all — Carlo and his wife; Danielle with her husband and daughter; the other son and a friend; and ourselves. We had an aperitif in the living room and came out to find the dining table laid with beautiful linen, crystal, china and silver. Carlo Urbani took his place at the head, and we began. Six dinner plates stood stacked before each person, and this was the cue to the number of courses. We took each from the top plate and then it was removed. Long before we got to the last plate we were eating the way a Marathon champion does the last five miles — pick 'em up and put 'em down, and come through gloriously if you drop dead. We continued to eat long after all appetite was gone.

That Martini, "like some sad emblem of a perished love," was a fine Alpha indeed, but arriving at Omega took time and fortitude. "Almost everything is from our own properties," said Carlo Urbani, and we began on the first plate with thick slices of sweet melon, complemented by thin smoked ham. Whatever else is said about Italy,

247

their fruits are the sweetest. The ham was not cooked, but delicately and deliciously cured with mountain woods. Dorothy was already inquiring about "receets," and Carlo Urbani was already shouting, "Encore, encore!" which came out wonderfully as Ong-cora. During the meal everything that anybody tried to say was punctuated by this hospitable yell. The second plate was dedicated to a *pâté de foie gras* through which black truffles had been delicately wrought. Bread was by each place on the cloth, and Carlo Urbani had opened wine as soon as we sat down. We had a chance to dally with the wine over the *pâté de foie gras,* and to our compliments on his choice Father Urbani said it was of their own pressing, and was the wine of the house — they did not sell any of this special quality. We lingered over this course, and had ample discussion of the delightful flavor imparted to the liver by the truffles — which was well worth ample discussion.

The third plate was for spaghetti with a sauce made with black truffles and mushrooms. I'm sure we were justified in supposing this would be the main item of the dinner — being in an Italian home and seeing the huge bowls of spaghetti that the serving girl toted in from the kitchen. So we didn't hang back when Carlo Urbani ordered her to heap us up; nor, after we had eaten the heap, did we demur at his ong-cora. Never, anywhere, was spaghetti more delicious. The sauce quickly and without reservation made me the world's leading truffle fan. We all ate and ate, and the serving girl carried out the empty dishes. The Urbani wine was exactly and positively right, and no glass got below a three-quarter tide but Carlo Urbani filled it again with the clear, amber pride of his vineyard. I reached across to pick up and look at the notes

Dorothy had made about the spaghetti sauce recipe, and found she had included some ong-cora.

We were now, roughly, at that point in a farm-home Thanksgiving dinner when everybody is utterly stuffed and Mother says, "Now, there is plum pudding, mince, apple, squash, pumpkin and raisin pie!" Out of politeness everybody has to have something, and feeble answers come. But nobody really wants more, and the best dessert is a nap.

So the next plate was for the roast lamb and chicken that came in orderly rotation around a vast silver platter, and with this we had a salad. Both black and white truffles were flowing like the wine, and their relative effects needed discussion. I suppose the truffles we saw that day would cost more than a pretty penny in a gourmet store back home, and the flair and finesse with which they were used, served and discussed had Dorothy's cookery ambitions in a tizzy.

By now the spaghetti was forgotten, and we could see that it had been merely a prelude. After the chicken and lamb we had a roast of pork, and with it a spinach mold. White truffles were used with the pork, and now Mrs. Urbani turned and asked me, since I had had ample chance to make a comparison, which I preferred — white or black? This was a tender query. She might as well have asked me which of her sons I thought the smarter. I had never tasted a truffle, and until that day had never seen one, and for nigh unto two hours I was slowly being truffled past all discretion, and now I was supposed to tell the wife of the world's leading truffle producer which way my preference leaned. Diplomats are trained for these things. I poised, thinking, and I said, "But they are so very different, the one from the other." She seemed pleased; I had thus far said the right thing. She leaned forward, and everybody was waiting for my answer.

"Yes," I said. "I think perhaps the black." Again, I had said the right thing. They all agreed with me. I was discerning, and a gentleman. But this is my taste. The black and the white truffles grow the same way on the fibrous roots of the mountain trees, but come at different seasons. The black comes first, along in the fall, and later in the winter the white matures. They do not have the set forms of the top-of-the-ground mushrooms, but look misshapen and are not an item of beauty. And they are not at all alike in flavor, so you will use the black with some foods and the white with others.

The next plate was for a torte — a special Urbani confection designed to honor both kinds of truffles, for one side of it was heaped with black mocha frosting and the other side with rich white whipped cream — from the Urbani dairy. It had candied cherries in a puff-paste base, and as I began laboring with it Carlo Urbani was already shouting, "Ong-coral" Truthfully, at the time, I expected to find truffles in the torte, but the mocha and cream were just symbolic. By this time I needed more wine the way America needs more taxes, but it did help down the torte which, under less stuffed circumstances, was delicious to a fault and would need no help.

The champagne, which now arrived, was not from the Urbani industries. Carlo Urbani made that clear. In this, Italy defers to the French. But through his truffle connections in France he had access to some interesting cellars, and he thought we would find this champagne adequate. He popped the first bottle while the girl brought in a vast silver bowl of fruit compote, beads of condensation on the outside to prove it had been chilled. I believe this fruit compote stands alone as the finest single food item I have ever forced between my teeth — it was a mix-ture of every delicious fruit to be had in that country, where fruit is fruit. I gladly took more when Carlo Urbani cried ong-cora, and probably gave too little attention to his select champagne. And like a fat pig ready for stick-ing, I vaguely heard Carlo Urbani, at last, say, "Cognac?" It was over. We had been at table three hours and thirty-five minutes, and the only thing I didn't get to do was wipe my hands on the long hair of a Nubian slave girl.

The cognac was superfluous. I think Danielle was some-what touched that her little girl came and perched on my knee and that somebody, anybody, approved of a daugh-ter. We effected a polite leave-taking, and dopey, sated, plump, burpy, stuffed and replete we ended our truffle hunt in Umbria. We shook hands all around, gratefully thanked the man who owns one thousand dogs, and in the early dusk of the Apennine Valley we wound down the river to Terni, where we found a room in the Hotel de Paris. The young man who showed us to our room said the dining room would not open until seven o'clock.

"Thank you," I said. "But we shall not require any supper."

Je T' Plumerai Le Gaz

Italy was to astonish us once more, and on our way to the Piedmont and France we pulled off the throughway at Modena and found a hotel that was so utterly clean that we still don't understand it. The place was waxed beyond belief, and when they tell about seeing yourself in a floor — it can be done. We could see ourselves in the floor, and it's an interesting angle. Even in nasty-neat Holland we hadn't seen anything like this. The place was so faultlessly clean that we sort of half agreed to stay more than the one night, just to give them extra business and to make up for all the places we'd found in Italy that were not. But we didn't, because the dining room didn't pan out. The dining room was just as clean as the rest of the place, and the linen and china beautiful. The waiters wore white ties, and pleasantly welcomed us, and advised us so we would be sure and have only the best. They brought an Italian aperitif that tasted like Dr. Twaddle's nonrefillable cough syrup, and suggested the ravioli, which was the specialty. It was pretty bad. We decided to push on.

Our conclusion is a simple one, and I suppose basically

sound: that Italy's big problem is her people. Somehow the magnificent scenery and gentle beauty of the country has not generated a salubrious sympatico. We willingly admit our lack of language was a barrier, and that without it we swam upstream. We grant that distant terracotta villages on rugged hills, surrounded by olive groves and vines, all reeking with antiquity, will be cherished always as lovely memories. We state without reservation that our finest meal abroad was at Scheggino. We know what weather can be in Maine, and we presume they were having a bad spell in Italy while we were there. Nobody, not even us, will quarrel about the arts and history and ancient landmarks. But we came to Italy happily and we left gladly. In spite of Scheggino, we can get better Italian food in Ashton, Rhode Island. When we came at last to the Suza Valley and found a hotel that advertised, "Ici on parle français," we were in the slipstream of France and we began to feel better. The landlady did speak French, but she was Italian, and when the eggs came to our table in the morning they had dirty shells. I've sandpapered too many eggshells in my life to like that. There's no need of it. We spent our last Italian money to buy tickets for the tunnel from Bardonecchia in Italy to Modane in France, and for lunch in a pub by the railway depot, our last Italian meal. The lunch was Italian, and so was the toilet. The country I have maligned no more than she disappointed us had the last word — we shall never forget that toilet.

We drove the VW up a platform and onto a flatcar, and the instructions said for us to set the brakes, leave the shift in gear, and not to get out or to turn on any lights. The instructions said nothing about praying. The tunnel is owned by the French, so they go frontwards into Italy and then backwards going home. With the locomotive behind us we were pushed twenty-five kilometers under the Alps and so left Italy.

When we emerged in France the most wonderful thing happened. A fine-looking customs officer stepped up and welcomed us to the French Republic and asked if there were any way he might assist us. Not once, in Italy, had anybody made such a gesture. He suggested perhaps we would like to buy some gasoline coupons. These are a good thing to know about, and you can save money with them. We never bothered with them because we never knew how long we'd stay in a country, and the coupons are good only in the country of origin. The disarming smile of the customs man was thus a little left of affability — behind him was a fellow selling gasoline coupons. "Thank you," I said, "but we bought some earlier in Calais." It was a lie, but it was clever. It probably saved us a long search, as normal penalty for not buying coupons, and with a look at our Green Sheet the customs man waved us past. I'm convinced the hardest country for an American to get into is his own.

We came down the mountain valley in a drenching rain, and so didn't go far. At St. André Le Gaz we pulled off the road into the village and I walked into the Hotel des Voyageurs. Soaked between the automobile and the door, I came into the lobby to find four men beering at a table, and a youngish woman at the bar. "Mouillé," I chirped, which should interest all high school French students who have learned to say, "Il pleut!" I have never seen a more universal and wholehearted agreement with a simple statement of fact, and they all began discussing the weather in such friendly fashion that I found myself ordering a round of beers in due time. I had gone into many bars in Italy where I could have and would have

254

gladly paid for a round, but nobody ever enticed me into it. Here, back in France, I was thick in the middle of good-nature in no time at all. I could see it was good here. The steamy alehouse was a fine place to wait out a rainstorm, and the lady had a room. After a most discourteous interval I chanced to remember Dorothy, sitting out in the VW until I would come back to get her, and I jumped up and said, "Ma bonne femme!" The men all laughed, and when I brought Dorothy in they rose to shake hands, pledged her a long and happy life, and welcomed her to the revelry. One of the men held an umbrella while I got the suitcases, and the woman toted our bags upstairs as if she was happy to do so.

I wonder if I can explain about the WC. This was down one flight from our room, and it was an interesting cubicle. It had red rosebud wallpaper, and the pipes had been painted pink. The pull-chain was long gone, and a length of wire had been twisted in to replace it. But on the wall there was a little sign that read: "This toilet is kept clean for your benefit; please leave it as clean as you found it. The Management. Member, French Society of Tourist Innkeepers."

But, you see, the toilet really wasn't what you'd call clean. It wasn't German neat, and it wasn't Italian nasty. It was passable, but it just wasn't up to the sign. And to us, coming back to La Belle France from ancient Latium, we found that sign most amusing. In Italy the dirty plumbing annoyed us — here in France a neatly printed sign took the curse off an indelicacy and we were in good humor.

It rained all evening, and a number of villagers came into the hotel to pass the time. The bar was like a steam bath. When I finally agreed, prodded by Dorothy, to stand on a chair and lead the ensemble in "Alouette," the success was much like my triumph in Munich. One of the men, a baritone, said he had once been to Quebec, and he recognized my hac-cent. "Alouette," if you don't know it, is the unofficial national anthem of French Canada. In a rough-and-ready translation it has to do with plucking a birdie, and it goes on and on. When you finish, heverybodee 'as hanodder drink. There is perhaps no other song so singable. In St. André Le Gaz it was a sensation.

At suppertime our hostess cooked and served us a meal to make up for all those we had never finished in Italy, and I said, "For breakfast, I'd like some ham and eggs." The beds were good, the hotel quiet, and the night restful. We came down for breakfast, and our lady brought me a great ovenware dish of thick ham slices covered with eggs, and it was piping hot and delicious. But she brought only the one serving. She had to go out and bake off another one for Dorothy, and she lectured me friendly-like on the poverty of my instructions — I might just as well have said "we" instead of "I would like ham and eggs," and then she wouldn't have made only one. "A thousand pardons!" I said, rising from my chair to kiss her hand, and we did have such a wonderful time in Le Gaz.

After we came away I found the key to our room in my pocket. We had not meant to take it, but there it was. It would be fun sometime to carry it back and apologize, and sing "Alouette" again, but in the meantime any tourists who might become as disillusioned as we were with Italy can borrow it. That particular room, in that particular hotel, makes a good place to revive. The key is hanging in our summer kitchen, on a prominent peg.

The White Knight of Roland

France has no great high-
way systems, but every road is a good road and every
turn offers excitement. We moved downward so we could
come along the Rhone and up the Saône to Burgundy,
and we had a small hope that we might intercept the
Yankee at Mâcon and do a service to the National Geographic Society by pepping up their story with a few im-
provisations. We had that last recollection of the Morrills
sitting on their suitcases in the airport at Stuttgart, and
something of a premonition that they had not been
headed for the fun we found. We learned afterward that
we didn't miss them at Mâcon by much, but we did miss
them. The Hotel Europa in Mâcon might remind one of
the old Bellevue in Boston, and we parked our VW right
by the front door on the main street and left it there for
three days. We inspected everything in the river, but
learned nothing of the *Yankee*. France is a country of
sections and regions, and I was having fun with my own
particular *patois du pays*. In Mâcon my French puzzled
everybody. "Where did you learn French?" they would
say, and I always said. "A Loyston!" Lewiston French
never did much for me until I landed in France, and then

257

I was glad for it. "C'est épouvantable!" they would say. We moved along up to Dijon and then into the wonders of ancient Burgundy until in Puligny-Montrachet we had a wine that can be had only in the very room of the very château where we had it. One may become Pope, or the leading hitter in the American League, but until he has had that wine in that room he has not lived.

This was no accident. In Brooklyn there is an import house which calls itself the Mons. Henri Wine Company, and the sales genius who generates enthusiasm for its products has the improbable name of Bill Callahan. Bill told me if I found myself in Puligny-Montrachet to look up Roland Thevenin. So just before we came to Beaune, which is the center of the incredibly lovely Côte d'Or wine region, we passed through Puligny-Montrachet and we saw a long, high masonry wall on which at least two gallons of paint had been required to letter the name of M. Thevenin and his enterprises. If I should hand Bill Callahan a million dollars, taxes paid, and a gallon of my own maple syrup I could never repay him for his introduction.

We didn't stop, then, but went on into Beaune and got a room at the Hotel Central, where for the next week we felt sorry for all the schoolteachers whose tour tickets insure them a swift completion of their appointed rounds. After a delectable dinner, warm hospitality, deep sleep and formidable breakfast we went back to Puligny-Montrachet and drove up to the ancient château of M. Thevenin as if we owned the place, hoping the name Callahan would mean something to a man who had no inkling that we were about to favor him.

These old châteaux in this region aren't much to look at from the outside. Square and looking very cold, they haven't much except age. Indeed, they always look uninhabited. I don't know if one is supposed to pound at the front door, even. I went to the back and a housemaid opened, and she was an unfortunate young thing who had been out of the room when looks were passed around. She had about as much glamour as a pail of whale manure. But nobody was ever greeted with more warm enthusiasm than I was. She acted as if I should come right in, take off my clothes and stay forever. The French she ribbled off was completely beyond me, and it took a long time for me to understand that M. Thevenin was not at the château, but might be found at his office in St. Romain. Thus we drove to St. Romain, a few kilometers away and off the main roads.

The geography of grape country is important to quality of wines, and between Puligny-Montrachet and St. Romain we saw about all kinds. Some vineyards were fairly flat, others ran up mountains. St. Romain is a thirteenth-century village, all walled, with a mountain almost directly over it, and when we came into the town not a soul could be seen anywhere. But the coat of arms of M. Roland Thevenin, a white knight, was displayed prominently on a wall, and inside a heavy oaken door I found a man. One of the sadnesses of our whole trip is that we never learned this man's name. It was simply the way it happened — he didn't introduce himself and nobody ever told us. He was a fine-looking man, and might have been right out of a haberdashery advertisement. He was, of course, M. Thevenin's right-hand man, manager and front man, and he proceeded to case us with finesse. I mentioned Bill Callahan's name, and after a cautious interval we were deemed proper, and St. Romain was ours.

This gentleman took us through the caves, previous to which he provided each of us with a *tastevin,* a little silver dish that looks as if it might be an ashtray, from

which one tastes, but does not drink, the wines. Now and
then as we walked the vintage dungeons he would pause
at a barrel, insert a syringe, and squirt us a sample, and
thus we moved along. We came at last to one cave deep
under the mountain, and far down the line of casks was
a stone arch that led nowhere. It was against the face of
the rock, and was sheer ornamentation in a place where
ornamentation had neither function nor need. In the
arch, laid on their sides, were bottles of wine going up
higher than I could reach. It needed no expert to see that
these bottles had been there a long time. No, said our
man, nobody knew the year — it was so long ago. This,
he said, was a cave the Germans had failed to find when
they overran France, and he chuckled. Remembering the
deteriorated wines in the Apostle Cellar at Bremen, I
asked if these wines in the limbo of St. Romain still had
character.

"Excellent character, as you shall see."

He reached down a bottle which we brought home with
us and had for Christmas dinner on our Maine farm, and
its character was notable.

Our man took us through the bottling plant, and explained the French system of controlling quantity and
quality — I suppose our American trustbusters would
like to take a crack at it, but the man said it was a good
system and he had no complaints. Sometimes when a
quota of a good wine is filled a vintner will have a great
deal of the same quality left over, and then it goes to
market under other names and if you know what you're
buying you can get some bargains. I said I was going to
mention that to M. Callahan in Brooklyn, and he said M.
Callahan already knows that. It was fun when this man
stepped to a cupboard and brought out a whole handful

of Mons. Henri Wine Company labels to show us. It's a small world.

Then our man said, "M. Thevenin is waiting to see you." We stepped across the narrow St. Romain street, walked through a rugged door ironed with hand-forged hinges, and came from the thirteenth century into our own. Concealed in the antiquities is a modern office with swivel chairs, neon lamps, electric typewriters and shapely secretaries in chic styles. M. Thevenin, impeccably dressed, was behind a polished executive's desk and he rose affably to greet us. I have seldom met a man who seemed at very first sight so well worth knowing. We stayed quite some time, and M. Thevenin answered all our questions in a quiet, literary French that took me back to college phonetics. He in turn asked about our tour, enlarged upon our impressions of France, and suggested a hotel in Paris that he believed was ideal — one he stopped at. I was interested that he knew the telephone number of the hotel without looking it up.

I don't know if the shade of my old French Lit. prof got some vibrations that day or not, but it should have. During the conversation M. Thevenin revealed himself as a poet, and said that his several small volumes had won him prizes and citations, one from the French Academy. When the name Ronsard came up I was able to toss off a line and he rose to it joyfully and said I must see his verses and his scrapbooks — which unfortunately were at the château in Puligny-Montrachet. Would we please come to his home on Sunday, take a bottle with him, and continue our literary mutualisms? Say at eleven hours?

The Hotel Central in Beaune is just off the market-place, and Beaune is the center of the Côte d'Or. The Hôtel Dieu, Beaune's hospital, is just behind the hotel and one of the best examples in France of medieval architecture. All manner of caves run under the city and at least every second door is a taste-and-buy. Once a year the Knights of the Tastevin gather for a ceremonial wing-ding, and while it doesn't approach the Bavarian beer blast it's quite something. The architecture of the hospital, exciting as it is, cannot compare with the architecture of the Hotel Central, which for some reason has no two rooms on the same level. Our room was cozy and looked into a street where all manner of interesting things went on, but we had to go up three flights and come down one and a half to get to it. The three other rooms on our same corridor were up and down from ours, by two and three steps. I never did figure it out. The dining room was excellent, and a full mirrored wall at one end gave an illusion of depth and numbers until we thought there was a mile of tables. One of the three waiters was "almost thirteen," and his job was to draw corks, which he did with such adroitness that we could see he had been doing it for years. In Maine a girl under twenty-one can't even ring up the sale of beer in a supermarket. I would say that a boy of that age already trained, in France, has a long and successful career ahead of him, and that he will always find Burgundy a fertile field. Until Sunday we had only to watch such things and to amuse ourselves as we wished.

The day we had gone to St. Romain had been overcast, and I thought we should retrace the route in sunlight. The day we started out was the same day some driving club had chosen for its road race, and we kept passing these low-slung racing cars drawn up along the road as we climbed from Beaune into the grapejuice hills. We wondered what was afoot. At one crossroads a platform had been set up, there was a radio arrangement, and we saw some men with checkered flags. Then, as we dawdled along admiring the scenery, there came a roar behind us and we looked back to see a swarm of these things, four and five abreast, coming at us. There was no place to go except ahead, so I got the VW in high gear and off we went. It was nip and tuck at times, and in one little village perched high on a crag we were lucky enough to catch a funeral party coming out of a church. Along we went, holding our own, and we descended so our ears popped, into a fine old village called La Roche Pot, where there is a wonderful old castle with wine cellars that we had intended to visit. We went past the castle so fast we never saw it. We came to the finish line at last, and while we didn't win we came in a very close third. We received an ovation, and then turned around and went back to see what we had come to see.

On the Sunday we jokingly told the waiter at breakfast that we were taking Communion with M. Thevenin, and he was much impressed that we knew this gentleman. At the château the homely maid welcomed us again and bowed us into the kitchen, where the only hearth fire we saw in all Europe was blazing. Magnificent copper utensils adorned the walls and the heavy overhead beams, and it was interesting that lights were arranged on them as if they were oil paintings. Mme. Thevenin greeted us, and light-haired and pretty she seemed hardly old enough to be the mother of the two grown children. Since M. Thevenin had been called away on a small errand she would show us through the château until he returned. Plain as the building is from the outside, its interior is beautiful and pleasant, and the furnishings old, comfortable and attractive — suggesting perhaps the Germans didn't find this, either. But you don't want to believe everything you read in the papers. Many French wine towns line up with a "sister city" in Germany, and for purposes of blending vintages they have close and profitable arrangements. I don't know, and a guess is a guess. And to prepare us for the literary conversations to come, Mme. Thevenin showed us a book of verses her husband had written for her, lovingly inscribed and beautifully bound. She was very proud. "When you are very old you can say that Ronsard celebrated you," I more or less quoted, and my professor must have had another tingling vibration. Madame smiled, touched my arm, and put the book back.

Not until we were home and I was looking in some books did we realize all that happened that day. That M. Thevenin came in shortly, and that the crystal wine glasses had female nudes on the long stems is remembered. I recall how expertly he drew the cork, and then spent two minutes sniffing and tasting the wine. And I know we sat two hours in the most enviable conversations — about wine and poems and books and abstractions. Mme. Thevenin would rise now and then to stir or add wood to the fire. I remember that afterwards M. Thevenin took us through his caves at Puligny-Montrachet, where he keeps his white wines, and that we had *tastevins* and saw many casks. We knew we were overstaying, but we apologized sufficiently and his acceptance was agreeable. It wasn't until I got home that I really knew.

The book at home tells me that without question the finest white wines to be had in all the world are those produced in Puligny-Montrachet, but that they must be tasted within the immediate château of the grower. They do not and cannot travel. The favored few, to whom the invitation comes, ever know this to the full. At the time it was pearls before swine, but now we know.

I sent one of my own feeble efforts to M. Thevenin, a modest volume he may add to his library, even if he cannot read it. I worked hard on the inscription, to let him know I appreciated everything. And I wrote, "From a poetaster to a poet." I thought that was moderately clever.

The Blues of Chartres

In the next few weeks we wandered all over France, and came one day to the Loire River, which we followed to the sea. This is the castle country and the tourist offices give you all manner of pamphlets. But there is a sameness to castles, except that you come to one where King Richard languished or, as now, the one where Queen Mary of Scotland liked to sit and watch her hatchetmen take a few Protestants apart, little by little, so they'd squeal good and loud. This one arrested our attention. Back in Scotland we had been amused that the present monarch is Queen Elizabeth the First. Because Elizabeth Tudor was mean to their Queen Mary they don't recognize her, and the memories of the Highlands are long and durable. But here in the Loire Valley, gazing down at the spot where the poor heretics went screaming to their doom just so Good Mary could have a little fun in her drab life, we got a notion the Scots have forgotten more than they remember. At Orléans we picked up the thread of that other famous woman, Joan, whose birthplace had impressed us in the north, and whose name had come up in the cathedral at Amiens. We

265

followed her into Paris, where she sits on a gilt horse. But our days were drawing nigh, and we had saved that wonderful experience for the last — Paris.

We came to Vendôme one evening in another chill rainstorm, and again Ronsard's name came up — as well it might because Vendôme is his birthplace. A sign over the bar in the restaurant said,

> *Mignonne, allons boire*
> *ce nectar pur de Ronsard . . .*

It took me a time to come up with it, but what Ronsard wrote was,

> *Mignonne, allons voir*
> *si la rose . . .*

They make a wine there which is named for their favorite poet son, and some adman had paraphrased a verse. I asked the waitress if I might have the sign but she said it belonged to the wine company. Instead she gave me a poster that reads, in French, "Notice! There are more old drunks than there are old doctors!" And so on. I brought it home and gave it to Bill Spear, our local G.P., and if you go in for some pills you will see it framed in his examination room.

Vendôme has a run-down old church which used to be a cathedral. But they changed the seat to nearby Chartres, and now the edifice in Vendôme is called a "widow-church." It's a shame some of the money that flows to Rome can't be diverted to set a little glass and chink a few fissures in Vendôme. The sight of somebody's old drawers stuffed in a church window to keep the cold out of the sacristy can crab a place. We felt that a modest appropriation could restore the former beauty and perhaps make Vendôme as attractive as Chartres, but we didn't noise this opinion around to get any reaction. Off in one of the old church buildings the town of Vendôme has a museum, and we stumbled on it one morning. A little man was sitting all alone as we came in, and he charged us a franc apiece, the same as the Louvre. I remarked that the rain must be bad for business and he said, "Catastrophic!" We had a lot more fun in this museum than we were to have in the Louvre.

There is one painting called "The Suitor from Nuremburg." The story seems to be that the cobbler's daughter is loved by a local jerk, but he can't get up his courage to ask for her hand. So while he's in the background this dandy from Nuremburg comes along and does just that. Snap the shutter right there. It's a huge painting, and the sweep of the rich, red cape on the Nuremburg boy dominates the canvas like an August sunset. The local clunk is outside looking on, and there are some other people as well as the old cobbler with all his tools and the very pretty young lady. We stood in front of the thing an hour, and kept coming back to see it again. Otherwise the museum has a collection of working tools from various trades, and a great deal of odds and ends worth dallying over. Some of the oils are reputed valuable. And they have the harp of Marie Antoinette. I never knew that Marie did any harping, but she had a dandy. It's in a glass case, and looks out of tune these many years.

From Vendôme we came to Chartres, and in spite of the chocolate episode back in Bremen with the expert, we found his glass in the cathedral disappointing. It's a matter of color and effect. The great red windows of Amiens are at least red. Here in Our Lady of Chartres we came into an interior that will vie with any mortuary

267

parlor in the land, and we felt as if we should have come lugging in our own caskets. The old artisans who turned out the famous blues of Chartres practiced an art which, I think, is fortunately lost, and they must have been a funereal lot. The somber, dismal, tomblike cast of Chartres strengthened our opinion that a little cash could well be diverted to the widow-woman in Vendôme.

Now we wanted to apportion our time so we would come to Versailles, and then to Paris, at proper hours, so we stopped in Le Perray at the Hotel des Tilleuls, where from one window we could see the office of security across the way and from another a real linden tree. The room was not the best we found, but the man and wife were good to us. The husband had been to the States once, and he would speak a few English words and then a few French words and thus make up a sentence. I was glad to find somebody else had mastered this technique. Dorothy talked food with them, and they gave her a bottle of Dijon mustard as a parting gift. At one point she said she missed a poached egg on toast, and he said he would make us some. His toast was a kind of zweibach, but his eggs were authentic.

The date of the eggs was November 8, and we planned to move along the ninth and come into Paris on the tenth. I called the Hotel Belfast on Avenue Carnot, mentioned M. Roland Thevenin, and they assured me I would have the best with all hospitality. So we came out of the Hotel des Tilleuls to get our VW from the parking spot under the linden, and found our area surrounded by police. They swarmed in front of the security office. There were armored cars, communications vehicles, and machine guns mounted on tripods on the sidewalk. There was even a portable kitchen. It seemed improbable to me that the French Republic was thus turning out to welcome us to

Paris, and since none of the officers paid the slightest heed to us we assumed this was presumptive. At any rate, we had a complete police escort all the way. At every hundred paces, all along the route, two officers tended out, standing looking at nothing and seeing everything, and as this is a good road and we could whiz right along the effect was that of a picket fence of policemen. We guessed what was going on, and at a filling station had it confirmed. This was the route to be taken by President de Gaulle when he came up from the country to participate in the Armistice Day exercises at the Arch of Triumph. We preceded him by just enough so we got the full benefit of his official security.

We came into Paris by the Avenue of the Grand Army, from Versailles, and were swept into the whirlpool of traffic at the Arch of Triumph. This is one-way, and it is the worst motor vehicle traffic to be found anywhere in the world. Dorothy was at the wheel because I was too scared to drive, and she made three mad circumrotations of the Place de l'Étoile before she shot out of the tangle like a rabbit before the hounds and bounded down Avenue Carnot. There was a parking spot exactly before the front door of the Hotel Belfast and we left our VW sitting right there all the time we were in Paris. Only a gun at my head and absolute lunacy would ever get me to drive around that circle, and every once in a while Dorothy dreams about it and sits up in bed screaming.

Ah, Paris!

M. le President de Gaulle safely arrived in Paris shortly after we did, and we walked up to l'Étoile on that Armistice morning to see him conduct the program. We had ample chance, in France and in Paris, to get some French opinions about this man and his policies, and we formed a general opinion which is triflingly at odds with what the American people are caused to believe out of misunderstanding, misinforma- tion, or the expediencies of party politics. He is far from universally adored in France, yet even those most willing to criticize him will apologetically add, "But he has been good for France." I suppose historically this may be his ambition, and a hit-and-run tourist has no right to talk to a few people and come away with convictions. I will say that the exercises at the Arch of Triumph were by far the most emotionally impressive public experience of my lifetime, and when the band played "la Marseillaise" I wept freely.

Everybody who has ever been to Paris has been to the Arch of Triumph, and it is one of the half-dozen great monuments of the world. The arch itself is 164 feet high, 147 feet wide and 72 feet thick. It is a four-way arch, and the larger archway sits so it faces the Avenue of the Champs-Élysées and the opposite Avenue of the Grand Army. The several avenues which terminate at the arch circle suggest the spokes of a wheel, or as the Parisians see it, a star. The square, which is round, is called l'Étoile, or "the star."

This monument lifts itself out of a circular area which is 131 yards in diameter, with lawns and posie beds. Then this is surrounded by a traffic circle, a round-about, which is 65½ yards across. Double that: a total of 131 yards. So it is 262 yards from sidewalk curb to sidewalk curb, with the Arch of Triumph in the center. But the sidewalks around l'Étoile vary from 85 to 100 feet in width, so you must add a maximum of 200 feet. The Place de l'Étoile is almost as far across as three American football gridirons, and takes up about ten American acres. I have a five-acre apple orchard, and I'd hate to spray twice as much.

So, when we walked up on the morning of November 11, we found this entire area taken up by military formations, and the sidewalks and avenue intersections all filled with people and everybody standing raptly awaiting the arrival of the president. There were many bands, and units from all the French armed forces. Directly before us were the second-year cadets from the St. Cyr Academy, the equivalent of our West Point, and away across on the other side we could see a detachment of cavalry — each horse as straight as each man. Under the arch, folds gently moving in the very light air, was an immense Tricolor that came just to the heads of the dignitaries standing under it. We decorously threaded through until we had a spot at the curb.

Walking back and forth, some of them still in the famous capes, were the policemen of Paris and of the National Gendarmerie. I thought it was wonderful that all the might of France could be drawn up symbolically in one grouped tableau, and the comic-opera French policeman had to stand guard. The policemen said nothing, seemed to see nothing, and paced back and forth unconcerned — there was nothing for them to do. The crowd was silent — not even a baby cried, and beside me a woman was holding two. Not a foot shuffled, and Kipling's roaring Paris was silent as the tomb. There wasn't a shred of sound. When de Gaulle came he was standing in an open military vehicle, hand at salute, and his chauffeur swung him half around the circle and under the arch. De Gaulle hardly looked, at that moment, like the great enemy of Huntley-Brinkley, and I wondered if our networks analyze so penetratingly as they claim. De Gaulle is six feet and four inches tall, and as an old soldier he had, at the time we saw him, done little fading away. His nose, brought to a great beak by the cartoonists, isn't quite that prominent and if anybody wanted to be pleasant toward him for a change he might be conceded a rather fine-looking, martial figger of a man. There was no fanfare by the band when de Gaulle arrived, and no applause or any kind of public outcry. The place and the occasion dictated silence, and silence prevailed. Having laid the wreath and made his remarks, de Gaulle soon reappeared and was driven down the Champs-Élysées, where great crowds were waiting to see the parade about to come. And the military delegations at attention around the Arch circle began preparing to fall in.

The youthful cadets of St. Cyr, brushed and tidied to the last notch, stood rigidly just in front of us, and they waited there while a band started off, and until the cavalry could get in line. This unit of horses was magnificent, with many trappings and bright metal, swords and plumes, and the rump of each horse had been clipped and brushed to make a checkerboard pattern. The officer brought these horses from the far side of the circle so for a time they stood just before us, immediately ahead of the St. Cyr cadets. Then, with every horseshoe ringing on the pavement together the troop clattered off for the parade — a beautiful display of horsemanship.

I noticed that many of the horses had fouled the pavement while they were standing in wait. But the cadets of St. Cyr didn't notice that. When their officer snapped off commands and they moved out to join the parade, they went directly across the spot lately vacated by the horses, and they showed what military discipline can do when you hone it to a fine edge. Not a cadet's eye looked down, not a foot faltered. Wherever the stride and the cadence took it, a boot came down. Some boots clapped on the pavement, and some squished while others went splutt, and off went the cadets of St. Cyr down the Avenue of the Champs-Élysées. There isn't a farmboy in Maine who didn't learn to skip as he ran barefooted through the pasture, and we would not make good French soldiers.

But it was a tremendous experience to see the Armistice Day exercises at l'Étoile, and if in the emotion and grandeur we were caught up a little I wouldn't be surprised. Late that night we walked to the subway that leads under the pavement to the Arch, and we came up for a close look at the place. The great flag was still fluttering, and under it an honor guard stood about the flagstone over the tomb of France's unknown soldier. A true profusion of flowers, and the perpetual flame. Among those standing at strict attention, holding many standards and Tricolors, was a group from the American Legion, and we were glad to see them.

Over and above the call of frivolity, we had one errand in Paris — to go to the American embassy and look up

273

Craig Ashe. He's a boy from home, and a Marine assigned to the Security Guard at the embassy. Except in London, on our trip, we had been able to avoid embassies and such, but one morning we walked into the Paris version and got the official reception. It's quite an experience. Anybody looking at all like an American who approaches is immediately assessed as another stupid fellow citizen who has lost his passport, or at best, wishes to lodge a complaint against somebody who cheated him on a taxi fare. The embassy is supposed to be geared to high-grade international relations, working on the balance of trade and the intrigues of dignified national interest, but it spends most of its time with people from New Mexico who left their passport on a train windowsill. Thus one who approaches is sized up, sorted and catalogued as to what he has lost or what bugs him or what he has had stolen. We thought the young man just inside the door looked greatly relieved when we said we were looking for Craig Ashe. It was Craig's day off, but he would be informed, and we left our hotel address and an invitation to dinner at his convenience.

Craig came the evening we got back from the flea market. Just the other day I was fixing something in my farm shop and I said, "Now, if we were in Paris I know where there's a whole sidewalk of these parts." The flea market of Paris is the world's greatest collection of junk. Mile after mile of anything and everything, and the day we went was one of lively trading, because they were holding a sale. But with us, as with so many other things, the fun of the flea market came unexpectedly from another direction. We rode out to the Place de la Mairie on the subway, and as we came up from under ground we saw a crowd going into a café and barroom, and we joined it. The place turned out to be a bookie joint, except that in

274

France this is lawful and government operated. The races being wagered were at Chantilly, and in a back room the clerks were taking the money and issuing the tickets. We never knew if we won or lost, but we took seats at a table and watched the exercises. In a moment we noticed that we were the only ones sitting down, and a waiter who finally saw us seemed surprised to find us expecting his attention. Yes, he had Ambassadeur, and he brought it. Precisely at noon the betting ceased, the door of the back room was closed, and everybody except us left the place. We had another Ambassadeur in the quiet of an empty house, and the clerk became talkative. He told us what to see, and look out for, at the flea market, and made us promise to come back and tell him what we thought of it. We did, and he had two Ambassadeurs at a table waiting for us when we arrived. So we lingered, and it was approaching dinnertime when we got back to the hotel.

There was Craig, with another Marine, and we went out on the town. I was interested that Craig seemed to know so little about Paris. He had acquired hardly any French, and except for some girlie shows and hot spots knew few of the attractions. Later that evening he took us around to the Marine barracks, and I could see why. He and his fellow Marines live in a good American dormitory with all conveniences and services you can find in Memphis, Tennessee, or Syracuse, New York. They live as Americans, eat American food, and keep comfortably apart from all else. A couple of days later we went back to the embassy so Craig could show us around, and I was disappointed that he wore no brilliant Marine uniform. He was dressed in a plain business suit, and there was nothing to indicate he was either a Marine or a guard.

No, he said — in France the security of all foreign property is a responsibility of the French National Police. There was really nothing here for a Marine to do. Oh, once in a while some internal disturbance, or maybe looking for a lost washroom key, but day in and day out the French Police handle everything. Hadn't we noticed the police outside the building? We had, indeed. They were lined up the way they had guarded our route into Paris. Across the way was a mobile arsenal, with radio communications, and Craig said it was amazing to see them go into action whenever some crackpot tossed an inkpot at the Embassy. I believe it. As of January 1, 1968, the Paris policeman no longer wears his comic-opera cape. This is probably too bad, but the decision to do away with the cape was made some years ago, and a grace period was allowed so those on hand could be worn out. A few were still used right up to the last minute. Along with the high-crowned cap, the effect of the cape was somewhat unpolicelike, if not frivolous. But only a fool would tangle with a Paris cop. We saw a few of them in action, and they are wonderful. We saw a bicycle tangle with a Citroën on the Rue de la Paix, and immediately the place looked like the filming of an Abbott and Costello movie. A policeman moved over, tipped his hat and bowed, took people by the arms as if he were ushering a wedding, and shortly had everybody properly disposed as if he were about to conduct a chorale of "In Excelsis Deo." Actually, nothing happened, but all I could think of was the corner of Tremont and Boylston Streets and the policemen I've seen there handling Boston's problems. The bicyclist and the motorist went over to a sidewalk café and took a wine together, and for a time the bystanders discussed things with the policeman. Then the policeman went back in the street and got traffic moving again, and it was difficult because the

276

Citroën and the bent-up bicycle stayed where they were until the bottle of wine was finished. I have never seen a traffic mishap more pleasantly disposed of.

Another time Dorothy and I were roaming the Left Bank and we wanted to taxi back to the hotel. We came to one parked across the street, but traffic was so heavy we couldn't get over there. We stood on the curb maybe ten minutes waiting for a break, and then along came a Paris policeman, his hands clasped behind his back under his cape, and he appeared not only to see nothing but to believe there was nothing whatever to see. He came up to us and deliberately turned and stepped into the flow of traffic. You never heard such a squealing of brakes, and like Moses dividing the Red Sea he strode across with us, like the Children of Israel, behind him. On the other side he turned away from us, and was gone before I could thank him. Traffic resumed and we took the cab. Over a hundred years ago Bill Nye wrote about the pleasure of being arrested in Paris, and I have an idea it would be an efficient and definite experience. Craig said as much. He said the U. S. Marine Security Guard at the Paris embassy has the best security guard in the world.

We walked Paris. When we got tired we'd take a cab or the Métro back to our hotel. We were so pooped come evening we know we missed a great deal of the celebrated night life that gets all the play, but the two percent or three percent of it that we saw is still pretty good for Maine farmers whose principal debauchery for a long time was a chew of spruce gum now and then. We saw enough so when people mention something we can say, "Oh, we were there!" We had a day in the Louvre, and so many rests at sidewalk cafés that I had to go back to American Express and change some more checks. The one attraction I know of that we deliberately avoided was the guided

277

tour of the Paris sewers. For some reason I have no regrets about this. And when we thought we had "done" Paris sufficiently Dorothy said, "Let's stay one more day to make sure."

"We'd like to stay another day," I told the hotel clerk.

"But you can't — we've already rented the room!"

"See what you can do, the name is Thevenin," I said.

So we stayed another day. We had champagne for the final touch, and as we drove slowly out of Paris towards Chantilly we absolutely ruined the entire morning for hundreds of other drivers who tooted crazily a fond *au revoir* — an odd thing because in Paris horn tooting is forbidden except in emergencies.

The Days are Shorter

We meant to go to Spain, but our time ran out on us. Now we must see Luxembourg, then through Germany to Switzerland, and back north in Germany to catch our boat for home. It's funny, but ten out of every eight friends back in Maine, winking and making sly smiles, ask me about the bosom exposures in Paris, and nobody has asked me about the broad grain fields of France. Near Soissons we crossed our previous Calais–Munich route, and pulled up at a VW station in Laon for the mileage check. This is where I found the barber with the pink hair, and it was a lovely touch as a farewell to France.

The VW man, as usual, had a suggestion for a hotel, and it happened to be right next door — on Avenue Carnot, the same name as our street in Paris. He helped lug in our bags, and a friendly lady welcomed us. Then we set out for barbering, and the first shop we came to was for men only. So Dorothy set out looking for a ladies' shop, and I went in. The extremely pretty and well-cosmeticked young lady who was receptionist removed my jacket in loving manner, and blushingly I asked for a *coupe*. She stepped behind a portiere, and immediately there came forth the most dreamy spectacle my eyes have ever beheld. He — and he was a *he* all right — had pink hair. He also had a crimson smock with embroidery and lace, and a pair of powder-blue rooty-tooty pants cut for beanpoles. These came to a near-miss right at the tops of his sharp-pointed orchid shoes. There exuded from him a warm flavor of jasmine and muscadine, with a restrained touch of lilac. He bowed without stint and ushered me into the operating room. Here, exactly like him but with other colors of hair, were three others, snipping away at patients, and they gave me an affectionate greeting as I took my place. The barbershop was a bower of delight. "You only pass this way once," I said to myself as I settled back, and as if of hemlock I had drunk I succumbed to the soporific perfumery and waited to see what came next.

The thing was a good barber. He had a delicate, caressing, fondling touch, and he whispered sweet nothings in my ear to make sure I was constantly happy. Before the services were over I concluded these fellows were all right, and that they believed these affectations belonged with their trade. I keep trying to tell Richie Baumer, my barber at home, about this and suggest to him that he might

279

try a few similar niceties and refinements, but he thinks I made it all up. Afterwards I went hunting for Dorothy, and I found her — resplendent in a gorgeous high-lift up-do that no respectable Maine woman would wear to a dog-fight, and which she had done over in the next town we came to. The VW made out all right.

As another fitting farewell to France we hit Longuyon the night before market, and we woke before dawn to the activity of setting up. From our hotel window we watched the farmers arranging their stalls, and the great vans opening out into awnings and tents. It was to be our last market in Europe, and we spent the forenoon. We haggled a little, but protested too much and didn't buy anything except some fruits.

Approaching Luxembourg the remnants of the old Maginot Line suggest the follies of war, and Luxembourg is a good place to pause and think on these things. The country is merely a "grand duchy," and its interest to us lay mainly in contemplating the mixed-up history since the first germanic tribes came there to start something. The place has only 999 square miles, with about a quarter of a million population — Maine has 31,000 square miles and about a million. So it doesn't take long to drive across Luxembourg. It's a pretty place with woodlands and hills and some fair-sized rivers. The iron mines are important, and mills to go with them, and farming runs largely to dairying. The unfortunate thing about Luxembourg has been its location, and even in the days of slingshots and hatchets the invading hordes came from all sides, and then other armies would come from the other side and they'd fight. There are several cities in the duchy, but the big one is also called Luxembourg and it is a modern, busy place with a good part of the old defensive wall still standing if you want to muse on the past. Luxembourg speaks French and German, and as you pass from west to east you find the dominant French giving way to the dominant German. This, too, we were to notice in Switzerland.

Coming out of Luxembourg into Germany we were held up by customs. The man took our Green Sheet and our passport and went into his booth, and we could see him talking with other officers. They gave the passport a real scrutiny, and after a man got through with it he'd take it again and give it another look. Then they called in some more men. We supposed there might be some border incident afoot, perhaps a police hunt for some bank robbers, and we waited not too serene. Finally four men came out to our VW, handed us the papers, and one of them said they had been much interested in seeing all the rubber stamps — all the places we'd been. "Eine gute Fahrt!" he said.

We wanted to see Kaiserslautern, where our army has its big base, so we swung that way and were sorry. This was a mistake. Miles after miles of installations; big, huge, expensive, unquestionably wasteful. We are committed in western Europe, and nobody questions that we must stay a long time — perhaps always. But through Kaiserslautern we fought heavy traffic of Buicks and Pontiacs, all bearing United States plates. And fifteen kilometers beyond Kaiserslautern, in the direction of Speyer, we found the perfect indictment of an American occupation. Deep in a valley, right beside a beautiful stream, we found an inn so fine we stayed three days. Not once, in that time, did anybody from our American military base come into that inn for a wine or a meal. I know very well that if I were stationed at that base fifteen kilometers away, I would long since have found that wonderful inn and made use of its hospitality. A pretty young woman waited on table and her husband was the cook. One evening, counting the football team and a factory party, the girl took care of over fifty people and never missed a shot. She ran about at full tilt, and even though we insisted we had plenty of time and were in no hurry she gave us every attention. We were the only nonlocals in the place, and we had more fun than anybody, and fifteen kilometers away thousands of American soldiers and civilians were eating institutional food and drinking Milwaukee beer and wishing they had something to do to pass the time. Dorothy said, "I can't understand it."

Headed for Basel we threaded the Badische Weinstrasse, and in the Gasthof zum Löwen in the historic town of Heitersheim I made more history. I lost the filling in a tooth. We had come to this place late in the afternoon, in a rain, and it was good to come and call quits for the day. During supper the landlady joined us, and some others, and we sat late in conversation because tomorrow was Ruhrtag. The landlady said everybody else would be gone, but she would get us our breakfast.

She did, and remembering the pleasantries of the evening before she outdid herself and made a mockery of the term "continental breakfast." She piled everything in the kitchen on our table and came to sit with us as we ate. I crunched into one of the concrete crusted hard rolls, and that did it. I picked out the amalgam, staring at it, and ran my tongue into the bottomless crater. And I was immediately aware of another void — certain technical vacancies in my vocabulary. What's the German word for *filling? Zahn* is tooth; a dentist is quite logically a tooth-doctor. I took the gamble that so often pays off in that language. "I have lost a filling," I said. The German word for filling is *Füllung*. No sweat.

"Have you pain?" she asked.

"No pain."

She made a telephone call and came back to tell me the dentist was occupied with an operation at the hospital, but would soon return, and I was to go to the office and wait. So our advance to Switzerland hung fire while I had a tooth filled, and with the possible exception of the French barber in Laon it was the finest feminine touch of the trip.

I scarcely got to the dental office when a beautiful woman wearing a white smock came into the waiting room and warmly, but firmly, shook my hand. She asked if I were having pain. "No pain," I said. She said, "Gut!" I've seen some good ones, but I honestly never saw such an attractive dental nurse or hygienist as this one. This one made Helen of Troy, Aphrodite and a midsummer night's dream one glorious moment all wrapped up in a handy package. I'm going to say she was in her forties, beginning to show some gray hair, and formed so congenially even her professional smock couldn't hide it. She was just right. She led me to the chair, adjusted my bib, and smiled at me so I glowed all over. I can give you her name. I can also show you her receipted bill, because she was the dentist. "In school," she said in German, "I studied English, but I have forgotten all of it. I'm sorry. Open, please."

Deftly, excessively gently, and while I was totally anesthetized merely by her proximity, she cleaned out the cavity and reloaded it. While she mixed the amalgam I looked about at her office. She had compact Seamens fixtures, unavailable to American dentists who would like to get some — they drool at the catalogue and curse the tariff barriers — and there was none of this overhanging shaft and pulley stuff that makes an American dental parlor look like a planing mill. The drill had a pull-out cord, and no evidence of turrets and gears. And there was

EUROPE ON SATURDAY NIGHT

no blinding overhead floodlamp which always hits your eyes more than your mouth — she had a tiny spotlight that came in on my lip and once it was in place I didn't know it was there. That night I sent postcards to all the dentists I know saying, "Boy, you should see this girl's equipment!"

She charged me DM20, which is $5.00. I lingered hoping to kiss her goodbye, but Dorothy said, "Come on, we're late for Switzerland!"

The Last Ten Francs

Switzerland needs no evaluation from us. Here the Helvetians were conquered by the Romans and the "nature of the place" created built-in consequences which led to the famous neutrality. Living in Luxembourg was like living in revolving doors, but the Swiss shut the door off and made everybody go somewhere else to fight. The Alps dominate, and it's pretty hard to move through Switzerland without noticing them. We did ask a few questions about the famous democracy of Switzerland, because our own New England Town Meeting is supposed to come close to it. But in New England it's been running backwards for some time, and I guess we have neither the passion of the Swiss for preserving purity nor the wisdom that comes from their geography. I also took notice of the gun laws. Home in Maine our constitution says the right to keep and bear arms shall never be questioned, but a lot of people are questioning it. In Switzerland they don't monkey around with the softening preliminaries to totalitarianism — there a man is obliged to keep and bear arms.

We thought we did notice in Switzerland a tinge of something that bothers us in Maine — taking tourists for granted. We had been told that the innkeepers of Switzerland are tops, and take great pride in professional perfection. Many of our overnight stops on our trips were in hotels where the tourist is not commonplace, and we gathered that we got attention and kindnesses because we were an exception. In Switzerland your every want is solicitously provided, but it seems to involve nobody in the inn personally, and kindness to guests is routine rather than spontaneous. We would not place the Swiss above some others as innkeepers.

The big event, for us, in Switzerland was changing money and buying some chocolate. We had been border-hopping until we had quite a bit of odd money, even to a Scottish pound. Since Switzerland is the money-changingest country, why not convert everything into German marks, which would last us to the boat, and after that we could use dollars? Almost every doorway in Switzerland has a sign saying they'll change money, so we pulled up at a kiosk and tossed everything on the counter. This was no bank, and we had none of the fun and fuss that went with changing money in a German bank. The woman behind the counter sorted lira from shillings, totted it up, and handed over the German marks — less her percentage. Then Dorothy said, "Oh, I've got one more!"

It was a French ten-franc bill — worth two dollars. And instead of taking money for it, she picked up a handful of picture postcards, got stamps for them, and said, "I'll take the change in chocolate bars."

"With or without nuts?" asked the woman.

"With nuts."

"All with nuts?"

"Yes, all with nuts."

Instead of almonds, the European chocolate bar has hazelnuts, and it also has something our domestic bars don't have — European chocolate. The woman wagged her head and went out back. She came in with an armload of chocolate bars. We have no idea what the postcards cost, or how much the postage was, and we have no notion of the price of Swiss chocolate in Switzerland. But nobody ever made ten French francs trot so far. We had about a peck of chocolate bars scattered about on our luggage, and presently we came back into Germany at Constance and stopped for the Green Sheet examination. The officer looked at the chocolate, gave our Green Sheet a look, and then he said, "Sprechen-Sie Deutsch?"

"A little," I said.

"Good," he said. "What will you do with all the chocolate?"

There flashed in my mind an occasion, years ago, when we were going to Canada to do some sightseeing. I had a box in the automobile, and we had five cameras in it. It made sense. I had two .35's, one loaded with color and one with black and white. I had a movie camera, a small Brownie that was more of an antique than useful, and my Speed Graphic. The Canadian customs man, when he found what I had, drew himself up to his full legal height and demanded, "And what are you going to do with all those cameras?"

I suppose he thought I was smuggling cameras, but it seemed to me a foolish question anyway, and I said, honestly enough, "Take pictures." I don't know what else you do with cameras. It was, of course, the wrong answer, and the fellow got real nasty about it. He ordered us to pull up in the parking space and he kept us there a long time and made an ass of himself. I wrote a letter about him to the tourist bureau at Ottawa, afterwards, and they thanked me and said they would look into it. So now, coming back into Germany, I got about the same question.

I suppose I could have told him about the ten francs, and how we bought some postcards, and how we thought we might get a couple of chocolate bars, but that we didn't know they were so cheap, and I suppose I could even have said, "We're going to eat them." But I laughed and said, "Souvenirs — would you like one?"

"It is forbidden," he said. "What is that?"

He was pointing at a gift-wrapped box on the back seat — our cuckoo clock for Terence. "A cuckoo clock," I said.

He burst into haw-haws. Every nutty tourist buys a cuckoo clock. "It was bought in Germany," I said. "I have the receipt."

"No matter. Where are you going?"

"To Hamburg, to sail for America."

"Has Germany pleased you?" he asked.

"Gern," I said.

He waved us along, and called, "Eine gute Fahrt! Gute Reise! Auf Wiedersehen!"

"Vielen Dank!" I said, and we began looking at the maps of Germany to find a route to Hamburg that wouldn't touch places we had already seen.

Turkey in Waiblingen

But we did go back to Waiblingen, and it's good we did because we drove over to Stuttgart one day to check our boat reservation and found that Hamburg was out. The man at the North German Lloyd office said everybody had been looking for us, and nobody knew where we were. He said the M.S. *Breitenstein* would sail from Bremen instead. He would telephone to Bremen at once and inform them that we had been found.

Good American holidays mean nothing in Europe. Thanksgiving was upon us, and back home our young folks were planning the usual farmhouse feast with roast turkey and all the fixin's, and we had promised, wherever we might be, to telephone that afternoon and join the party. Somewhere between Constance and the seaport we ought to find a special place, worthy of the occasion, where we could join, so far away, in the national gratitude for health, prosperity and the harvest. "I'm thinking," Dorothy said, "of Waiblingen."

I said, "Nur mit Humor dein Sach bestellt; dann lacht dir froh die ganze Welt."

"That's the place," she said.

So we came back to Waiblingen two days before Thanksgiving and everybody was delighted to see us. The shops were already decorated for Christmas, bright holiday lights were strung across the streets, and every bakeshop was featuring chocolate Santa Clauses. Nobody, anywhere, can beat a German shopkeeper at prettying up a show window, and at Christmas they let go altogether. There was one toyshop across the street from the Hotel Stern with an electric train in the window, and I had to fight my way through two hundred children to get near enough to see it. The friendly tone we remembered from Waiblingen was now gay with Christmas in the air. Advent wreaths were prominent, and on our dinner table was the traditional snatch of evergreen with a red candle.

But Waiblingen couldn't keep our minds off the farm. Never before had we been away on Thanksgiving. We thought about Ellen and Kathy laying the tops on mince and apple pies, and grinding the suet for the bag pudding. The boys would pick over the woodshed and find just the right logs for the roaring holiday fire on the hearth. One of them would have gone to the Green Front and paid three or four dollars for a bottle of ordinary white wine that the burghers of Waiblingen wouldn't allow in the house. And the old tom would be laid out in splendor and one would hold while another stitched and his great gaping breech would be tightened over the beechnut stuffing. Potatoes to mash, turnips to cut, squash to steam, onions to cream, and cranberry sauce. A big bowl of fruit, a bowl of nuts. Dorothy said, "I hope they remember to bring out the pewter candlesticks — they are always on the table." Everything at the farm would be the same as always — except for two wandering parents of unknown whereabouts. They couldn't possibly envision us arriving in Waiblingen, she in a German hairdo and I with my French socks, chocolate bars and cuckoo clock. But we could picture them — when the great feast was spread Johnnie would say the words and we could almost hear him asking the Almighty to give us safe journey home, "Wherever they are!"

But except for thoughts of home we were in no pain. The dining room was maintaining its high standard and the landlady had lost no skill at the Dinkelacker fountain. We shopped, and came back to the hotel to rest and refresh ourselves. And on Thanksgiving morning when we came down to breakfast I told the landlady, "Today, in America, is Thanksgiving."

"I have heard of that," she said. "This is the day all Americans eat turkey."

"That's right, and our family is at our home eating turkey and we are here."

"I have never seen a turkey," she said.

Now God does move in most mysterious ways His wonders to perform. That morning, in Waiblingen, a huge American-style supermarket was opened, with free balloons for the children and everything, and we went into it, and in the very center was a case of frozen poultry, and right in the middle was a Virginia turkey. That turkey cost less in Waiblingen than he would have in Virginia. There was only one turkey in the whole display. We carried it back to the hotel and gave it to our landlady. At last she had seen a *Trutthahn*.

We haven't the faintest idea what she ever did with it. We had a hope that she might thaw it out and have it cooked for our dinner, but remembering our experience in Munich with Frau von Itter and the Cacklebird we were pretty sure an oven roast was unlikely. I would guess that eventually they cut the turkey up and fried it, and

290

probably decided it wasn't fit to eat. But whatever happened to it, a chambergirl presently brought us a note. The landlady has toused around until she found somebody who "knew" English, and the note was the result. It said, exactly:

> *Please at 13 hours*
> *Schickens and pommes frites*

This was our invitation to Thanksgiving Dinner in Waiblingen.

Dorothy got out her Bavarian suit with the lace shirtwaist, and I put on my black suit with the vest. When we came down to the dining room, precisely at one o'clock, the landlady and her two waitresses stood in line and bowed, and every guest in the dining room rose. Our table had a centerpiece, and the usual glassware of the house had given way to ringing crystal. The chicken and fried potatoes were complemented with salad and other vegetables and I'm sure the Neckar wine had been sent out for on purpose, and was not from the hotel's cellar. Each time we sipped every other glass in the dining room was lifted toward us, and all eyes were on the Americans who were celebrating their great national *Dankfest*. We lingered, they lingered, and the afternoon meal ran on until everything had to be explained to dinner guests who came in.

We were in no hurry whatever, because allowing seven hours for time difference we didn't plan to telephone to Maine until midnight. The landlady showed me the telephone, high on the wall in a back corridor where they stored beer. It was nice and cool there. And by nine or ten the landlady and Dorothy had cemented such a complete rapport that they were sharing champagne — it was a Sekt

291

that came in small bottles just big enough to fill one glass, and the row of empty bottles was already alarming. Dorothy's German and the landlady's English had now reached high intellectual planes, and kept getting better all the time. The overseas operator understood me the first time, and it was fun to listen and hear *vier-fünf-vier-tzwo* ringing in the kitchen back home. We talked for $28.00.

But Thanksgiving in Waiblingen was not over. The landlady found more Sekt, one of the waitresses began telling smutty stories, and the cook came in from the kitchen. The guests had mostly wandered home, but a few still stayed to make sure we weren't lonesome. When we did start up for bed Dorothy stopped on the stairway and said, "You know — I have a mixed-up feeling about to-day."

"Sekt is a shorter word for it," I said.

"I don't mean that. I mean — there were those youngsters sitting around the table back home, wishing we were with them for Thanksgiving, and I don't feel that way at all."

"We had a good day."

"No, you don't see what I mean. I mean, I missed them, and they missed us. But instead of wishing that we could have been at home with our family — I spent all day wishing our family could be here with us!"

"I know what you mean," I said.

And probably a hundred times since we've come home, Dorothy and I will be sitting in the big front room with a fire going, and either listening to the radio or reading some books, and all at once she'll look up and say, "Wonder what they're doing in Waiblingen tonight?"

I wonder.

And Auf Wiedersehen

After Waiblingen we had only to wait out the on-or-about at Bremen, so we kept to back roads and moved north. I wanted to swing into Paderborn to see the weathervane, and pay my respects to the sensible people who live there, and had something of the old feeling about Hamelin Town. Paderborn was so much bigger than I had expected that the pleasant little tale of the weathervane lost much of its charm — it's a much better story if it might come from a quaint, quiet little place. A few years back some restoration work was done on the old Paderborn church, and a prominent German artist-craftsman was commissioned to design and make a new weathervane for the steeple. He did, and it was put up with appropriate ceremony.

But it was one of these things where somebody says, "What is it?" and the artist answers, "If you don't know what it is, you're stupid!" But the artist hadn't made allowance for a fairly basic consideration — that a weathervane is supposed to function by telling people which way the wind blows. The good folks of Paderborn could look up and admire this supreme example of creative impressionism, and evidently they were glad to support the arts, but they couldn't figure out how the wind lay. Enough of this is enough, so one day they had a local blacksmith pound them out a plain, old-fashioned, gilded weather-cock, and they took down the work of art and put up the simple rooster, and he stands there on the steeple today telling everybody where the breeze is. I thought this deserved my attendance, so we drove quite a distance out of our way to come to Paderborn and look up at the church and say, "Well done, good people of Paderborn."

The wind, that day, was westerly.

In Neumarkt we found a hotel room with two wash-bowls and no water, and I went down to inquire. The man came up to our room and showed us that the faucets didn't work, but we could get water by turning the shut-off valve by the floor. Very simple.

Then in Schloss Neuhaus, where an interesting old castle is now a military barracks, we got involved in the family concern over a youngster's broken leg. When we came in, the hotel owner told us things might not prove too pleasant, as their little boy had been playing soccer in the schoolyard and ended up with a badly broken knee that was requiring surgery. Thus the operation of the inn revolved around the operating-room schedule and visiting hours, and we might not get good attention. We gave him a bar of Swiss chocolate to take to the young man and Dorothy offered to help in the kitchen — which he thought was kind but funny, and he said this wouldn't be necessary. He came back from the hospital with good news and took care of his Saturday night trade in relieved spirits. It was the usual Saturday night, lingering, and when we left the dining room to go upstairs we found the back entry of the hotel full of bicycles. A tangle of wheels and handlebars with just room enough to turn around the newel. Many of the evening's guests had pedaled to the inn, and having freely imbibed felt themselves in no condition to drive home. They had walked home and would come in the morning to reclaim their bicycles.

They also returned in the morning to come to church. Our sleep was from hour to hour, because all night the great bell in the church tower clanged the time, and the front door of the church was exactly twenty paces from the back door of our hotel. And in the morning when the sexton hung on the great ropes and burst forth with the summons to mass we were almost thrown out of bed by the racket. We dressed, and when we went down to breakfast we climbed around the bicycles and found the door to the dining room locked. The other door, to the kitchen, was also locked. The back door, opposite the church, was locked. We had been locked in all night with a bevy of bicycles. We went back up to our room, but presently a great pounding came at the back door, with some shouting, and it roused our landlord so he opened up. The men had come to church, and now that church was out they wanted a drink and their bicycles. Back in Maine it is illegal for a taproom to be located within pious and statutory distance from a holy edifice, and a morning snort on the sabbath is strictly forbidden. I guess, though, you can stand a bicycle overnight without breaking the law. After they got the bicycles untangled I went out to pace off the distance from bar to church, thinking that might be a good thing to know.

We found Bassum a Christmasy town with a bright-lighted community tree directly in front of the Hotel Stadt Bremen, and we holed up there to sort our things and get ready for sailing. The man and wife who run the hotel were very fine to us, and they had a small boy who came to our table every morning to shake hands before grabbing up his briefcase to run to school. His mother and father protested that they spoke no English, but after we got home we had a letter from them in excellent English thanking us for some postage stamps we had sent to the boy. We thus came back to the Hotel Bremer Hospiz, and when our fair-haired friend of the hot chocolate welcomed us exuberantly we told her we had been to see the famous blue glass of Chartres. She said, "Zo!"

The North German Lloyd man telephoned us every few hours to say that "on" was still "about," and told us to be ready to bring our automobile for its official cleaning promptly — but he didn't know just when to tell us to bring it. This turned out to be a joke. The United States Department of Agriculture has a strict ruling about "foreign soil." During our trip we tried to keep the VW clean, and had done well at it up to the last couple of weeks. We'd struck some mud and slush on our way to Bremen, and because I knew we had to pay twenty-five dollars to have the car officially washed and the proper papers certified I didn't go into a garage with it. So when we came to Bremen our VW was rather a mess. Then the man from North German Lloyd telephoned again and said the time had come. We drove, after full and lingering farewells at the Bremen Hospiz, to the North German Lloyd office and a young man took our VW to be washed and certified.

He came back shortly and the VW was fully certified, but it hadn't been washed. It looked to me as if they had run a damp sponge over the windshield. But they gave me papers in triplicate attesting that all foreign soil had been removed and the vehicle was ready for import, U.S.A. I guess some of the dirt got back to Maine, all right, and has mingled with our Maine acres.

In the Overseas Harbor we found the *Breitenstein*. She is larger than the *Wolfgang Russ* and our accommodations more spacious, but in general the two ships are about alike. Having enjoyed so much our previous visit to Bremen and the time we spent with Herr Schröder of the Lagerhaus, we were pleased to be sailing from Bremen instead of Hamburg, because now we could watch the miracle docks operate, and seeing the *Breitenstein* take on cargo was a great thrill. For one thing, we were to carry almost all of Germany's Christmas mail to the United States, and trainload after trainload of boxcars got shunted to our pier. Men would open the door of a car and out would cascade the mailbags. Sling-nets hoisted the bags aboard and dumped them in the holds, and then other men would jump up and down on them to make sure they were packed tightly. What bothered me in particular was the thought of all the cuckoo clocks there must be in those bags, and I thought now and then I could hear a cuckoo complain. When the last mailbag had been rammed into place they laid planks on top and hoisted aboard five automobiles, of which ours was No. 4. It's quite something to see your own automobile on a sling, the dockside crane yanking it over the yardarms and then dropping it like a plummet into the hatch. But the crane operators of Bremen control their derricks with the finesse of a maiden lady doing tatting, and just as our VW must surely smash to bits the cables tightened and it rested as gently as a snowflake comes down.

We also saw some of Herr Schröder's container business. Several of the great metal boxes went into the holds, but we took eight aboard on the deck. These were lashed down with steel cables, and were put aboard with a huge floating crane that came alongside under its own power to do the job. By this time we'd met our officers and steward, and the first mate told us such equipment couldn't be afforded at Brooklyn when they came to unload, so they would rig their own derricks and save money. But in Bremen the crane was so cheap they couldn't afford to rig their own derricks. He also said after one more voyage the *Breitenstein* was going to a shipyard and would be converted to all-container service. No more loose mailbags.

By the gangplank was a small blackboard hanging on the rail. It had the departure time on it, but every hour or so somebody would come and erase it and put on a new time. But at last "about" became "on," and a tug moved alongside, the pilot came aboard, smoking a *Bremen pilot* cigar, and we were ready for the homeward cruise. The steward came to me and said, "Now, I have scotch, rye, bourbon, gin, rum, brandy, Asbach, Kirschwasser, Steinhager, five kinds of beer, plenty of wine and some champagne — is there something else you would like to have me get before we sail?"

Alas. If our reputation as lushes had been whispered to him, he was overconcerned. I said we were homeward bound, and would soon return to a staid, pious, abstemious society where strong drink is considered raging, and that we had ten days at sea in which to taper off into sober citizens, and I felt the supply he had enumerated would suffice unless we ran into an emergency. He said he thought all possible emergencies had been foreseen. I said it sounded so. He said to push the button if we wanted anything.

On this trip we were five passengers. Walter Naujoks, a young man coming to America for the first time to work and live, who has since written to us that he is happily disposed and has no intentions of returning to Germany. A young lady, Luise Myohl, who had been in the States before as nursemaid and housekeeper, and was coming back to marry her widowed boss. Her family came to see

298

her off, and it was a tearful farewell, and in Brooklyn her betrothed met her at the boat and it was most joyful. And a charming lady of unestimated years who was named Elvira Dreshman and was going to run an antique shop in the Midwest. She was introduced as *Frau* Dreshman, but in German, at her age, this needn't presuppose that she was married. We didn't ask and she didn't say. And unlike the company on the *Wolfgang Russ,* this one was completely capable in English.

And so were the officers. Captain Hermann Poppe was a blustery-looking coot who wasn't blustery at all and had a good laugh when something struck him funny. When we said we had lingered in Bassum everybody laughed, because that is where Captain Poppe came from and evidently it is a local joke in Bremen. The chief engineer, Wilhelm Kaspar, was an older man, quiet and not overly forward with the passengers. On a German vessel a chief engineer has gone as far as he can, and will never climb higher, but a chief mate can still aspire to a command. Ours was Chief Mate Lothar Lange, who took to us and made the voyage far more than ordinary.

There was a pang to leaving Bremen. Ours was an utterly happy experience, even in retrospect with Italy, and now it was over. It was a once-in-a-lifetime affair, and we knew as we watched the great steeples on the *Dom* of St. Peter's stand above Bremen and grow smaller and smaller that it was not *auf Wiedersehen,* but goodbye forever. The great busy harbor took no ceremonial notice of our going, but kept pushing and loading and tooting, and the face of the grain elevator, and of the Lagerhaus, showed no emotion. We could see the little building where the toy harbor is kept. It grew dark almost at once, and the Weser was now deep and wide indeed. We came to the lights of

Bremerhaven, and a Greek passenger liner was at the Columbus Quay and it was true — we couldn't see the passengers because they were getting off on the other side.

So we left Germany, and Europe. The next morning we were *not* butting down the North Sea toward the Channel with our cuckoo clock, chocolate bars, VW and probably some cheap tin trays, because the North Sea and the Channel were as smooth as glass. Britain here, the Low Countries there. This very way, some of it, my ancestor had voyaged back in the 1600's, already seasick. He must have had a weak stomach.

Auf Wiedersehen and *gute Reise!* Breathes there a man! There was soon a faint misty outline that was said to be the end of England, and later another that was said to be the end of Ireland. It was, anyway, the end of all Europe, and the next we would see, apart from ships that passed, would be Nantucket Lightship — outpost of North America. Home.

Welcome to Brooklyn

We never did figure out why our ancestor hated the sea. The Atlantic remained calm and the *Breitenstein* methodically churned along. And with Steward Habben attentive we had no complaints. He brought me three books he thought I might like to read —

Huckleberry Finn, Sherlock Holmes and Stewart Holbrook's *Holy Old Mackinaw.* The last had another title on it, because in the paperback they wanted it to sound sexy, but that's what it was — the history of the American lumberjack. Each evening the lounge was jolly, and after a couple of days at sea Chief Lange brought down his tapes. The lounge had a radio and we had listened to German, Dutch, French and English stations until we got beyond their signals, but now we couldn't pick them up. The Chief was a recording hobbyist, and he had one tape of the rousing drinking songs we had listened to all over Germany — all oompah. I asked him to make me a copy and he did — it came to us soon after we got home and we play it once in a while and wonder what they're doing in Waiblingen.

The first evening he brought his tapes down we sat until after midnight, and the next morning before breakfast a tap came at our door and the understeward, Reinhard Blume, bowed us good-morning and said we were expected in the quarters of the chief mate for hospitality. It was the morning-after bit — if you have had a pleasant evening continue it. We found Chief Lange in his room, Christmas greens and a red candle on his table, his recorder playing soft music. He had cookies laid out, and Blume brought some beers. Not since Hamburg had we beered at breakfasttime, but we pledged Herr Lange happy days and made out as best we could. The photo of his wife on his desk showed a very pretty girl, and he grew weepy-eyed at the thought of spending Christmas in Philadelphia while she was in Bremen. It's impossible to tell any good American joke in German, because of the word order, and it's almost as impossible to tell such a joke to a German who speaks English. But we tried to convey all the Philadelphia jokes we could think of. How they close

301

on weekends. And the one about the raffle — first prize was a week in Philadelphia, and second prize was two weeks in Philadelphia. He smiled politely, but it wasn't a success. We thought that probably, after he had spent Christmas there, he would get the point and laugh later. When it was time for Herr Lange to go on watch we shook hands and Dorothy and I returned to our cabin and slept all day.

I can't imagine and I don't care to find out what it's like to approach America by jet propulsion. On the *Breitenstein* the approach was several days in the making. On the chart where Chief Lange stuck a flag each afternoon to show our position we saw one day that we were just south of Cape Sable. We had already seen a seagull — one loner who came swinging over and gave us a look. The next morning we had a flock of them and they stayed with us. We couldn't see Cape Sable, but I went to the lounge and turned on the radio, and in boomed CBC-Halifax. I had to smile as I thought of my friend Mac-Donald, who programs CBC-Halifax, sitting in his studio. There we were with absolutely nothing else in sight in 360 degrees of wide ocean, and if we hadn't been tuned in nobody would know CBC-Halifax was on the air. It seemed like a vast waste of signal just to reach the Provinces.

Nantucket Lightship is the first homecoming evidence of America. Sitting anchored smack in the navigation lanes, just about two hundred nautical miles east of New York harbor, here is one of the six or eight most important navigational beacons in the world. Not a very fancy vessel, she seems beautiful to the eyes of returning wanderers, for she is the outpost of home — something to surge the emotions long before there is any chance to gaze upon the Statue of Liberty. Fifty miles northwest would be Massachusetts, or Nantucket Island, and another twenty-five miles or so the Cape called Cod. The ocean was still as vast as it had been for a week, but Nantucket Lightship meant we were almost there.

The *Breitenstein* came out of the morning to pass within a mile, and I complimented Captain Poppe on his navigation. He said thank you, and Chief Lange smiled. When you have a mate you don't navigate, you don't have to. And now we could pick up a lot of radio stations — Boston, Newport, Hartford, and that evening late we got WQXR from New York. For the first time in four months we heard about Vietnam, urban renewal, integration, schoolteacher strikes, and all the other burning issues so important to Americans.

We would come to Brooklyn by night, pause for quarantine, and dock at dawn. Chief Lange said we would not have a good view of The Lady, but if the weather were clear she might appear briefly and he would call us. So just when there was dawnlight enough, but not too much, Blume rapped on our door and called, "Statue of Liberty!"

Even when all you can see is the tip of her torch over the end of an island, the Statue of Liberty is the greatest sight that can grace the eyes and touch the heart of an American. Nothing is more emotion-packed. Walter Naujoks came out on deck to stand with us, and we quickly saw that the effect on him was comparable. She beckoned him to a new home, new opportunity, new life. Of all the symbols of all abstractions, I think this is the one. No American who goes a-traveling ever comes all the way home, but at his first sight of the Statue of Liberty he comes the closest. It was just the tip of her torch.

Again, there was no hurry about leaving the ship. No pursers and stewards pushed us along. We had a good breakfast and said our farewells. At dawn the docks of Brooklyn looked bare and abandoned. No great fields of cranes stood up at attention as in Bremen and Hamburg.

But the crew of the *Breitenstein* broke out the ship's derricks, and before we finished eating they had much of the mail ashore and forklifts were trundling it to the trucks. "It is expensive to use American facilities," said Captain Poppe.

Then Dorothy looked overside and saw our son and wife and grandson on the dock. "Come up the gangplank!" she yelled. "We want you to look at the German toilets!"

And Herr Habben came then to say, "This is Mr. O'Hagan, the American customs officer."

We shook hands with Mr. O'Hagan in wondering manner. We had crossed so many borders without a hitch. Our most complicated had been the British, where they are still fighting the Common Market, but it hadn't been any great trouble. There was once the men had held us up a few moments to look at the rubber stamps on our passport out of idle curiosity, and once the man had laughed at our chocolate bars and cuckoo clock. But mostly it had taken five to eight seconds. And now we were to penetrate the high walls of our own native land, and deal with our own kind — and how was it to work out? Mr. O'Hagan said, "I take it you are a schoolteacher."

"No," I said.

"Well, I was looking at your declaration, and this is the way all schoolteachers make one out."

We had, indeed, listed every purchase and attached every receipt. "If I'd known that I'd-a done different," I said.

"No," he said. "I like it this way."

He was courteous, kind, and absolutely honest to both us and Uncle Sam. But it did take a lot of time — more than it took us to enter ten other countries combined. He finally snapped a rubber band around his book, signed his name to a sheet and said, "You owe me sixty-two dollars."

That included the duty on the VW, which was now entering as a secondhand vehicle. I paid him, and he let us go home. The youngsters had their own automobile, and our VW was on the dock with its pint of North German Lloyd gasoline. So they pulled up at the first filling station while we tanked.

It was the first credit-card drink of fuel our little car ever tasted, and as the attendant handed me back the charge card I absentmindedly said, "Danke-schön!"

He said, "Whajasay, Mac?"

It Wouldn't Be the Same

Full of Flatiron Pond trout we had left Maine on a summer's day, bound for Montreal and the great adventure. Hardly full from a Howard Johnson hamburger we came home to Maine over the bridge at Kittery, and there was snow in the air as we saw the sign that says, "Hi, Friend — Welcome to Maine!" The man at the tollgate on the turnpike cautioned us to stay below thirty-five miles an hour because it was slippery, and I looked at our VW speedometer to see where that jibes with European kilometers. It would take a time, no doubt, to get used to Maine customs.

The farmhouse, when we came through the woods, was ablaze with lights and our daughter and husband had been holding a rousing homecoming feast until the rest of us should arrive from Brooklyn.

The very first thing we did when we came into the house, the both of us, was to go to the cupboard and take down glasses, and run the spring-water tap in the sink. "To home!" we cheered. It was the best drink we'd had in four months.

And then what could we say? How do you tell people in Maine about the Löwenbräu tent where twenty thousand people were seated at tables? We found, of course, that we had been on a trip that was ours, and ours alone, and that the happy experiences of Europe were in our hearts and memories and we had no easy communication. That view from the Skotterup Kro. The man with a thousand hounds and the torte the color of truffles. The nauseous stench of Venice. The gendarme on the Left Bank. The light on Baker Street. That foolish frozen turkey clunking on the dark wood of a Waiblingen bar. The lawyer with no coat on. Those farmhands drinking our health in the steam of a rainy night at the Hotel des Voyageurs. A bottle of wine with Poet Thevenin, and *kuchen* with Artist Lemm. The miles of begonias and the tall dark spruces of Zuflucht. The marble riprap along Alpine roads, and a German shepherd tending his flock in the snow. Chocolate bars and Chartres, and a beer with the Herling cousins in Neu Wulmsdorf. The policeman in Gifhorn who disrupted a whole convention so we could park, and another policeman in England who turned and walked away. Campers at Dunkirk, an aperitif by the flea market. Queen Mary's frivolities by the Loire. It tumbled on and on. We said it was good to be home, and our family said it was good to have us home.

We were good travelers. We left our Maine and our United States at home and we journeyed amongst other

peoples with courtesy to them and credit to ourselves. As
far as we know we offended nobody, and we met many,
many who seemed glad to see us. And we had done exactly what we meant to do — we had seen the folks between the airports and the bus stops, people who live there
about as we live here. It wasn't many evenings until
Dorothy looked up and said it for the first time, "Wonder
what they're doing in Waiblingen tonight?"

We've got a pretty good idea what they're doing in
Waiblingen tonight. I told a fellow I'd like to be able to
take a few friends and drop in at the Hotel Stern for supper some night — just as if it might be only down the
road. Why, he said, that's no problem. All I'd have to do is
get party rates on a swoosh-plane to Stuttgart, rent a car to
Waiblingen, and just pop in and pop out. It wouldn't
cost as much as you'd think, and it would take only a couple
of days.

No. Waiblingen is far away. We know. We were there.

After we were home a time I got a letter from a man
named Taylor in the sales tax division at our statehouse.
He wrote to say that the "presumptive evidence" indicated
that I owed $56 use-tax on the VW sedan I had brought
from Germany. This was now due and payable.

Well, this wasn't quite so. The Maine use-tax law ex-
empts items that have been in use outside Maine for three
months prior. From the VW factory at Wolfsburg, or as
we like to call it, Foylesbeersch, back to tax-minded Maine
had been well over this free time. I owed the state nothing. I dropped him a polite note, and Taylor came back
to say that I was mistaken, and that unless I coughed up
he would be forced to take steps, pointing out that he
worked hand-in-glove with the Attorney General, no less.

I wrote him again, not so politely, but he was adamant.
I never paid it, and after a time he quit. But I was bitter

about it. We had maneuvered that VW all over Europe without fifteen minutes elapsed time, inclusive, in any involvements over taxes, registrations, licenses, duties, imposts and insurance. We hadn't even won a parking ticket. But now, in my state by my own people I was being bullied into a tax the state clearly and by its own records knew I didn't owe. Hi, Friend — Welcome to Maine!

Would we go again? No. We'll settle in for our old age with our happy memories, and our collection of beer glasses for which we have no brew. It wouldn't be the same if we poured Narragansett into a Dinkelacker glass. Our souvenir bottles of akvavit, Kirschwasser and Ambassadeur are empty and on the shelf for décor. Along with the bottle that came from deep under the hill in St. Romain. We have kept one bottle of Oktoberfestbier from Munich, but it will never be opened and I hope some day it will achieve the age and the value of those Apostle wines in Bremen. No, we had our trip and it was ours all the way — and how could we tell anybody about it? We haven't even any pictures — and if we had made some pictures one of them would have been that view out the window that day when Dorothy said, "Now, this is what it's like in Europe!"

That's what it's like in Europe, but rooftiles seen through a toilet window don't make such-a-much to throw on a screen.